# THE VOICE

## Other Books by Curt Smith

# THE V⚾ICE

MEL ALLEN'S
UNTOLD STORY

CURT SMITH

**THE LYONS PRESS**
*Guilford, Connecticut*
An imprint of The Globe Pequot Press

Copyright © 2007 by Curt Smith

The Lyons Press is an imprint of The Globe Pequot Press.

10  9  8  7  6  5  4  3  2  1

Printed in the United States of America

ISBN: 978-1-59921-094-0

Library of Congress Cataloging-in-Publication Data is available on file.

For J. Roy Goodearle

(1925–2006)

◆

Sometimes I feel that I will never stop; just go on forever;

till one fine morning I am gonna reach up and grab me a

handful of stars, swing out my long, lean leg, and whip three

hot strikes burning down to the heavens; and look over at

God and say, "How about that!"

— poet Donald Hall

◆

# Contents

◆

# Acknowledgments

"Manners are of more importance than law," said the British prime minister Edmund Burke. Mel Allen majored in the latter, and mentored in the former. At one time The Voice was America's *nonpareil* sportscaster. He was a childhood hero, later friend, and "nature's nobleman."

This book has tried to be, as Mel might qualify, respectful but critical, neither putdown nor paean. I have done 105 interviews; heard hundreds of broadcast hours; and researched at, among other sites, the National Baseball Hall of Fame and Museum, Library of Congress, *The Sporting News*, and in a cycle of irony, University of Alabama, where I wrote Allen's 1984 speech accepting a Distinguished Chair.

The author Willa Cather wrote, "A book is made with one's own flesh and blood of years. It is cremated youth." This book etches mine—and Mel's. It explores his 1964 firing by the New York Yankees. It etches a man riven, driven, and exposed. It compares past and present: what I felt, growing up in Caledonia, New York—pop. 2,188, and 300 miles from the nearest big-league park—*v.* what facts tell me now.

The first fact is Allen's effect on a—mine, Baby Boom—Generation. I have spoken with household names in sport, art, and politics: George Will, Sean Wilentz, Juan Williams. They loved recalling The Voice: at age fifty-eight, say, felt eight evoking him. This is not an inconsiderable gift.

The second conclusion is Allen's art at peak. Many Voices have done myriad sports events. None eclipsed Mel on postwar baseball.

Similarly, none—not Graham McNamee, Bill Stern, nor Cosell as in Cosell—crashed so suddenly, or returned from the living dead. Leonard Koppett wrote, "I can imagine a world without baseball, but I can't imagine wanting to live in one." Mel could not imagine such a world. Its loss broke his heart.

"Having made it on his own . . . he has been made to realize how vulnerable a naked man . . . can be in a hostile world that over and over again savages him for no reason he can define," wrote an author. Savaged, Allen showed heroic grace. "A critic blasts Sinatra," broadcaster Bud Blattner said, "and Frank slugs him." Mel replied stoically and courageously, without hate or spleen. He fought the fight, came back, survived.

If a Voice is good enough, lasts long enough, and has an easy familiarity, he becomes an extended member of the family. Harry Caray seemed deliciously truant. Byrum Saam made English a second language. Allen felt baseball a winnowing force for good. I am not sure that he was right—only that he never doubted. Will muses: "I write about politics, mostly to support my baseball habit." Mel never tried to break it, nor could had he tried.

Paul Fay wrote a book about John F. Kennedy, *The Pleasure of His Company*. I am grateful for these Voices's company: Nat Allbright, Red Barber, Bud Blattner, Jack Brickhouse, Jack Buck, Harry Caray, Joe Castiglione, Jerry Coleman, Tom Collins, Bob Costas, Roy Firestone, Joe Garagiola, Earl Gillespie, Curt Gowdy, Hank Greenwald, Milo Hamilton, Merle Harmon, Ernie Harwell, Waite Hoyt, Ernie Johnson, Ralph Kiner, Larry King, Tony Kubek, Vince Lloyd, Sean McDonough, Ned Martin, Jon Miller, Lindsey Nelson, Ed Randall, Pee Wee Reese, Phil Rizzuto, Chris Schenkel, Lon Simmons, Charley Steiner, Chuck Thompson, Pete Weber, Bob Wolff, and Jim Woods.

I also wish to thank writers Maury Allen, Stephen Borelli, Bob Broeg, Jack Craig, Bob Dolgan, Joseph Durso, Jay Gallagher, Doug Gamble, Michael Gershman, Stan Isaacs, Leonard Koppett, Doug Lippincott, J. Anthony Lukas, Jack Mann, Bob McCarthy, Phil

Mushnick, Jim Ogle, Scott Pitoniak, David Plaut, Rob Rains, Harold Rosenthal, Richard Sandomir, Bill Schulz, Leonard Shapiro, Morris Siegel, Ken Smith, Larry Stewart, George Vecsey, Paul White, George Will, and Juan Williams.

I am indebted to past and present major league and minor league officials: Bob Allen, Marty Appel, Howard Berke, Glenn Geffner, A. Bartlett Giamatti, Jim Healy, Larry Lucchino, Laurel Prieb, Joe Reichler, Bud Selig, and Brent Shyer. *This Week In Baseball's* cast was helpful: John Bacchia, Geoff Belinfante, Steve DeGroot, Mark Durand, Roy Epstein, Warner Fusselle, Terry Kassel, Mike Kostel, Jim Rogal, Jeff Scott, and Bob Smiley. Other interviews include Tom Gallery, William Gavin, Bill Glavin, Ron Howard, Richard Nixon, Jimmie Reese, Lou Schwartz, and Sean Wilentz.

The Latin phrase *primus inter pares* means first among equals. It describes the Hall of Fame's Bill Francis, Senior Researcher; Jeff Idelson, Vice-President, Communications; Jeremy Jones, Manager of Recorded Media; and Pat Kelly, Director, Photograph Collection. I also wish to thank Kent Stephens, College Football Hall of Fame Collection Manager; Kristin Strohmeyer, Hamilton College Reference; Steve Gietscher, Senior Researcher, *The Sporting News*; and the University of Alabama's W. S. Hoole Special Collections Library: Clark Center Jr., Curator; Donnelly Lancaster, Archival Access Coordinator; Tom Land, Institutional Records Analyst; Jessica Locher-Feldman, Public Outreach Series Coordinator; and Marina Klaric, Archival Technician. I am especially grateful to Mel's gracious family: sister Esther, brother Larry, and sister-in-law Margie.

Ken Samelson will never forget his Mets 1986. This Red Sox fan will not forget Ken editing the manuscript with superb insight and care. The Lyons Press Associate Publisher Eugene Brissie made the book possible. Andrew Blauner guided it from pre- to postgame show. My wife, Sarah, endured rainouts and extra innings. Our children, Olivia and Travis, each a Ballantine Blast, supplied the Seventh-Inning Stretch. I also wish to thank friend and counselor Phil Hochberg and audio/video archivist John Miley. The facts and opinions herein, of course, are mine.

I do not know "How about that!" in Chinese. I do know the Chinese proverb "One generation plants the seed. Another gets the shade." Mel planted the seed for generations' love of baseball and its ally, the English language. To this day we still get his shade. ◆

# Prologue

he philosopher Plato said, "Before we talk, let us first define our terms." Vin Scully made baseball a child's sun, moon, and stars. Harry Caray spun existential pleasure. Red Barber forged an alchemy of look, sound, and feel. They were not, however, the best to broadcast the game.

At his peak, that was a lonely, valiant, and ambitious man who had all, lost all, and against likelihood, came back. Many preferred Mel Allen to being at the park. Others prayed that laryngitis would silence him forever. He likely sold more cigars, cans of beer, safety razors, and Americans on baseball than any announcer who ever lived.

Except for the Equator, everything begins somewhere. Mel began with a voice—to sportswriter Huston Horn, "an indefatigable, hinged-in-the-middle tongue"—that a florist must have decorated. In Omaha, hailing a cab, he said simply, "Sheraton, please." The cabby's head jerked around like a swivel. Bob Costas grew up on 1960s Long Island. "His voice should be in a time capsule—how baseball was for us."

Allen rose and fell like a buoy off Long Island Sound: riveting and inexhaustible, tying Alexander Scourby and James Earl Jones. In 1955, *Variety* magazine named his "one of the world's 25 most recognizable voices," akin to Churchill's and Sinatra's. It was then, Mel said, as his manner spoke of propriety and a modesty, not newly formed, that was neither bogus nor offensive, "that I knew mine was not unpleasant."

The Voice wed rhythm and tempo and similes and allusions: dash, syntax, and detail, his 6–4–3. Johnny Mize "is a sentimental hero, in any case." Phil Rizzuto was "an exponent of the [shortstop's] art." Cameramen on the roof drew an "uneven fringe of shadow," phrase and mood falling lightly on the ear. He was musical, histrionic, and touched by unpredictability—also sweet, much-wounded, and as artless as they came.

Once Mel spied two teenagers kissing at Yankee Stadium. "That's interesting," he said, "he's kissing her on the strikes, and she's kissing him on the balls."

Now-colleague Rizzuto shook his head. "Mel, this is just not your day." For a long time, most of Allen's were.

"Hello there, everybody!" turned national idiom; a home run: "White Owl Wallop" or "Ballantine Blast." When Hank Bauer doubled, Warren Spahn sawed batsmen, or bad-ball hitter Yogi Berra begot good, "How about that!" followed. You felt the sunlight, dusk, and heat; fielder crouched, batter cocked, and pitcher draped against the seats; above all, a surety that there was nowhere you would rather be.

In 1957, Allen became the first sportscaster profiled on CBS Television's prime-time *Person to Person*. Host Edward R. Murrow sat, cigarette in hand, one knee upon the other. Suddenly The Voice appeared, in a rowboat, paddling toward his Bedford Village, New York home.

"Where are you, Mel?" the host said, laughing. "How about that! Mel Allen and his yacht."

"Hello, Ed," he said.

"Pull hard on the left oar—you aren't going to make it," Murrow said.

"Oh, I'll make it," Mel said, nearing the dock.

"What are you doing in a boat like this at night?" Allen didn't miss a beat. "Well, isn't everybody doing this sort of thing?"

It never occurred that he would not sail with the wind.

◆ ◆ ◆

In 1939, Mel was named Voice of the New York Yankees. By 1964, he had aired 18 pennants, 12 world titles, and nearly 4,000 games; to *Sports Illustrated*, "the most successful, best-known, highest-paid, most voluble figure in sportscasting, and one of the biggest names in broadcasting generally." At high tide, Allen did 21 World Series, 24 All-Star Games, 14 Rose Bowls, CBS Television's *Mel Allen Sports Spot*, NBC Radio's *Monitor*, and nearly 3,000 Twentieth Century Fox film newsreels and short subjects, saying, "This is your Movietone reporter." Up to eighty million heard him each week.

Gigs tethered Army-Navy, Blue-Gray, and East-West football; *Jackpot Bowling*; heavyweight boxing; Triple Crown racing; and Little League World Series; ten-time *The Sporting News* Announcer of the Year; three-time National Sportscasters and Sportswriters Association best broadcaster; and first Voice to enter Cooperstown (Class of 1978). At one time or another, Mel graced each U.S. network: ABC, CBS, Mutual, and NBC's Red and Blue. Said film critic Jeffrey Lyons, raised in Manhattan, "He could make the telephone directory sound like the Sermon on the Mount."

"You're like shit," Ralph Houk told Howard Cosell in 1963. "You're everywhere." Yearly Allen filled about 600 TV, radio, and motion picture hours. For a quarter century, depending on your view, he was a Saladin, chatterer, or surpassing personality of the big city in the flesh.

"Write 'Good luck, George,' and add my name," said a bartender, insisting that Mel sign a $5.00 bill.

"This is illegal," Allen noted, scribbling.

"For this, I die," mused the keep.

"He did things no one else could," said the Mets Ralph Kiner. Antipodal, raconteur Tex O'Rourke sniped, "Mel is Alabama's answer to the babbling brook." A viewer telegrammed during the 1958 World Series: "Shut up, you Yankee-lover!" It arrived four hours *before* Game 2.

Take Costas, twist Al Michaels, and add Chris Berman, Curt Gowdy suggested. "That's how big Allen was" to a 1950s and early

'60s shabby-genteel boy in Upstate New York, as big as Ike or JFK. Beach, yard, sunporch, or car: The Voice, said a writer, was "forever linked with the golden age of baseball on the air." A bystander could walk down the street, a hundred windows open, and not miss a pitch.

"Freeze-frame the age," said 1952–64 NBC TV colleague Lindsey Nelson. "The Yanks season was one platform." October built another. Till 1976, team Voices did the network Series. Allen aired each on 1947–63 radio or TV. "Welcome to this country's greatest sports event!" he blared. To many, the Classic *meant* the great actor of our baseball time.

"If Mel sold fish, he could make it sound as if Puccini wrote the score," wrote the *Los Angeles Times*'s Bud Furillo. Tom Gallery was 1952–63 NBC sports director. "I always thought there was a theater and exuberance about Allen that brought a special drama to the occasion."

Before long, Mel's life acquired a drama of its own.

"I hadn't thought of him in years," National Public Radio's Juan Williams said in 2006, "but the name, it's still mythic. Gosh, there was no one like him." In 1957, Juan, age three, moved from Panama to New York. "Allen was my assimilation." Then, one day in 1964, near his apex as an institution, Mel's prepotency crashed. Movietone ended its newsreel division. NBC removed Allen from the "Granddaddy of Them All," the Rose Bowl. In December, without even an announcement, the Yankees released him. "They never even held a press conference," said The Voice. "They left people to believe whatever they wanted—and people believed the worst."

Thirty years later color still flushed his face. "The lies that started were horrible, that I was a lush or gay or had a breakdown or stroke or was numb from taking medications for my voice." Lacking any explanation, *Sports Illustrated* wrote, "Allen became a victim of rumors. He was supposed to be a drunkard, a drug user. Neither rumor was true, but he couldn't fight them. It was as if he had leprosy."

F. Scott Fitzgerald wrote, "There are no second acts in America." Overnight, disappearing from the playing fields of America, Allen despaired of a second chance. Childless, unmarried, he began a decade of banquets, voice-overs, peewee baseball, and other curiosa, becoming a nonperson, for reasons he never grasped nor understood.

July 1968, Minnesota hosts Cleveland. Interrupting broadcast partner Harry Jones, Mel began a treatise on geography and literature. "This is the land of 10,000 lakes. They have these picturesque names," he said, *reciting* them.

Jones tried to retrieve the game. Instead, Allen paddled to Lake Superior, site of Henry Wadsworth Longfellow's poem, "The Song of Hiawatha."

Did Harry know the poem? he asked. Wearily, Jones muttered that he did.

"Let's see now, how does it go?" Mel mused, repeating its first thirty-seven lines.

Jones glared. Years later Nelson relived the good-bye song. "Was Allen blackballed? A strong word, but yes." Added Barber: "He gave the Yankees his life, and they broke his heart."

An unknown 1940s and '50s admirer had sent one red rose a day. The Voice's garden now looked bare. "I've written since 1959 about every famous name in sport," said the *New York Post*'s Maury Allen. "No topic's caused more mail than why the Yankees fired Mel." This is the first book to explain why.

At the time, hearing dry-as-paint pretenders, you recalled the hypothetical, what might have been. Then, in 1977, Mel began hosting *This Week In Baseball*, eventually, sport's highest rated TV serial. Each Saturday he etched players, isolated in his attention, talking *sotto voce*, a semi-Marceau at ease.

"For years he was a forgotten man," wrote William Leggett, "but it has all come back to him in abundance"—rise, ruin, and rebirth.

To many, he seemed to have never left.

Allen's coda became the rest of his life. "Kids knew him from *This Week*," said executive producer Geoff Belinfante. "Older folks remembered the salad days. Everyone had a frame of reference"— Mel, as Rorschach test.

Once, comparing presidents, historian Stephen Ambrose wrote, "It must have been an awful thing to be Richard Nixon." It must have been awful to be The Voice when life as he defined it withered—also great to later grasp millions with him, with him because they loved him, and sense himself complete.

Recall a grand and painful, stirring, then despairing, and ultimately redeeming life. ◆

# Yesterday Once More (1913–1936)

t is wistful, even wishful, that adults change magically. "Give me a child until he is seven," said Saint Francis of Assisi, "and you may have him afterward." Put one way, we rarely stray from DNA. Put another, as Al Gore malapropped, "Leopards don't change their stripes." Allen seldom did.

Before his death, Mel yoked "Dear Heart," "You've Gotta' Have Heart!," and "Heartbreak Hotel." Aptly, he was born February 14, 1913—Valentine's Day—in Birmingham, "The Cradle of the South," to Russian émigrés Anna Leibowitz and Julius Allen Israel.

Julius's father, William Israel, reached America at thirty-five, settled in West Blocton, Alabama, and built a dry goods store. "It was a tough place," mused Julius, the fourth youngest of eight children. "The meanest guy there was an outlaw named Bart Thrasher." Slim and striking, Anna left the Ukraine at thirteen. At twenty-one she married Julius, February 25, 1912, in Minneapolis.

Mom clasped good works, prayer, and belief that God guides life. Dad prized work, fondness for the familiar, and reverence for everything American. "Pious folks," the magazine *Park East* read. "Allen's devotion to them caused him to model his conduct on theirs." Its nub was respect for age. "One thing drilled into me," Mel said, "was to defer to older people." Ironically, if not a genius, the oldest of three children was a tad ahead of type: Melvin walked at nine months, talked in sentences at one year, and read box scores at five. "Like me, he loved baseball," said Julius. "I just didn't want it putting limits on tomorrow."

In 1900, 8,000 cars had been an oddity. By 1913, four million once-playthings-for-the-rich swelled the middle class. To George Eastman, new color photography was a "mirror with a memory." The new president, an ex-Davidson baseball player, added piety and zeal. "We are not put into this world to sit still," claimed Woodrow Wilson, inaugurated eighteen days after Mel's birth. "We are put here to act."

In 1912, Julius moved his store to Johns, a mining town 18 miles from Birmingham. The Israels acted to lend a hand. "Mel'd tell stories," said *This Week* associate producer Bob Smiley, "about Jews coming to Johns when they were short." To reach it, you passed scrub and stream and soil flanked by skies shot by Ansel Adams. To Allen, the road into back country had a romantic *Saturday Evening Post* glow. Rural Alabama was the world.

"A drowsy, dreamy influence seems to hang over the land, and to pervade the very atmosphere," Washington Irving wrote of the Hudson Valley, with its lush and humming earth. Mel somehow felt Johns's witching power. Chickens littered farms. Friends raised pigs. Allen's first game was "The Pig Chase," chasing them to holes where he fell, once nearly drowned, and was rescued by a neighbor.

At night train whistles forged "child's dreams," as John Connally said of another Southerner, Lyndon Johnson, "[that] could be as wide as the sky and his future as green as winter oats because this, after all, was America." It was a hope The Voice never wholly lost.

We are all a product of time and place. There is no hoax in retrieving Allen's to note that hitting fungoes, citing averages, or trading the American Tobacco Company four-color playing cards, he and friends thought of little else.

Each year began with games of pepper in cold and rain. Mel played back-lot center field, shortstop, and second base. "I was pretty good," he said, accurately. "Quick, decent arm. When I was eight, I played hardball on a team of teenagers." Siblings Esther and Larry were born in 1914 and 1920, respectively, "More than them, I just loved the game: couldn't wait for school to end in May."

Morning pickup games tied grass stain, bruised wrist, and broken window. "Sometimes," Anna drawled, "I think Mel was born with a baseball in his mouth." At lunch, he consumed pictures in big-league guides and annuals. Bylines bound Damon Runyon, the Carl Sandburg of the short story, and Grantland Rice—"Grannie," the courser of the press box—and Ring Lardner, *le pere grand* of the *Post*'s "Alibi Ike." All met, said Allen, in "Johns' leading john."

The Israels' home lacked indoor plumbing, electric light, and telephone. "One of Daddy's sisters, Rose, married a furniture store owner," said Esther. "They lived at the top of the hill and we were at the bottom." At four, Mel took the Sears and Montgomery Ward's catalogs, staked the outhouse, and scanned photos of bats and gloves. Inside, Mom and Dad read text: "How I learned baseball, and to read before kindergarten."

One day in 1920, the barely first-grader began reading aloud a Birmingham *Age-Herald* editorial endorsing James A. Cox for president. "My hair stood up on end," said Julius, stunned. "I had known all along that Mel was brighter than most, but he'd never let on just how smart he was. He was always such a modest and"—cross his heart—"quiet little boy."

The tyro skipped four early grades, graduating elementary school at age 11; high school, 15; college, 19; law school, 23. "Most years," said his brother, "Mel'd start with books a little or lot beyond his age."

Spying them, Julius imagined theft. "These aren't your books!" he said. "They're for an older kid."

Mel never corrected him—"too humble," said Larry, and busy with baseball. Outside of class, he reveled in accident of birth. "What a time to follow the game. Every part, I liked."

In 1908, vaudevillian Jack Norworth wrote *Take Me Out to the Ballgame.* Next year Philadelphia's Shibe Park forged baseball's first steel and concrete plot. By Mel's birth, eleven new sites reflected the grid of city streets. "Each fit on an urban parcel," said author Michael Gershman. "Ballparks assumed a symmetrical form as they took on the lines of their property."

Fenway Park became a shooting gallery. Gappers owned the Polo Grounds. At Crosley Field, homers struck a laundry. Each seemed extended kin. "You'd see some relatives twice a year," said Allen. "Pie Traynor or Ty Cobb, I'd read about, get to know 'em like family." Their park was the street where he lived. The effect, like his voice, turned heads.

In 1921, a new player swung. "TV is picture plus caption," said Nelson. "Baseball radio's a different beast," debuting August 5, on KDKA Pittsburgh, America's first commercial radio station.

Harold Arlin, twenty-six, bought a ground-level seat, put a scorecard on a wooden plank, and used a telephone as microphone. How did the Westinghouse Company foreman sound that afternoon? Few live to say. Western Pennsylvania had several hundred radio sets. Which, if any, heard? Speakeasies, raccoon coats, and Clara Bow fused. Film's Rudolph Valentino faced a future with sound. Arlin faced tomorrow with a larynx and a prayer.

"No one had the slightest inking if this'd take off," said Allen. "Then all of a sudden we saw the effect." In 1925, 10 percent of Americans owned a radio. Sixty-three percent did by 1933. By fit and start, the wireless ferried prose to Braves Field, Sportsman's Park, and Griffith Stadium. Its problem was geography. Fancy America as clock: Baseball's read 12 to 3.

"Every pre–World War II team was in the Northeast and Midwest quadrant," said Allen. "Tough luck if you were me. No regular-season coverage, just the Series," even that evolving slower than autumn in Alabama. In 1921, Westinghouse aired its first: KDKA to outlets in Newark, New Jersey, and Springfield, Massachusetts. By October 5, 1922, radio "for the first time carried the opening game directly . . . to great crowds [estimated five million] throughout the eastern part of the country," wrote the *New York Times*.

In May 1923, a professional singer walked up lower Broadway on lunch break from jury duty, entered the AT&T Building, and won a WEAF audition. That October the baritone called the Series. Stations from Washington to Massachusetts, said the *Times*, "will radiate the contests simultaneously with WEAF . . . connected with special land wires to microphones controlled by that station." Mel would later conjure Graham McNamee's born-for-wireless voice.

The Classic ended Monday. By Saturday, WEAF got 1,700 letters. "Given how new radio was," Allen gaped, "we're talking a zillion letters now." McNamee aired foreign visits, coronations, and at least ten sports, including football, horse racing, and marbles. In 1923, Calvin Coolidge addresses Congress; 1924, the Democrats nominate John W. Davis on the 103rd ballot; 1927, Lindbergh returns from Paris. The natural did each. "How do you do, ladies and gentleman of the radio audience?" he began, closing, "This is Graham McNamee speaking. Good night, all"—radio's first great name.

"Today you can hear baseball a lot of ways," The Voice observed in 1995. "Then you had radio, which meant network, which meant Graham." On January 1, 1927, McNamee aired the National Broadcasting Company's first Rose Bowl. Eventually he did twelve straight Series. "You must make each of your listeners, though miles away from the spot, feel that he or she too is there with you in the press stand, watching the pop bottle thrown in the air; Gloria Swanson arriving in her new ermine coat; [John] McGraw in his dugout, apparently motionless, but giving signals all the time."

In 1929, a reporter yapped, "McNamee, will you pipe down?!" Hearing the Series, Mel began to laugh. "Jiminy Cricket, some writers hated broadcasters becoming big names." Graham's last Classic was 1934, "opened by the umpire who will howl 'play ball,'" he said. "Wild-eyed rabid fans" jammed the stands. "All hint of rain has been dispelled." Next year Kenesaw Mountain Landis drenched McNamee's parade. "The Commissioner chose Series broadcasters," said Allen, "and thought he'd got arrogant."

Baseball's Pinza never called another game. It was a feeling with which one day Mel would empathize.

In 1994, PBS Television's *The American Experience* profiled Ronald Reagan. He "evoked a simpler place, a simpler time," it said of 1910s Illinois. "Small towns. Patriotic values. Family and community. An idealized America that no longer was, that perhaps never was." Reagan was born in 1911, on the one and only road of rural Tampico, "in circumstances so poor that years later, while visiting his birthplace, he visibly recoiled." Father Jack was a shoe salesman, always seeking his big break. From age four, Dutch, as his parents called him, "lived the life of a gypsy. Every year a new town, new neighbors, friends left behind. Dutch had nowhere to go—except within."

The Voice went within his family. Anna wanted him to be a cantor, like her Dad, "really, Birmingham's first Jewish leader. I got my voice and love of stories from him." Abraham Leibowitz sang at European synagogues. "I hoped that Mel'd be a singer or concert violinist" until he nearly severed the left forefinger paring a peach. Mom declared that her eldest would now play coronet.

Instead, Julius carted them to Sylacauga, Alabama, back to Johns, and later Bessemer, a large steel-producing city, opening a ladies apparel shop. Anna ran a family, modeled clothes, and made hats for, among others, touring actress Lillian Russell. Luck ran south—literally. One farmer bought goods with a deed to land in Florida. "Who'd ever use that thing to live in a swamp?" Julius said, losing it. Mel laughed: "Today it's prime real estate—Miami Beach. He was a wonderful guy, always chasing the Golconda."

Bessemer's economy caved after World War I. Dad sold his store, moving to Cordova in rural Walker County. The Ku Klux Klan had half-a-million members in Indiana. The Deep South had many more. "People began to boycott our new store," said Mel. "The Klan had a blacklist." One night the sheets rode. Noting a doctor's shoes, Anna twitted him next day. "My, didn't you look wonderful sitting so straight in your saddle?"

A hernia and bleeding ulcer put Julius in a hospital. Several Klansmen visited with a bouquet. "Isn't this a great sight?" Mom said, casing the room. "We have a Jewish intern, a Presbyterian minister, in a Catholic hospital—and the Ku Klux Klan." Shopping for Passover, she entered a Cordova store. Around its stove sat a mayor, preacher, and lawyer.

"How's Mr. Israel?" one inquired.

"He's fine," she said.

"Out shopping. You expecting some company?"

"Yes."

"With Mr. Israel in the hospital, is it a man?"

"Indeed it is," she burned. "I am told it's Jesus Christ, and there's only one house in town noble enough for Him to stay."

The business went belly-up. Surprisingly, several Klansmen asked the Israels to stay. "We've come to know you," one said, "and you're a different kind of Jew."

"There's only one kind," snapped Anna. Mel took to selling men's clothing on the road.

"For a decade Dad became a traveling salesman," he later said. "It wasn't easy. We'd always be moving": Greensboro, Toledo, Detroit, Birmingham. From eleven to fifteen, The Voice went to four different schools.

Baseball was the constant: an itinerant's link to the outside. At 2½, Mel saw his first game, in Birmingham, with Pop. "Allen, who liked to talk even then," said the *New York Daily News,* "came home chattering to his mother about peanuts and popcorn." Mom couldn't grasp missing meals, saving money for a glove, or at eleven batboying in the Piedmont League. "The Greensboro Patriots," Mel explained. "Jim Turner was a pitcher. Later [1942] he joined the Yankees, like most pitchers having a long memory of my time on the bench."

After school, Allen delivered dry cleaning on roller skates. Daily, he posted scores on the cigar store blackboard. "Even then, baseball!" Anna said. "Never enough time for music or class." One day the school principal knocked on her door. "My God, he's been expelled!" she thought. "Let me fall down dead on this spot and I will welcome it." The principal had come not to expel but praise. Said Larry: "Mel had been elected by citizens to serve in Raleigh as North Carolina lieutenant governor for a day."

Before long the Israels trained to relatives in Detroit. "Joe Louis now lived there, having come from Alabama," Mel said. "He became the Brown Bomber, and me the Voice of the Bronx Bombers." Daily, he heard the Tigers Voice say, "Good afternoon, boys and girls, this is [Edwin] Ty Tyson speaking to you from Navin Field," with its steep seats, rightfield overhang, short lines, and gaping alleys. Soon "there wasn't an afternoon," wrote the *Detroit Free Press*'s Bob Latshaw, "that you could avoid his voice."

Flat and dry, Tyson—"He's the one who got me hooked on broadcasting," said Allen—pealed the "[born in] Tyrone [Pennsylvania] Tradition." Leon Goslin—"Goose"—flapped his arms while chasing pops. Hank Greenberg became "Hankus Pancus." Charlie Gehringer was a strong, silent type: "The Mechanical Man." Roomie Chief Hogsett asked for salt. No answer. Finally: "What'd I say wrong?" Charlie: "You could have pointed." At twelve, Mel pointed at getting in for free.

"For a while I sold soda for admission. That didn't last long; I wasn't strong and the case was too heavy." Worse, a boss saw him eyeing the field. "He fired me. I was a lousy huckster." One day Allen ripped a finger with a rusty nail and took antitetanus serum. A Tiger homered. The Voice fainted: weak, or a Yankees fan? "The drama and serum didn't mix."

In 1948, retiring Babe Ruth's number, Mel introduced the cancer-wrecked superstar at Yankee Stadium. In 1926, for the only time, he saw Babe play.

Ending the eighth inning, Ruth caught a fly, smirked at teammates, and entered the dugout—"the *Tigers* dugout!" boomed Allen—for the top of the ninth.

"Where were the umpires?" a writer said.

"Babe wasn't due to bat. Anyway, this was the Sultan of Swat. He could do anything he liked." Detroit led, 10–2. New York batted around. Ruth then left the dugout, got a stick from the Yanks bench, and—"this is the God's honest truth"—went deep.

"Yankees win! The crowd couldn't believe it," said Mel, head bobbing like Louis Armstrong's. "But then, neither could I."

Mark Twain vowed to go to Cincinnati for the Apocalypse because it was always twenty years behind the time. "Its certain stately and also sleepy quality [John Gunther]" also lulled Alabama. Mel often revisited where, caught between puberty and adulthood, he grasped the "Forgotten Americans. Farmers. Shopkeepers," said a writer. "People with an inbred respect for authority and an unyielding belief in the American Dream." First, though, he went to college, then removal to a city where prose and baseball merged.

Tennessee Williams called the 1930s "that quaint period when the huge middle class of America was matriculating into a school of the blind." Unknowingly, in 1928 Allen matriculated at a school for his voice: the University at Alabama at Tuscaloosa. "I'd lettered in three high school sports, but I couldn't win one in football here because I was smaller than older kids." Known as Skyrocket—"I got kidded about my age [fifteen]"—the freshman tried baseball. The first day eight balls went through his legs. "I have been sympathetic to victims of such experiences since."

Mel became baseball student manager—"my consolation prize"— a political science major and speech minor, and A– student, missing Phi Beta Kappa because of a C in mathematics. In Illinois, Reagan's father opened a "Fashion [Shoe] Boutique." Allen's moved to Tuscaloosa "because there wasn't enough money to put Mel in a dormitory. All I could afford was to put a roof over his head."

Saturday night The Voice sold shoes at Brown's Dollar Store. "On a good night I'd take five dollars home. Then my parents got worried I was into too much": intramural baseball, annual magazine, sports editor (student newspaper and annual), debate (facing

Georgia, Georgia Tech, and LSU), and drama (Black Friars, similar to Harvard's Hasty Pudding Society).

Shakespeare said, "The play's the thing." The lead in *Hamlet* ultimately decided that he required a different type of resume. "Since both the baseball field and stage seemed beyond me," Mel said, "the idea of portraying the spellbinding attorney for the defense caught on."

He did "these extracurricular things because I liked them." Later they forged a career impossible to guess at or foretell.

In 1932, Allen graduated, entered university law school, and began $5.00-a-week clerking. Unemployment topped thirteen million. More than 25 percent of the workforce was out of work. Every state had either closed its banks or reduced their capacity to act. America crossed Dogpatch and Dante's Lower Room.

On March 4, 1933, Franklin Roosevelt took office. "First of all," he countered, "let me reassert my firm belief that the only thing we have to fear is fear itself." Seas didn't part. Curtains, however, spread. FDR still stirs the New Deal and Good War and "headmaster's admonition," wrote John Dos Passos, "the bedside doctor's voice that spoke to . . . all of us." At the time, Mel was mesmerized. "I'd hear him on radio coming out of the library, or in a professor's home. It was like a blanket, warm and reassuring," bundling a listener against despair.

FDR dubbed Al Smith "the Happy Warrior." Mel would have been happy to tie tort, brief, and case. "I began clerking because I needed the money," he said. "But I also thought it was my ticket to a law firm." Then, in August 1935, Alabama's and Auburn University's radio football Voice, leaving ten days before the season, bought a ticket out of town.

Desperate, the Birmingham CBS outlet affiliate called Crimson Tide coach Frank Thomas. The former Notre Dame quarterback flashed a canary smile. "Don't worry. We got somebody who knows the game [writing Thomas's radio show script] and can broadcast football here."

Mel grinned half a century later. "I'd started doing public address announcing," tying yard and time and substitution. "All Frank knew was that I'd done PA"—to Thomas, radio—"so that he responded in the affirmative." It was a point upon which The Voice would never double back.

At twenty-one, he had never called down a down. "I wasn't really interested, but it was a sure $5.00 a game if I got the job. Only thing I knew 'bout football was what I'd learned from McNamee and Ted Husing," CBS's 1930s icon. "Everybody patterned themselves after them." At WBRC, Mel, wowing the station manager, re-created part of Graham's 1927 Alabama-Stanford Rose Bowl. "I won the audition," and then, "'course, I found out later I was the only one *to* audition."

Allen memorized each roster, was "so green I didn't know you had a spotter," and the first Saturday "pulled a rock": Losing a play, he called third down, second. "So while they're in the huddle, I made up a phantom play and ran it into the line for no gain." Despite its size, the 1,000-watt outlet "got complaints about the five-down sequence. I've never tried to take an audience since."

Listener Pete Jarman Jr., didn't mind. "I enjoyed Melvin Israel's broadcast of the Alabama football game and sincerely hope that he will broadcast more," he wrote, "since he will evidently possess much talent along the line." It led to a $1,800 speech-teaching fellowship: better, Mel jibed, than $5.00 clerking. "At midterm he'd say, 'As of now few of you'd pass,'" mused brother Larry. "It made 'em work." One student found class less ooh-ah than off-tackle. Fifty-five years later Mel found a log in his Connecticut basement.

"Look at all those A's!" *This Week In Baseball* writer Warner Fusselle whistled of Paul (Bear) Bryant.

"Yeah," Allen laughed. "They stand for absent."

Bryant graduated in 1936. Mel earned his degree, passed the Alabama bar, and got a permanent teaching post. That December he borrowed Dad's Ford, drove thirty-six hours nonstop, and took five ex-classmates to New York City. "I'd never been East, figured

I'd use Christmas for vacation. Get a little hayseed out of me, make some money."

In New Haven, he dropped Burt Levey, got a $20 fare, and visited Yale Bowl, where McNamee made third and one seem Odysseus *v.* Hercules. "I walked out in the middle, surrounded by 70,000 empty seats on a cold New England day." Taking Irving Berlin Kahn, the songwriter's nephew, to Newark, The Voice crossed the Hudson to a Husing-arranged audition.

"He'd heard me on Tulane-Alabama football, and I was intrigued by wild stories like in a windowless room you had to improvise for an hour." Instead, Allen read a symphony program to "see if I could pronounce composers' names." He got a telegram New Year's Eve 1937: "You have the job." Be careful about what you ask. "Gosh darn, it was a lark. I hadn't thought of broadcasting."

Mel returned to Birmingham, where Julius now owned the Lady's Wear Shop. CBS's offer made him and Anna hit the roof. Sacrifice, odd jobs, law school's grind—for *this*? "Just plain foolishness," said Dad. "After what you have been through, to throw it all away talking on the radio."

The network persisted. "Finish your teaching, then come up," a producer told Allen. "If it doesn't work, go home."

Finally, he yielded. "My aspiration extended to nothing beyond a six-month stopgap, after which I would return to Birmingham and start studying the case of *Jones v. Smith*."

Pop knew better: "You'll never come back. Not if you go to New York." Mel's trek lasted sixty years.

"I love France," wrote Montaigne, "so dearly that even her faults are dear to me." Driving north, Allen sensed that from Alabama he would never wander far away. ◆

# Stargazer (1937–1948)

t twenty-three, Columbia's new announcer had black hair, chestnut skin, and a frame as thin as a post. He put forth irony, a fluent phrase, and a graceful front when under pressure. The rookie was expert at social intercourse, had an open face, and wed beguiling word and boyish gesture. Such amalgams are hard to find.

Mel underplayed his talent: pizzazz, courtesy, a dramatic lilt. Broadcasting's fuel is likeability. His already ran on charm. "He wanted to please, worked like hell, and lacked meanness," said Husing, who didn't. The plowboy would cow Babylon on the Hudson; Caucasian, air a 1986 rap hit; Orthodox Jew's pipes, fill the Mormon Tabernacle. "A unifier, easy for different people to approach," 1953–56 Yankees Voice Jim Woods added. Most fell for his nice-guy air.

In New York, Allen "sensed that his name was more redolent of the CCNY gym than the outfields of mid-America," wrote J. Anthony Lukas. Problem: "This was an overwhelmingly Christian nation," Mel noted, pulling him to assimilate into a vaguely Protestant Anglo-Saxon cast. Solution: Call yourself Melvin Hall, said a friend, after a campus building. Frank Thomas urged Mel Thomas. Taking Dad's middle name, Melvin Israel became Mel Allen: the former, son explained, "not euphonious enough or easy on the ears."

Julius blew a cork, then softened. Mom, too: Mel would be home by 1938. Remaining, at any rate, was the cantor's core. Anna's father chanted the Kol Nidre; his grandson, "How about that!" An aide noted, "Less than his folks, being Jewish was only one part of his makeup. Mel was really the ultimate achievement-driven man—more American than ethnic." Reagan's youth spun an optimist; Allen's, a brooder and a worrier.

In 1953, he won a "best sportscaster" award. Congratulating him, Lindsey Nelson found The Voice blue. "It's nice, but what if I don't win it next year? They'll say I'm slipping." Dad said later, "What Mel needs is the swelled head he deserves." A partner sensed his fear "that there was only one direction left—down."

Raised in a stoic home, Allen viewed intimacy with distrust. Self-control was protective, masking kindness: thus, fear of being used. Many felt they knew the practitioner of the small town's civilities and codes. Few did. "So effervescent on the surface," said Nelson. "You had to look beneath" the man who, scoring confession, treated pain like a locked-up room.

"Mel's essence," his mother once said, softly, "is to do." To do meant treating rhetoric like the buckle of life's belt.

At eleven, I went downstairs one Sunday, turned on the console, and began listening to *My Fair Lady*. Awaking, my mother charged from her bedroom to say that I was never to hear Eliza Doolittle again.

"Why?" I asked. "We're always listening to Broadway records," including Mel's offstage game voice in 1955's *Damn Yankees*.

"Then put on the others," she said. "I don't want you listening to this."

Much later I found the reason: Rex Harrison's frequent use of a single syllable, *damn*. Anna would have nodded. "There were things you didn't do," Allen said. "Brag, condescend," or—God place the mark—profane.

Alabama's W. S. Hoole Special Collections Library contains Mel's annual law curriculum, Party Principles and Practical Politics, Holy Scriptures, and Yiddish Holiday Prayers and Books of the Bible. "Language," he would say, "puts you in control. You could draw a word picture on a World Series or Rose Bowl for sixty, seventy million people." Entering a living room, The Voice treated you like a guest.

On May 6, 1937, he interrupted *The Kate Smith Hour* to report the *Hindenburg*'s crash, then understudied Ted Husing and Robert Trout, did ads for Fred Waring, narrated daytime soap operas like *This Day Is Ours,* and hosted *Calling in CBS Foreign Correspondents,* including Edward R. Murrow and Charles Collingwood. "In college I fell asleep to big bands on radio." Now Mel opened the network at 6:00 A.M., parsed organ pieces on the nightly Wurlitzer, and introduced dance music. "Each night from eleven to one the networks changed bands" every half an hour.

"How do you do, everyone?" he said on Saturday. "For the late dancers, CBS offers Benny Goodman and his orchestra coming to you from the Manhattan Room in the Hotel Pennsylvania in New York City." The outside marquee read: "Welcome, Mel Allen."

In black tie, he eyes the bandleader: "And now what do you say we call the old *Saturday Night Swing Session* to order? What's the start going to be?"

"You just said it, Mel Allen."

Face alight, Mel swings his arms. "Well, all right then. Cut loose with the downbeat."

Once he mispronounced the ballroom Sammy Kaye was playing in. "You should have seen the stare. Hell, he was too corny for me, anyway." A friend mentioned Guy Lombardo. "Never liked him. Give me Goodman and Glenn Miller. They didn't make me dance." Later, Mel's accent turned antebellum: "Maybe as you get older you refind your roots." His voice then was clear and quick, language-in-bloom crossing place or class.

"Melvin Allen speaking," it began. "This is the Columbia Broadcasting System. Hello, there. We've been waiting for you. It's time to play *Truth or Consequences.* Say, are you the life of the party? Can you roll peanuts across a floor with one ear and carry a tune with the other? Can you step out of character and dress at the same time? Then meet that prize-winning pixilator of front-parlor pastimes. The *Truth or Consequences* man, Ralph Edwards."

Edwards grinned the smile of a man who could kiss babies, wear hats, and glad-hand with the best. "Where'd you get that one, Mel Allen?"

"It's just exactly like you wrote it, Ralph."

No one scripted the 1938 Kentucky Derby, International Polo Games, or Howard Hughes's record flight around the world. "Mel was the first to get an [July 14] interview," said Larry. Police cordoned off the aviator: Improvising, The Voice shed a barricade. Another scoop lit the day Husing called the Drake Relays from a church steeple. Subbing, Mel did the Vanderbilt Cup Auto Race— "NBC had exclusivity, so we were bootlegging coverage"—from a plane above Long Island.

At seven, Allen witnessed a man severed by a propeller in Bessemer. Now twenty-five, still afraid, he reached the airport "thinkin' I'd rather be low-down than high-up." Mel then saw his engineer's young daughter: "happy as a clam, can't wait to get in the air." Shamed, the greenhorn decided that "if she can fly, so can I"—in a DC-3, ad-libbing fifty-two minutes about boat races, tennis matches, anything he saw. Darkness delayed the race. Finally, rain postponed it. The producer had the pilot land. "He went up a kid from a turntable department," wrote Ron Powers. "He came down a star."

At twenty-five, Mel aired that fall's Series. "For some experience, they put me with [play-by-play] France Laux and Bill Dyer." CBS flagship WABC began *Mel Allen on Sports*. Recalling Alabama, "They said to keep from getting rusty I could do football," airing its first telecast (Fordham-Waynesburg State) over RCA's experimental outlet, W2XBS (later WNBC), from Triborough (later Downing, now Icahn), Stadium, September 30, 1939. Jim Crowley coached Fordham. Frank Leahy assisted. Vince Lombardi built one of its Seven Blocks of Granite. Said Allen: "Talk about your living legends."

Next week Manhattan hosted St. Bonaventure. "No spotter. We didn't know if cameras were on, or anyone was watching." Few players knew the game was televised. To Mel, even a mob wouldn't have killed the law: "I was going back to 'Bama." U.S. Tobacco Company then bid $50 for CBS's *Pick and Pat Minstrel Show*, introducing singers like Jo Stafford and Perry Como. The job paid $45. "Put together, I'm making almost $100 a week." Soon Allen began *Grand Central Station, Harry James, Glenn Miller,* and later *The Chesterfield Supper Club.*

A photo shows "horse-opera clowning at a CBS announcers party," said the *Daily News:* The Voice, in cowboy hat, western shirt, and spurs, "cavorting with the cast." Numbers clicked. "The most I'd be making clerking in Alabama was $10." Before long Allen added the Big Ballpark in The Bronx to the Ballroom at the Waldorf.

Memory, said Alexander Chase, is the thing we forget with. Mel never wished to forget this time. On soft, springy-green afternoons, the ex-batboy drove uptown to the Polo Grounds and Yankee Stadium, found an empty section, and whispered play-by-play. "I'd done football, but I'd sit and say, 'God, I'd give anything to broadcast here.'" As we shall see, God answered through soft soap, not hard sell.

In June 1938, anything worth pitching was worth repeating. The Reds Johnny Vander Meer no-hit Boston, 3–0. Four days later Ebbets Field debuted at night. "A bunch of us went from CBS to see baseball under the lights," said Mel. Vander Meer, from New Jersey, was the starter. "They even gave me a night. That's the jinx. You don't get past the third inning." Brooklyn couldn't get past selling out. "Ticket lines stretched around the block. Meanwhile, I'm warming up, sit down, up, down, up again."

Play began seventy-eight minutes late. The Dodgers were still hitless in the ninth. With two out Leo Durocher lined barely foul. Cincinnati skipper Bill McKechnie sauntered to the mound. "He wasn't about to take him out," said Allen. "Everybody'd been in an uproar since the sixth." Leo flied out—Vander Meer's second straight no-no. "Talk about a bonus. Some times every day I thought I was seeing history."

Much of New York's, alas, could only be seen, not heard.

◆ ◆ ◆

In 1934, the Big Apple's three teams inked a five-year radio ban. Much of baseball twitched with fear: Who would pay if you could hear for free? In late 1938, the National League named Reds president Larry MacPhail to save the Dodgers from insolvency. His first act was to use the wireless.

MacPhail hired a distant relative of writer Sidney Lanier from Cincinnati. "He believed in [radio's] promotional power . . . he became sold on it," said Walter Lanier (Red) Barber. The General Mills Company put Brooklyn on WOR: live, from Ebbets; away, by wire, "re-creating" a game Red never saw. WABC aired the Yankees and Giants home schedule live. "Then you'd do in studio," mused Mel, "whatever road games they had space for."

By now, the re-creation was a rite like gloves left on the field between innings. A stick on hollow wood simulated bat *v.* ball. The sound track included background murmur. Infielder: "Come on, babe, bear down." Manager: "Don't give in!" Fan: "You couldn't hit my *house!*" Not much was real. Reality: It didn't matter to Arch McDonald.

Since 1934, the Senators "Rembrandt of the Re-creation" had tied "right down Broadway" (strike), "ducks on the pond" (baserunners), and "There she goes, Mrs. Murphy" (Senators home run). Upon a key save, catch, or "our boys" hit, Washington, brace thyself: The ex-butcher, crophand, soda jerk, fight referee, oil rigger, and patent medicine man sang a hillbilly ballad, "They Cut Down the Old Pine Tree."

McDonald filled a People's drug store three blocks from the White House. "He'd stand beside a second-floor window with these homey sayings," Mel laughed. "Folks on the sidewalk'd roar." Like clockwork his Nats dredged the second division. Paying $400,000 for Jints/Stripes rights, General Mills lured him to New York. "People there knew his reputation," said The Voice. Arch, in turn, knew Wheaties, a broadcast imperative of the time.

"General Mills," mused Allen, "liked announcers who'd done games elsewhere in their style." Going deep begot "It's into

Wheatiesville!" A batter rounded second base. "Man, what Wheaties does for you—Vitamins A through Z!" The dugout greeted him: "Wheaties—go get 'em! Man, look at that reception! You eat Wheaties, too!" The Old Pine Tree did, year after year.

"McDonald was country, not at all like New York," wrote the *Washington Star*'s Morris Siegel. General Mills didn't care. He could shill the Breakfast of Champions. Surely, that would suffice. "I couldn't wait for Arch to get here," said Allen, nor replace him at Griffith Stadium. "Wheaties asked me to audition. Several days later they said, 'Mel, go down to Washington.'"

For a moment he nearly forgot how the Senators swam in catatonia and disarray.

At twenty-six, The Voice readied for Georgetown and Embassy Row and Lafayette Park: too, Opening Day's bandstand of nostalgia, faith, and myth. "All that ceremony, the bands, President Roosevelt throwing out the first pitch," Mel said of his unorthodox, overhanded lob. FDR was "that man," hated by "economic royalists," a "traitor to his class." Other classes, loving him, gave Roosevelt forty-six states in 1936 to Alf Landon's two. "As Maine goes, so goes Vermont," jeered aide James Farley. As McDonald went, so did Mel.

One day in 1939, Walter Johnson entered Nats owner Clark Griffith's office, having thrown a record 110 shutouts, pitched 55⅔ straight scoreless innings, and ten times won 20 or more games. Something about him lured warmth and adulation. "He captured the imagination of the public as no pitcher before or since," said Mel. "The Babe Ruth of the mound." Seeing him, Clark's bell went off: the Big Train, on Nats radio! "It's a thrill to lose out to Washington's biggest hero. I lost my job before I called a pitch."

In May, McDonald's sidekick began a Yanks Ivory Soap commercial. Allen heard him at the WABC studio. "And now, ladies," said Garnett Marks, coyly, "I want you to get up close to your radio set. I want to talk to you about Ovary Soap." Misspeaking, he laughed, failed again to say "Ivory," chuckled, failed again, and was fired.

The Voice settled in—this time for real. "Guess which soap I still use?" he beamed half a century later. On June 12, Mel manned CBS's coverage of the Hall of Fame dedication. Postmaster General Farley attended; Landis bought the first sheet of stamps. That November McDonald cut a path back to Washington. "He might or might not have worked in New York," said Griffith. "Arch didn't like it enough to find out."

By 1940, his number 2 "won [McDonald's] job against the competition of most of the country's outstanding baseball announcers," read the *Times*. "Only 27, [Mel] is the nation's youngest big-league radio reporter"—and among "the 13 [under thirty-one] most successful men in the country" given the New York Advertising Club's "Order of the Rake." In every way, as Allen, raised up by the calendar, so far, so fast, too fast, he worried, for his own good, became Voice of the *New York Yankees*, a season of excess dawned.

"Thinking back, I still sometimes don't believe it," he said, slowly. "A guy made a mistake and gets canned. Arch dislikes his new city. They pick me to succeed him. Sometimes I sit around Yankee Stadium and it hits me. Everything worked out—everything *had* to—for me to get a chance."

Nick Mileti was the Cleveland Indians 1972–75 owner. "My years in college," he stated, "were the finest of my life. What was unusual was that I knew so then." Allen knew. He did not know that the getting that was good was about to get even better.

Between 1939 and 1948 nine big-league teams won at least a single pennant. The other seven made the first division. Hailing and prizing the time—last to have a .400 hitter or the Indians win a World Series; first, black big-leaguer, one-armed outfielder, and postseason playoff; first/last, "Subway [sic Streetcar] Series" west of the Mississippi and batter hit safely in 56 straight games—you recall stories in which baseball has been rich. None told more than Allen—since most involved the Yanks.

"People said rooting for the Yankees was like rooting for U.S. Steel," wrote Robert Creamer. "Nonsense. There's nothing as wonderful as a team that wins." In 1990, the HBO network aired *When It Was a Game.* "In a 29-year span from 1936 to 1964, the Yankees won twenty-two pennants and sixteen world titles . . . without a doubt, the most successful and recognizable team in all of sport. Once a player put on the pinstripes, no other uniform could possibly fit as well."

Already a Yankee to his pinstriped underwear, Mel loved their then-71,699 seat Basilica on City Plot 2106, Lot 100, in the southern Bronx, bought for $600,000 in 1921 by Jacob Ruppert and Till Huston from William Waldorf Astoria. "Even before '39, I'd sat there a hundred times." Steel girded three decks. A Roman facade trimmed the upper. The grandstand wrapped home plate beyond the bases. Bleachers trimmed the fence. The effect was august: Allen referenced *The* Yankee Stadium.

"From the plain of the Harlem River it looks up like the Great Pyramid of Cheops from the sands of Egypt," wrote *Literary Digest.* Mel's take was workaday. "From wherever you started, it was worth the trip." Roads knit The Stadium to New Haven, Rye, and Valley Stream. The number 4 subway train, on elevated tracks, glimpsed interior shadows, long and short distances, and high and low walls. Bull pens split the bleachers and grandstand. An overhang screened flys. Backdrops vied: from centerfield, home plate; box seats, apartments, and water tower; "my booth," said Allen, "folks filling the distant rows."

Numbers would change, said a friend, when one plus one equaled three: 301 feet (leftfield pole), 402 (left side, left-center bull pen gate), 415 (right side), 457 (deep left-center), 461 (center), 407 (deep right-center), 344 (right side, right-center bull pen gate), 296 (right pole). It paid to pull: Wall heights were 4 feet, lines; 8 feet, near the pens; 14½, right-center. One shape fit all. "You'd see a pitchers duel, then next day a slugfest," said Mel. "Anything could happen." With the Stripes, it did.

◆ ◆ ◆

Their "House That Ruth Built" opened April 18, 1923: Bombers 4, Boston 1. Himself went deep. "Babe's drawing power erected the park," wrote Joseph Durso. Ruppert "tailor-made it for his pokes."

The Voice saw humor everywhere in life's absurdities and possibilities. An exception was his hero-worship of Yanks lore, fact, and fib. In 1943, they had Mel accompany Ruth to events in the Tri-State area. A guest is said to need no introduction. That was *literally* true of Babe. "I'm sitting in his Cadillac and he's speaking in his outgoing personality like he knew me for years." It was, Allen said, like talking to God.

More sensual than theological, Ruth bound brass and guile. "In truth, as the years pass," wrote Ron Fimrite, "[he] does not seem so much mortal as part of our mythology," inherently tied to glut. Breakfast might mean two steaks, beer and bourbon, a dozen eggs, and slab of ham. "Boy," mate Joe Dugan said, "when he hit one, you could hear it all over the park. The sound when he'd get a hold of one—it was different, that's all." Babe played harder, hit longer, and cursed better than any player of his time.

"I knew his records by heart by the time I got there," said Allen. They bespeak a hyperbolic/larger is finer/Ruthian bent: suspension (five, 1922), fine ($5,000, 1925, for insubordination), salary ($80,000, 1930), slugging (.690, career), and homers (season, 60; career, 714). The big guy—6'2" and 215—was a big-gamer (ten Series, .326, 15 taters, and 33 RBI). "What I didn't know was all the stories." Most still make Ruth's coffin rise.

Superstitious, he slumped for several weeks. "So Babe stuffs me into a locker with orders to stay there, then homers twice," said 1930–31 roommate Jimmie Reese. "For four days, I stood in that hot box until the streak ran out."

Freed, he crashed into Babe on a fly. Mates tended Ruth. Reese lay in blood. "I was praying. If the big ape doesn't get up, I'm thrown out of New York."

Instead, the sunny-dark superstar threw him to a manager, Philadelphian by birth and Victorian by bent. "Like so many players," said Allen of Joe McCarthy, "I was in awe."

Marse Joe never played in the majors, but played them like a bass. "Twenty-four years managing, never out of the first division," wrote the New York *Herald Tribune*'s Harold Rosenthal. "A .614 percentage—all-time best." The Yankees 1931–46 skipper won eight pennants and a record seven Series. "A lot of Irish in him," Mel said, "and was a stern disciplinarian. But I also found him fair." Temper menaced jobs, arms, legs, and jaws. Few doubted that Joe was hard.

"To someone breaking in, he was incredibly accessible. 'Don't worry about Murderers Row. We win on defense two ways'": Yanks gloves hurt a rival; harried, its fielding fell. The Bombers also knew the rules. A two-men-on-base pop neared the mound. Frank Crosetti whistled, Joe Gordon slowed, and Tommy Henrich trapped it. "By delaying the infield fly, they got a double play."

Allen fixed his soft, large eyes. "Pride, dignity. McCarthy instilled it in his players. If a guy wasn't hustling, another'd say, 'You're taking money out of my pocket, you so and so.' They took their lead from Joe."

"What's the score?" McCarthy bayed at a player in the dugout.

Another, sitting, stretched his arms. "Where the hell do you think you are, a canoe?"

Joe threw out a clubhouse card table. Slurring a black patron, infielder Ben Chapman was cashiered. "Didn't matter what he was hitting," said Mel. "Joe rejected him as a Yankee."

Some called McCarthy push-button; others, a paladin. To more, Allen became baseball's Zelig, especially with the man Marse Joe felt a son.

In 1923, superscout Paul Krichell returned to The Stadium after seeing Columbia's Lou Gehrig play Rutgers. "I think," he told general manager Ed Barrow, "I saw another Ruth today." Gehrig pinch-hit for New York June 1, 1925. Next day first baseman Wally Pipp braved a headache; whereupon manager Miller Huggins put Lou at first; after which the Iron Horse scored and drove in 100 or more runs, including a league record 184, thirteen straight years. "Every day, any day," said mate Bill Dickey, "he just goes out and does his job."

Gehrig's 1938 was his worst year since 1925: .295, 29 home runs, and 114 RBI. "Just a slump," Mel thought. "We figured he'd get over it." In 1939, Mary Martin sang "My Heart Belongs to Daddy." John Steinbeck wrote *The Grapes of Wrath.* Mickey Rooney huckstered *Huckleberry Finn.* The Yanks won Opening Day, 2–0: Lou's and Ted Williams's sole same-game. Gehrig made a boot, hit into two double plays, and swung like still frames of a motion picture. One day a ball was hit between first base and the mound. "Lou muffed it, all thumbs, no coordination. Something was wrong."

The homestand ended Sunday. "I knew I ought to get out," said Gehrig later. "I came up four times with men on base, and a hit any time would have won the game. But I left [five] on." That night, at home near New Rochelle, he mulled the enemy within: amyotrophic lateral sclerosis, a hardening and collapsing of the spinal cord. Monday the Stripes trained to Detroit. Next morning Lou waited for McCarthy in the lobby of the Book-Cadillac Hotel. "You'd better take me out," the captain said.

"Oh, Lou, you'll get over it," said Joe, heart breaking. "Come on, let me put you in."

Lou refused: It was over. "I can't go on like this." Shuffling, he took the lineup card to home plate. "Ladies and gentlemen," pealed the PA announcer, "this is the first time without Lou Gehrig's name in the Yankee lineup in [a bigs record] 2,130 consecutive games."

The crowd gasped, then stilled. Mel teared in the WABC studio. In the dugout, Lefty Gomez, crying, put an arm around his friend. "Aw, come on, Lou, cut it out," said the cut-up pitcher. "It took 'em fifteen years to get you out of the lineup. When I pitch, often it only takes fifteen minutes."

◆ ◆ ◆

John F. Kennedy called the presidency "the vital center of action." Baseball's—The Stadium, The Home of Champions—has housed 37 of 39 Yanks flags, all 26 world titles, 37 Hall of Famers, and its Gettysburg Address.

On July 4, 1939, the team retired number 4 between games of a doubleheader. McDonald was master of ceremonies. "Some may think I've been given a bad break," said Gehrig, "but I've got an awful lot to live for." The peroration wed sweetest song and saddest thought: "I consider myself the luckiest man on the face of the earth."

Later a *Daily News* photograph garbed Mel's home: YANKS SPLIT, LOU WEEPS, WHILE 61,808 FANS CHEER. It showed McCarthy, hat off; Gehrig, head bowed; Clark Griffith, weeping; but not baseball's Hertz, grasping Avis. "It shocked people when Babe hugged him. A rift had developed because of Lou's mother and Babe's wife. Each let the feud grow," said Allen, citing a story from 1931.

One night Reese and Gehrig played Babe and Harry Rice in bridge. "Lou was a conditioning stickler," said Jimmie. At midnight, he led by $1.25. "'I quit,' Gehrig said. 'I'm going to bed. We've got a game tomorrow.' Exhibition was all."

Ruth reddened. "You quit, I'm going to tear the [score] sheet up."

Gehrig: "What do you think, Jimmie?"

Reese: "Anything you want."

Lou: "All right, we'll play one more game," winning. Down $2.50, Babe again vowed to tear the sheet. Lou finally called his bluff.

Ruth "had to have the final word," said Mel. Reese died in 1994. The Bambino never paid. In 1940, Gehrig took a job with New York City, on occasion taking a limousine to the park. Word quickly reached the players. "'Lou, Lou, the Captain's coming,'" said Allen.

Once Gehrig sat alone on the bench with Mel during infield practice. Turning, he patted The Voice's knee. "You know, I never got a chance to hear you broadcasting 'cause I was always playing," he said. "But I got to tell you, it's the only thing that kinda keeps me going."

Allen excused himself, found a runway, and sobbed.

◆ ◆ ◆

Gehrig died June 2, 1941. Eighteen days earlier Joe DiMaggio singled at Comiskey Park. Soon every radio, corner bar, and paper sang his streak. Ultimately, DiMag's season rivaled Joe Wood's 1912, Mickey Mantle's 1956, or Mark McGwire's 1998. Amazed, Mel was not surprised. "I'd seen him at Yankee Stadium, day after day."

In 1936, the rookie tied .323, 29 homers, 125 RBI, and great center field. "I get credit," laughed Gomez. "Before me, they never knew he could go back on a ball." Joe caught a Hank Greenberg belt behind the centerfield flagpole. In 1937, Hancus Pancus hit another not even No. 5 could reach. "I was there," The Voice said, "and couldn't believe it—first in center's seats."

DiMag led the league in runs, homers, bases, and slugging— but could he bunt? "I don't know," barbed McCarthy, "nor do I intend to find out."

The Giants would have liked to. Instead, the Yanks won a second straight World Series. Next year they swept Chicago: CBS's Mel, doing color. By coincidence, The Stadium staged the 1939 All-Star Game a week after Gehrig's ode. Six Bombers started, including DiMaggio, homering. Said Allen: "pinstripes on parade." Joe tethered 30 homers, 126 RBI, and .381—last A.L. righty to clear .380. Was there ever a more hull-up man?

"God, you're beating the Browns 22–1. Why are you running around like a lunatic?" DiMag was asked.

"Because maybe there's somebody here who never saw me play."

Wright Morris wrote of Norman Rockwell, "His special triumph is in the conviction his countrymen share that the mythical world he evokes exists." Mythical or magical? The Yankees rarely had to choose. In 1939, they took a 3–0 game World Series lead. The closer jammed Cincinnati's tiny boomerang build on a brickyard at Western Avenue at Findlay.

New York hit in a 4-all tenth. "What happened next," said Mel, "was never explained." Charlie Keller dazed Reds catcher Ernie Lombardi in a collision. "The ball came up [on a throw] and hit

Ernie in the cup. Folks think he slept. Actually, he was paralyzed, the ball rolled away, and the pitcher didn't back up": Stripes, 7–4. Next year a fan had a brainstorm. "Have Lombardi sell coffee. He's a walking advertisement for caffeine."

Walking on the field, said Joe D, "we felt the other team didn't have a chance." Barber and Bob Elson, each a prim and orderly lector, called the schnooze in Mutual Radio's first year of Series exclusivity. "I could wait," Allen said of making October as winsome as a smile.

For a long time—1931–65, to be precise—the commissioner, radio/television network, and sponsor, usually the Gillette Company, chose play-by-play and color men for the Series and All-Star Game. Elson—"The Old Commander" (Navy 1942–45)—did the 1930–39 Classics. "Judge Landis was my friend," he conceded. "It gave me the inside track."

Gillette feared a slow track in 1940. "I'm not sure these clubs [Detroit and Cincinnati] will sell safety razors," said its ad czar, A. Craig Smith. Interest might demand southern expatriates. Smith had a team in mind.

On October 2, the Voice of the Yankees, twenty-seven, and Mississippi-born Voice of the Dodgers, thirty-two, of whom a Brooklyn taxi driver groused, "That Barber, he's too fair," broadcast their first game together, later speaking of common memory, distant youth, and yearning for time to stand still. "Even now, talking great announcers," said Vin Scully in 2006, "you start with them."

Red and Mel shared six World Series (1940–42, 1947, 1949, 1952). Often likened, they differed, too. Barber was white wine, crêpes suzette, and bluegrass music. Allen was hot dogs, beer, and the United States Marine Band. Like Millay, Red was a poet. Like Sinatra, Mel was a balladeer. Reserve was Barber's rosary: "Never yell. Never raise your voice. When the crowd yells, shut up." The Voice cheered even a hard-hit ground ball. "The noise pushed you up. When it shouted, so did you."

Red chatted on the small of his chair. Mel frayed its edge—"You couldn't get into a game if you leaned back"—filibustering for hours. Barber's three-minute egg timer reminded him to keep the score: "Report, not care or root. These are not the rights of the professional announcer." The Voice cleaved: "Of course, I wanted the Yankees." Many deemed Mel a Valiant. Others, aping Irving Howe, said, "We know the nightmare is ours." Ultimately, you favored one or the other.

Barber was "a professional *southerner*," said Nelson. "He used their phrases—'the catbird seat,' alien to Brooklyn—and worked at being a personality." Allen, on the other hand, was "as Southern as Uncle Remus." A pop fly became "a can of corn"; waist pitch, "thigh high"; full count, "three and two, what'll he do?" Even "How about that!" was regional, not personal. "A common Southern expression," Mel said. "It amazed me that the rest of the country came to think I invented it."

John Hutchens was then-*Times* book editor. "Barber was a good straightaway announcer. Allen had some screwy phrases." Future *Washington Post* writer Leonard Shapiro grew up in Flatbush. "There was only one way to feel about Mel. You hated him." Nat Allbright later re-created games on the Brooklyn Dodgers Radio Network. "Red was aw-shucks. Allen had a certain something that made you want to listen." Raised near New Haven, Red Sox Voice Joe Castiglione heard each. "You can have all the reviews you want, but Mel was the country's most famous announcer."

Barber was "less melodramatic," said Pittsburgh's Bob Prince. "Allen had a tremendous flair, just grabbed you." The disparity hid irony. Red was "a loner," contrary to his cornfed image. The Voice was "opposite to his persona in a different way: easily hurt, with a sensitivity you didn't see." Colleague Jim Woods felt Barber a rationalist; Allen, emotional, sentimental. "Red had a larger ego," flouting another stereotype, "yet more religious. After a game, he'd go to his room. Mel would table-hop"—a friend-seeker ardent in his ardor to be liked.

"Mel had a more exuberant sense of fun. Red's humor was, well, sometimes you wondered, '*What* the hell'd he say?'"

Woods asked, "What you been up to, Red?'

"Oh, I've been killing rats."

"How do you do that?"

"You see, you kill one here and you kill one there."

Of Woods's buzz cut, Enos Slaughter cracked, "I've seen nicer heads on a possum." Evoking Barber, Jim aka The Possum bared buck teeth. "Red's a friend and I *still* don't know what the hell he meant."

In 1978, like Mel, the Redhead made Cooperstown. "Through the years," said Associated Press's Barry Wilner, "the great baseball one-two punches have been Ruth-Gehrig, Snider-Hodges, Aaron-Mathews, Mantle-Maris, Mays-McCovey. Perhaps the greatest tandem in the sport, however, never hit a home run or ran the bases . . . two men who at times were more familiar to the people they broadcast games to than the names of the players on the field."

Red or Mel? Hope or Crosby? "Either way you got greatness," said Lindsey Nelson. That was also true of The Voice's team.

"Unlike an actor, whose lines have been written for him and who has memorized them, though with a privilege of throwing in an occasional ad-lib, in our profession you are describing it as it happens," said Allen of *ex tempore* material. "The great writers have an opportunity once an event is over to sit down and compose their thoughts . . . Ours is one [where] a script is being written with every word."

Nineteen-forty-one's made faces harden, strangers jabber, tension creep. It began lightly, as if to confuse the audience. In February, Yanks rookie Phil Rizzuto entered Ed Barrow's office to sign a contract. "I didn't know Barrow. I did know that the man being shaved by a guy whom he kept calling Goulash was Barrow."

Phil sat silently till Goulash finished shaving. "Young man, what is your trouble?" Ed barked.

"Mr. Barrow, I'd like a little more money, please."

"I give you this and no more. If OK, sign. If not, get the hell out of here." Rizzuto signed, winning seven Series from 1941 to 1956.

"You forget Scooter was so small as a player," said DiMag. "Maybe it's because his reputation later got so huge." That March, Joe, Dickey, and Red Ruffing gave him the cold shoulder. Upset, Phil asked Gomez if he had done something wrong. Relax, Lefty told the 5-foot-5 shortstop, "They're not snubbing you, they just haven't seen you yet."

June 29, 1941: Stripes take the lead for good. June 29: DiMag hits safely in an A.L.–record forty-second straight game. July 3: His homer breaks Wee Willie Keeler's bigs consecutive game streak (44, 1897). Any day: Les Brown and his Orchestra, playing, "He'll live in baseball's Hall of Fame. He got there blow by blow. Our kids will tell their kids his name—Joltin' Joe DiMaggio."

Hits kept coming; dots, connecting. "Some people could outdo Joe in every department of the game," said Allen. "But he was always way up there, plus what never appears in the box score: leadership." In a close game, Mel often saw Phil turn around to look at center field.

On July 17, the future three-time MVP, Mr. Coffee, and Greatest Living Ballplayer played in Cleveland. Twice third baseman Ken Keltner made a sprawling stop. In the eighth inning, "Sixty-seven thousand [67,648] fans here at Municipal Stadium . . . to see if Joe DiMaggio can keep his fifty-six-game hitting streak alive!" said Mel, recreating. "Jim Bagby on the mound works the count to one and one. A runner on first base. Here's the pitch. Joe DiMaggio swings! There's a ground ball to short to Lou Boudreau. He flips the ball to Grannie Mack for one out. The relay to Grimes at first . . . It's in time for a double play! Joe DiMaggio's fifty-six-game hitting streak is stopped."

For the heck of it, he hit in the next sixteen.

New York clinched in Game 136, baseball's earliest terminative. The World Series again blared two broadcast Dixiecrats. Both knew its cast. On September 25, the Dodgers won their first flag since the last full year of Woodrow Wilson's presidency. Said Mel, by contrast, "We were sort of used to winning, not that it became routine." 

In Brooklyn, the Classic further crazed a Flatbush of the mind. "Just being there was amazing," said then-rookie shortstop Pee Wee Reese. Players rode the subway. Backslapping filled the street. "You joked with people on a first-name basis. Ebbets Field was like entering a bar and saying, 'Hi, Ben,' or 'How you doing, Joe?' The damn stands were on top of you"—a Gestalt, even now.

Most of 32,111 seats had a good view—if you weren't behind a post. Left-center field draped the pitcher. A cement wall/scoreboard/wire screen decked right. Housewife Hilda Chester waved a cowbell in the bleachers. Behind first, straw-hatted Jake the Butcher roared "Late again!" of a pickoff. The Dodger Sym-Phony was a faintly musical group. "Their specialty," said *Newsday*'s Steve Jacobson, "was piping a visiting strikeout victim back to his bench with a tune *The Army Duff.* [Because] the last beat was timed for the moment the player's butt touched," he might belatedly sit down. "The Sym-Phony still had that last beat ready."

Until 1898, the borough was an independent city. Incorporated into New York, it still felt like a Nation-State. "Manhattan had skyscrapers, wealth, and fame," said Red. "The only way Brooklyn could strike back was with their club, for which fate had favored me." If "a million people saw the Bums, ten million heard Barber," wrote Robert Creamer. "You could walk the length of the beach of Coney Island," said the *Daily News*, "or the length of any Brooklyn street, and never lose his voice."

Red's mound became a "pulpit." The pitcher "tied the hitter up—turned him every way but loose." The sky "is a beautiful robin-egg blue with, as the boys say, very few angels in the form of clouds." Patter wed "tearin' up the pea patch" and "rhubarb on the field" and "FOB: Full of Brooklyns." A field was "the sun garden"; bat, "a dirty brown-looking stick"; score, "as tight as a brand new pair of shoes on a rainy day." Said Creamer: "The language he used . . . became part of everyone's speech."

MacPhail knew how "radio [made a game] played by two teams," said Red, "a contest involving personalities who had families, troubles, blue or brown eyes." The first Dodgers-Yanks Subway Series commenced October 1: Stradivarius or Gatling Gun, the mikemen fenced above the field. Games 1-2 split. The event crossed into Brooklyn: game and lead, Stripes, 2–1. "We're down but not worried," puffed manager Leo Durocher, "'cause we're home and got that crowd." Next day Flatbush led, 4–3, in the ninth. Hugh Casey got two Yanks, went 3–2 on Henrich, then "threw, if you're in Brooklyn," said Allen, "the pitch from hell."

Strike three eluded Tommy, umpire Larry Goetz, and catcher Mickey Owen. "It's rolling back to the screen," Mel reeled. "Tommy Henrich races down toward first base! He reaches it safely! And the Yankees are still alive with Joe DiMaggio coming up to bat!" DiMag singled. Keller doubled off the rightfield wall. Dickey walked. Joe Gordon doubled: 7–4, New York.

Owen vaulted hidebound into baseball's galaxy of goats. "The condemned jumped out of the chair," a writer said, "and electrocuted the warden." A day later the Bombers won their fifth world title since 1936. The Cathedral of the Underdog played a tired and humbled dirge.

In 1940, Joe Bolton and actor J. C. Flippen were Mel's Giants and Yankees analyst, respectively. Another actor's contract mandated a week off each October. "Bill Frawley'd be at the Series, loved to talk baseball," said Larry Allen. "He even talked about joining us. We laid out the pros and cons." As TV's Fred Mertz, Bill collared a curmudgeon's dream. In 1942, Allen—"[already] known as 'Colonel' to millions of fans throughout the East," said *TSN*—collared Columbus's Triple-A announcer.

"Hey, come on board," he told Connie Desmond. The Victorians called cloudless spells "Queen's Weather." Diction, command, and a golden voice lit Desmond's, who then joined Barber in 1943. Connie said: "I never thought of replacing him. Why would he leave?" In 1953, the earth turned flat: sober, Desmond might have succeeded Red. Instead, he took the future—and flushed it down a flask.

The Yanks history wrote much of 1942's. An Army Emergency Relief exhibition jammed The Stadium: Walter Johnson threw batting practice; Ruth hit the seats. "At the Waldorf-Astoria," Allen's notes record, "[I] was co-auctioneer with [ex-Mayor] Jimmy Walker and Red Barber . . . sold Yankee-Dodger-Giant players for $124,000,000 in 30 minutes." A record nine Stripes made the All-Star Game. The 106–48 Cardinals won their league. Reading any of New York's thirteen English-speaking dailies—"They had, how shall I put it, an attitude," said The Voice—you barely expected St. Louis to show up.

The Series started at Sportsman's Park. Allen readied, "microphone close to my chest, as was my custom, hoping to call the play a split second before the roar." He imagined "one solitary fan— Ralph Edwards taught me this—who I pictured sitting a few feet away from me. In my mind, that one guy was my audience. I was talking to him."

At breakfast, The Voice had read a *TIME* magazine article, "Fifty Million Ears." In U.S. drugstores, "lunch wagons, barbershops, parlors, and pool halls, over 25 million radio listeners will cock their ears to listen to three men [Mel, Red, and Bill Corum]—the sportscasting trio that broadcasts the World Series." To Mel, the "solitary fan" seemed a brood.

He forged a Jimmy Carter smile. "As you know, I like to talk, but now I'm terrified. I bumble along before I get my wits." The Series began on cue: Stripes, 7–4. The Cards then plucked four straight. Wrote Frank Graham: "The Yankees have finally found a team they can't frighten half to death just by walking out onto the field, and taking a few swings in batting practice."

He did not mean the team at Coogan's Bluff.

The Yankees being the Yankees, it was easy to forget that Mel then called another club. "The leagues staggered their schedule so that both teams were never home at the same time. When the Yanks were away, I'd go uptown and do the Giants live."

Allen took a cab, car, or Independent Line D subway train to the 155th Street station. The Polo Grounds had a wacky name (polo was never played here; 1891–1957 and 1962–63 baseball was), burlesque shape (bathtub, or rectangular), and patchwork of girders, pigeon stoops, and roofed bullpen shacks. "In lower stands, protective screen in back of home plate can be visual nuisance," *Sports Illustrated* later wrote. "Field boxes along foul lines distort view of diamond." In the first-tier press box, Mel had the best seat in the house.

"Centerfield bleachers are binocular territory": 505 feet, later 483. Phone booth lines (left, 279; right, 258) earned the snarl "Polo Grounds home run." A 21-foot overhang made left field closer. "Actually," said Allen, "because of the ball's trajectory, it was only 250." Drainage reeked. The outfield sloped. Drives vanished in each corner beyond the boxes. "If the old-style parks meant personality," said Harold Rosenthal long after it became an apartment complex, "this park was the person of its time."

The Jints had personalized the past quarter century: 1930: Bill Terry hit .401. 1932–38: Five times Mel Ott led the league in taters. 1933–37: Carl Hubbell was 115–50. The team won, among others, the 1917, 1921–24, 1933, and 1936–37 pennants. "It was the Broadway actors club," mused Allen, "going back to [ten-flag manager] John McGraw." A larger time was ending, though he could not know so then.

In 1938, the Third Reich crushed Czechoslovakia. Next year it gutted Poland, starting World War II. "Never in my lifetime," wrote Roosevelt, "have I seen things moving . . . with more crosscurrents." The Jints were not immune. One game they hit seven homers. Another, shortstop Billy Jurges chided umpire George Magerkurth's home run call. N.L. head Ford Frick decreed screens inside each pole. "The first modern foul pole," said Barber. "No longer would umps have to guess."

On August 13, 1939, Mel called five of another seven Giants dingers. Terry, now manager, suspended second baseman Burgess Whitehead. "Next day he shows up in full uniform at Yankee Stadium," said Allen, "and asks to work out." McCarthy refused. Whitehead rejoined the Giants, jumped, and was resuspended.

"Some guys never learn," chimed The Voice. Perhaps he was alluding to America's then-isolationist core.

Slices of spring training: The Yanks left Florida, played in Texas, and parked their train at the station. "There was a close play, the runner slid, and Dickey didn't wait for the call." Like Mel, the catcher bolted for the train. "To this day I don't know whether the guy was out." In 1940, the Giants decamped for Atlanta, where Terry, from Memphis, decided to play hookey.

"I'm going home through Alabama," he told Allen. "Want a ride?"

"Goldarn, home," said The Voice. "So began the wildest ride of my life. They had a narrow two-lane road, 150 miles, with a lot of curves. Bill's going 75 or 80. He might have hit 90." Not knowing if "I was going to Heaven or Hell, I knew I wasn't going to Birmingham." He got to the Polo Grounds April 16—Opening Day.

Nazi dominoes soon littered Europe. The Jints littered the second division. Once Mel misdated their last flag, leading a listener to write. In every way, Allen pined to please. "Thanks a lot for your card in which you corrected an erroneous statement," he replied, "due entirely to lack of thought rather than to lack of knowledge." Postscript: "I hope to see you at the Polo Grounds on Mel Ott Night."

In December 1941, Ott became player-manager, replacing Terry. The Polo Grounds housed the 1942 All-Star Game: Mel, doing Mutual. One day the Giants and Phillies stranded a record thirty runners. Allen worried about GIs stranded at Bataan and Corregidor and Burma and Oran. "Like most guys, I felt guilty. I couldn't wait to go."

Signed by Mutual, Mel missed the 1943 Series, joining the infantry September 1 at Camp Croft, South Carolina. Two days later he emceed a Joe Louis boxing match. Next year, ex-catcher-turned-major Hank Gowdy shipped him—"I was a private. Very private"—to Fort Benning, Georgia, broadcasting by Armed Forces Radio shortwave. "I tried to boost troop morale talking about our weapons," like the M-1 rifle. Gunfire simulated combat. "Thank goodness they used blanks."

At Casablanca, Roosevelt and Churchill demanded "unconditional surrender." Cairo plotted stratagem for the Pacific Theater. Teheran named date and commander for the Normandy invasion. At Fort Benning, Allen heard FDR's D-Day prayer over network radio. "I had a lot to be thankful for," he said. Bandleader Glenn Miller's plane disappeared December 15, 1944. "We were friends from my time at CBS. Because of a [scheduling] conflict, I couldn't go on his tour." Leaving the infantry also saved Mel's life. "My outfit made the first [1944] assault at Anzio, and nearly all were lost."

After the war, he met a one-legged survivor. "I'd worry about things and forget priorities. Then I'd remember him."

In 1944, Barber's worry was Gillette, offering Yanks and Giants radio. "My [Brooklyn] contract had a year left. They said, 'Break it. We'll pay legal bills.'" Irate, Red stayed. Gillette hired Bill Slater and Don Dunphy, who would have settled for a close shave. "They got so beaten in the ratings that Gillette dropped their broadcasts, got out of New York radio entirely, after that one telling year."

In 1942, the Redhead's aide launched three years in the North Atlantic, Atlantic, Mediterranean, and Caribbean. Released in 1945, 6-foot-4, 275-pound Al Helfer vaulted to The Stadium. "He drank triples without any apparent effect," said a writer, "sometimes wore a cashmere cardigan that cost the lives of a herd of goats," and fell to Barber like a lamb.

Perhaps Red was intractable; Bums radio, invincible; Mel, irreplaceable. "Sure, I wanted my job back," Allen said, "but I wanted more to get out. Not just for baseball; for other things, too." In January 1941 the CBSer had aired FDR's third inaugural from the U.S.

Capitol. Wind whipped the imperial city. To stay warm—"Hell, keep lips moving"—The Voice borrowed a cinnamon coat with a giant fur collar. Most onlookers wore high-hat garb. "Suddenly, a Secret Service guy grabs me by the neck, knocks me to the ground," saw the mike, and pulled Allen to his feet.

In April 1945, Roosevelt, sixty-three, died of a cerebral hemorrhage. Hitler shot himself in a bunker in Berlin. The Axis surrendered. Douglas MacArthur signed Japan's surrender. "We have had our chance," he said. "If we do not devise some greater and more equitable system, Armageddon will be at our door." Decision stood at Mel's.

"When you leaving?" Jints owner Horace Stoneham asked at the bar of Toots Shor's restaurant, New York's then-baseball distillery, in late 1945. His ex-mikeman shrugged. "I don't know," said Allen, on furlough. "Depends on how soon they start releasing troops."

Horace liked to drink, and did not discriminate, boozing alone, with strangers, and with friends. "Well, Mel," he sloshed, "if you get out in time for '46 [he would, discharged January 20, 1946, as "Staff Sergeant Melvin Allen"], would you like your old job back?"

"Sure, love to." Allen stopped thinking about the Yankees "and 'bout jumped twenty feet in the air."

Larry MacPhail, Dan Topping, and Del Webb had just bought the Stripes, Yankee Stadium, Triple-A parks in Newark and Jersey City, and leases on other minor-league fields from Jacob Ruppert's estate for $2.8 million. "[In 1921] Ruppert had paid more for The Stadium's 10-acre parking lot," wrote Joseph Durso. "His people were hot to sell." In particular, MacPhail, still a colonel to George C. Marshall, burned for radio. "We can't keep sharing a station with the Giants. People lose interest." His '46ers would carry every game.

"We're going on our own. What you do is strictly up to you," MacPhail told Stoneham. "One more thing. To make sure Brooklyn doesn't run this town, every game'll be live [including away]"—a bigs, and costly, precedent. "No more Western Union, or re-creations. Every pitch of every inning, from wherever it is." Soon MacPhail inked 50,000-watt WINS Radio, dumped Helfer and Slater, and phoned his former Voice at Crosley and Ebbets Field.

In 1945, Branch Rickey, Walter O'Malley, and John Smith bought 50 percent of the Dodgers. "Mr. Rickey said, 'If something overwhelming comes along, I am willing to be overwhelmed,'" mused Barber. MacPhail overwhelmed. "The most successful team in sports. The great stadium in The Bronx. Total continuity, as we had in Brooklyn. A three-year contract for $100,000. And history in the making—no more wire reports, use my own eyes, my own mind." Pause. "Plus MacPhail, which would complete our cycle."

Rickey set out to snap it. "He offered me a three-year contract, matched MacPhail's salary offer, and it came down to this: I had a civic involvement with Brooklyn. I had roots. I loved the borough and it needed me." Red loved its calliope of a park, how humanity gripped Flatbush, how he seemed its symbol. "I loved the personal dealing with everyone. And I admired Rickey." Torn by conscience, Barber stayed.

MacPhail phoned Allen, who called Stoneham, who again proposed Shor's.

"My problem is simple," said The Voice. "MacPhail wants to talk. He's going to offer me the Yankee job."

Horace mixed Scotch and solace. "Then you may not *have* a problem, and the reason is because I *do*."

"What do you mean?"

"MacPhail has a station and he needs a broadcaster. I have a broadcaster—you. But I don't have a station and may not be able to *get* one. Keep your appointment . . . "

"But I have a moral obligation," Mel interrupted. "I promised I'd do your games."

"I can't guarantee you a thing—and you can't promise to do games that may never air."

Stoneham flushed his glass. "As of now, you no longer have a moral obligation to anyone but yourself." At that moment, Allen knew that he was the Voice of the Yankees yet.

In January 1946, Mel typed an informal biography for once/again-parent CBS. "1939: Dartmouth Carnival. [Boning up, he studied skiing for a week. "We don't ski in Alabama."] Garden basketball, daily sports shows, International Polo matches at Meadowbrook, horse racing, boxing, National tennis single finals, sports quiz, *Choose Up Sides.* 1940: the Presidential campaign, election returns, and a call-in show with foreign correspondents. 1941: Inaugural and college football [through 1943] . . . Southwest, South, East, Middle West, and Pacific Coast teams . . . college. 1942: Army-Navy charity game. Giants and Dodgers 1939–40 (NFL) and All-American Conference (AAFC). Yankees and Giants 1939–43, Yankees home and away 1946 [salary $17,500. Later, Allen's top was 1,400 percent higher]. Series 1938–40–41–42 and All-Star Game 1939–43. Sports shorts, Movietone Newsreels," commencing 1946.

In World War II, Mel read about players for whom obscurity was too fine an end. "The game on the field was recognizable," Douglass Wallop wrote, "but many of the players were not." In 1946, deliverance toured the bases. Baseball broke its attendance record. Six A.L. teams set a single-year high, including the Yanks 2,265,512. "Five straight years they'd attract two million," wrote Dick Young. "Nobody'd done it before."

Lincoln coined the "blessed hush of history." The Stripes' history resumed April 30. Bob Feller no-hit them, 1–0, on ninth-inning outs by Henrich (to Mel, "Old Reliable," after a Louisville and Nashville train through Birmingham), DiMag, and Charlie "King Kong" Keller (Maryland '37, a then-odd college man). "Mc-Carthy did things his way," noted Allen. Now he and MacPhail snarled.

"Sometimes I think I'm in the greatest business in the world," said Marse Joe. "Then you lose four straight and want to change places with a farmer." In May, he retired to a farm near Buffalo. That month The Stadium's night debut drew 48,895. "Ruppert thought lights bush. MacPhail saw cash," wrote the *Daily Mirror*'s Ken Smith. Another paradigm: the DuMont Network's $75,000 for Yanks television. "We had one staff, not today's three [cable/free TV/radio]," said Allen. "I'd go down a ladder, do several TV innings, then breathe." Even a volcano needs a rest. "I wanted an aide, and knew that [Washington's] Russ Hodges had a law degree. I called McDonald, and Arch said he'd fit right in."

The two counselors clicked, touting old-shoe chivalry. "Mel became extremely popular returning from the war," a writer said of 1946. "Even the least likely rookie was called 'Mr.'" By July their agency began two-way and -voice ads. "At inning's end I'd ask something," said Allen. "Next inning'd start, Russ'd answer. Love those spontaneous ad-libs."

Once Mel changed the riddle. His aide gave a scripted answer. "It made no sense, which was the idea. Hodges'd get tickled and run out of the booth. The agency didn't know what to do with us." It did nothing. Russ's sole flaw, said The Voice, was not teaching him how to hit.

"It got so we could read each other's minds." They read through 1948, when Russ joined the Giants. "While Barber gave his listeners corn-fed philosophy and humor," wrote Wells Twombly, "and Allen told you more about baseball than you cared to know, Hodges . . . told it the way it was."

In 1946, it was that the Red Sox had never lost a Series. Enos Slaughter gets a Game 7, 3-all, eighth-inning single. Harry Walker then bats with two out. "Here's the pitch. There goes Slaughter! It's in there for a base hit!" said Mel, later re-creating. "Leon Culberson fumbles the ball momentarily and Slaughter charges around second, heads for third." Culberson threw to shortstop Johnny Pesky—at this point, views cleave—who was/not shocked to see Enos running and did/not pause before relaying. "And here comes

Enos Slaughter rounding third, he's going to try for home! Here comes the throw and it is not in time! Slaughter scores!" St. Louis, 4–3, game and year.

For Boston, the play began a half century of Murphy's Law (if something can go wrong, it will) *v.* Law of Averages (life is fair; things even out). A life larger than nearly anyone's waned in 1947. By April 27—his Day, at Yankee Stadium—Babe Ruth, "in and out of the hospital for throat cancer," could barely talk. Mel, emceeing, stood behind Ruth's trademark camel hair coat and matching cap. The ovation volleyed, rolled beyond the outfield, and crashed against the tiers.

"Babe, do you want to try and say something?" asked Mel, hands cupped.

Ruth croaked, "I must." Quavering, he hailed "the boys represented here today in your national pastime—the only real game, I think, in the world, baseball"—then shuffled toward the bench.

"Good luck, Babe," said Francis Cardinal Spellman, Roman Catholic Archbishop of New York, a year later. "I just wanted you to know that any time you want me to come to your house for Holy Communion, I'd be glad to do it."

Ruth smiled. "Thanks, your Eminence. That's just great, but I'd rather come to *your* place."

As a player, said Phil Rizzuto, "Babe'd sit there with that big cigar. When he wasn't going to bat, he'd stay in the outfield and talk to people in the stands and eat hot dogs." Broken, his shell watched 1947's Gibraltar.

In 1945, Rickey signed the big leagues' first Negro. Jackie Robinson debuted April 15, 1947. "I was there," said broadcaster Larry King. "Jackie just seemed to glide." Barber probed his soul. "I'd been one of the first Rickey told because I was the Voice, and I was from the South." He thought of quitting. Later Jackie hailed Red's healing. "If there are any thanks involved," Barber replied, "I thank him."

Chapter two of the Bums-Yanks serialized novel began September 29. "We'll beat 'em," vowed Pee Wee Reese, whose optimism soon abjured. New York beat Brooklyn twice. The *Daily News* then beat up on the Series: "the worst we ever saw," wrote Jimmy Powers. "It took exactly four minutes short of five dismal hours to play the first two alleged games." Game 3 spun a 185-minute, 9–8 Dodgers parody. Next day the Stripes led, 2–1, after 8⅔ innings. Improbably, starter Floyd (Bill) Bevens had ceded ten walks and no hits.

Form demands ignoring an at-work no-hitter. "What I did or didn't say wouldn't influence what happened," said Allen. "But players think you jinx it by talking. It's part of the romance, one of the things that separates baseball from other sports, like the seventh-inning stretch or the biggest difference, the lack of a clock." Game 4 was timeless.

Mel called the first 4½ innings: "I respected the tradition." Inheriting the mike, Red, "a reporter," he huffed, "not a dealer in superstition," leaked Brooklyn's line score: one run, two errors, no hits. Allen gasped. "I'm not being critical, but I couldn't believe he'd violate history. Nothing could stop Red's bid for perfection in the booth." Below, shucking perfection, Bevens would settle for a no-hit game.

Pinch-runner Al Gionfriddo stole second base with two out in the ninth. On a 3–1 count, Yankees manager Bucky Harris walked potential winning run Pete Reiser. Cookie Lavagetto pinch-hit for Eddie Stanky. "The pitch," Red said. "Swung on, there's a drive hit out toward the rightfield corner! Henrich is going back! He can't get it! It's off the wall for a base hit! Here comes the tying run and here comes the winning [3–2] run!" on Brooklyn's only hit. Box seat: $8.00. Sensation: priceless.

New York won Game 5, 2–1. Next day married a record Series crowd (74,065), longest regulation time (3:19), and sublime denouement. Brooklyn led, 8–5, at The Stadium: DiMaggio up, two out and on. "Swung on. Belted! It's a long one!" cried Barber. "Deep into left-center! Back goes Gionfriddo! Back, back, back, back, back, back! He makes a one-handed catch against the bull pen! Oh, Doctor!" DiMag kicked dirt near second. "In all the years I saw him," said Mel, "it was the only time he showed emotion on the field."

Exhausted, the Series schlepped to a 5–2 Yanks clincher. David Halberstam termed Lyndon Johnson "the president most reeking of human juices." Baseball's was Larry MacPhail, quitting after the final out.

"The players were clearly distinguishable," *The Sporting News*'s Harold Parrott wrote of August 26, 1939, "but it was not possible to pick out the ball." It *was* possible to pick out Red, in the second deck, behind third base, baptizing bigs TV baseball. He hawked Ivory Soap, Mobil Gas, and General Mills, holding a bar, donning an attendant's cap, and pouring Wheaties, respectively. "Yes-suh," Barber drawled, "that's a Breakfast of Champions."

Making history, baseball was flying blind. "No monitor, only two [W2XBS] cameras at Ebbets Field," said Barber. "One was by me, the other behind the plate, and I had to guess from which light was on where it pointed." Ultimately, few had to guess where baseball was pointed. In 1946, fifty-six million radio receivers dwarfed television's 17,000. "TV's potential was still around the corner," said Allen. For the wireless, '47 was Pickett's Charge.

By 1948, TV sets hit three million. Barber nearly died of a hemorrhaged ulcer. In September, he was phoned by A. Craig Smith, having once asked Red to abandon Brooklyn. "When I wouldn't, he tried to kick me off the Series. Thank God the commissioner named Voices, not him." Smith schmoozed like nothing had occurred. "The world's changing, and you're the only guy who can make it [Gillette TV] go." Barber balked, then caved. "Every hour I worried I'd hemorrhage again and cough up blood."

Ten million watched Indians-Braves. On Mutual, forty million heard a boom box, age thirty-five. In 1946, *The Sporting News* publisher J. G. Taylor Spink named Mel the "top [American League] broadcaster," encoring in 1947. The *Times*'s Radio Honor Roll agreed: "His dispassionate and unemotional repertorial ability is altogether too rare in sports announcing." In April 1948, Birmingham held "Mel Allen Day," awarded silver goblets, luggage, and a record player-radio, and gave a key to the state's largest city: of thirty-two then-honored, the only 'Bama-born.

Telegrams vied: Barber, Bill Stern, Harry Wismer. At Rickwood Field, 5,000 filled a Yanks-Southern Association Birmingham Barons exhibition. A barbecue at the farm of local stockholder Al DeMent fed team writers, Yanks players, and skipper Harris.

Allen beamed: "What's better than coming home?" Increasingly, home meant New York.

In December 1939 Anna and Julius had moved to Jackson Heights, Queens, then to a Riverdale, The Bronx apartment. "Mel'd lived in the YMCA, and Ralph Edwards briefly on a bench in Central Park," said brother Larry. "That's how poor they were," finally renting a flat with Andre Baruch. "Moving out, Mel kept after Mom, Dad, and me to come up to New York. Finally, we said yes." Larry became Mel's "statistician," wrote the *Daily News*'s Pete Coutros. "He does an occasional inning at the end of the year." Only Esther, married to neurological surgeon Daniel Kaufman, lived elsewhere (Long Island's Lake Success).

A *News* bio dubbed Allen unhip, unboutique, and a becoming fusspot: less Oscar Madison than Felix Unger. He liked film, ate at odd hours, and was prone to vomiting. On the road, Mel put pajamas on at 10:00 P.M. "Well, I need a good night's sleep," he said. Awaking, Hodges noted, The Voice was "a bundle of nerves."

Once the Yanks George Stirnweiss popped up a 3–1 ninth-inning pitch, leaving the tying run on third. At 4:30 A.M., Russ awoke to groans in the next bed. "Mel, should I get a doctor? What's the matter?" he said, turning on the light.

"I just can't forget about that 3–1 pitch to Stirnweiss. Don't you think he made a mistake swinging?"

Russ stared. Allen rose, gobbled shrimp—"I'll eat it in any form"—and gorged on approbation. Harry S. Truman threw out Opening Day balls left- and right-handed—to Yogi Berra, "amphibious"—April

19 at Griffith Stadium. Four days later the Yanks feted The Stadium—and their public face and voice.

"I throw out a ball, a borough head gives a speech, some fan's honored," noted ex-Mayor Fiorello La Guardia. "It doesn't matter, Mel's there." He began: "Hello there, everybody! In the twenty-five-year history of Yankee Stadium, thirteen pennants and eleven world championships have been won by the Yankees." Harris raised the title flag. Commissioner Albert B. (Happy) Chandler gave watches, rings, "and another award to . . . the Most Valuable Player in the American League in 1947," said Allen. "Ladies and gentlemen, Joltin' Joe DiMaggio."

The Voice was "mighty proud" to "acknowledge the presence of the man who won the first game ever played here in Yankee Stadium. With Whitey Witt and Jumping Joe Dugan on base, he hit his first home run of the 1923 season—the first in fact ever hit in Yankee Stadium . . . George Herman (Babe) Ruth!" Chandler then gave Mel a "[*TSN*] trophy," Dan Daniel wrote, "the most elaborate award yet given on a baseball field." Mel hoped that it redeemed Julius's nomadism. "Maybe the trophy can make up for the trouble he may have had bringing me up as a youngster."

New York governor Thomas E. Dewey—"an authentic giant," said broadcaster Lowell Thomas: a cinch to retire Truman—threw out the first ball. "I thought of that during the [1948] presidential election," said Allen. "Truman and Dewey, the two first-ball pitchers," one soon the hero of every dog that was under.

Truman's leitmotif was "Give 'em hell!" The next day profanity clubbed The Voice. Accidentally sharing WINS's program channel, a telephone caller started swearing at the operator.

"Allen, you bastard, get off the line," he said on hearing Mel. The broadcast went black, resuming three minutes later.

The same voice then began talking to a woman.

"I won't be home this afternoon."

"What, again?" she said.

"Oh, I'm just going home with the boys."

Mel, who rarely swore—"Dad gum" was an epithet—could be heard in the background: "I could spit."

Again WINS left the air: this time, for thirty minutes. Reemerging, it conveyed a chant. That summer an Indian lined to right. "It's going, going!" yelped Allen, braking a caution light. "It was one of those rainbow-type drives that sometimes sail back in," he said. "Then, seeing DiMag and Henrich drop their gloves, I continued, 'Gone!'" At break, he told Hodges, "Criminy, I sounded like an auctioneer on that one." On June 13, The Voice, again Zelig, fixed an un-Yankees-like glitch.

"Incredibly, a year earlier the club had forgotten to retire Babe's number. He was dying, so they needed to move fast." Ruth was so weak, Rizzuto said, "it took two men to lift him." In uniform, he leaned on Bob Feller's bat like a cane. "Ladies and gentlemen," Mel bayed, "the Bambino, the Sultan of Swat, Babe Ruth." Again the ovation stretched to Coogan's Bluff.

Allen "thought back to Lou in 1939" and 1947. Once more he asked if Ruth wished to speak.

"Not much," Babe whispered. In 1957, Mel told Ed Murrow, "I shall never forget it, nor shall I ever forget him."

*The Babe Ruth Story* opened July 26, 1948, its hero attending the premiere. Few confused him with William Bendix, the film's No. 3. "It showed Babe hitting his sixtieth home run in 1927," said Allen. "The fact that I was only fourteen years old and yet the film had me announcing gives you a rough idea of how bad a movie it was."

The real Ruth died August 16, at fifty-three. Next month the Yanks would finish third, not reslumming there till 1959. "Even in death," mused Mel, "Babe drew the usual SRO." At The Stadium, pilgrims touched his bier. Outside St. Patrick's Cathedral, thousands jammed Fifth Avenue. The heat mimed a greenhouse in the famed and crowded church.

Former mates Dugan and Waite Hoyt sat sweating in the first row.

"Lord, it's so hot in here I'd give my right arm for a beer," Dugan said, quietly.

At that moment Babe's casket passed. "Yeah," murmured Hoyt, "so would the Babe." ◆

# The Wonder Years (1949–1952)

n 1948, Ernie Harwell, thirty, left Triple-A Atlanta for Brooklyn. He swelled New York's Southern colony of Allen, from Johns; Hodges, Dayton, Kentucky; and Barber, Mississippi's pine and clay. "I'm asked why so many guys were from the region," said Harwell. "I say we were too lazy to work. Actually, we grew up in a Southern atmosphere, without outside excitement," of oral density and a siren past. "On the porch Dad and Mom and Uncle Fred and Aunt Ethel talked about the people of their town"—the local banker and beauty parlor operator and who married whom. Their rhythm became radio baseball's, mythy and sweetly rural.

The listener could picture bag, position, batter, and pitcher. A Dodger might hit to left-center field. "Mentally, you saw it all at once—runners, fielder chasing the ball, shortstop with the relay, catcher bracing," mused Harwell. "Football is better packaged for the screen": baseball, mind. Mel nodded: "On radio you chose your direction, but on TV you had earphones on, the director saying they were going to cut away to some cheesecake in right field, or a mother holding a baby, you know what I mean."

Radio was a sonata. Television was still life, deadened by statistic. The polarity hurt baseball's first "simulcast": 1949's Allen, simultaneously on each. "Some TV guys said, 'Don't talk too much because people can see what's happening.' Pull back, and anger folks on radio. Keep blabbing, and get letters about TV." In the end, Mel threw up his hands. "People think what they're gonna' think."

It was clear what the two media thought about the other. Radio had been an immovable object, selling as many as 165,000 sets a month. Slowly, TV became an irresistible force, vending seven million in 1950. "There was a ferment, a transition," said Mel. "Everything was primitive. For example, you could only tape a TV program by shooting its actual picture": a process termed kinescope, often fuzzy, like the age.

New York's primacy was plain. "What happened on our broadcasts swayed the game." Also clear: Some Voices would more easily adapt. Barber turned smaller than on radio. Allen became TV baseball at midcentury.

Mel called the 1948 Red Sox-Indians playoff for WINS and WOR despite a cold, viral pneumonia, and laryngitis. Still sick, he broadcast the Series. Next month *The Sporting News* threw a soiree at Shor's. "We are competitors in the business of telling the fans what has happened," emceed Dan Daniel, "and Allen tells much too much for the comfort of the writers." One reason: a mix of grace, verve, and cadence. Related: At one postwar date or another, Mel did college basketball's National Invitation Tournament; tennis tournaments; indoor track and field; Tony Zale-Rocky Graziano welterweight fight; Westminster Kennel Club dog show; NBC college, Columbia, Notre Dame, Rose, Orange, and Sugar Bowl football; Triple Crown color; and WOR *Mel Allen's Popsicle Clubhouse.*

A *Daily News* cartoon sketched him, in suspenders. "Football, baseball, boxing, track and field, basketball, Mel Allen, crack radio announcer for the Yankees, has broadcast every sports event in the book. That's why he's an expert on the air—and your favorite sportscaster." Text: "And there goes the ball game, folks! Tommy Henrich has just slammed out a home run off Bob Feller!"—The Voice, as ubiquitous as your nearest double feature.

By 1949, every other American saw at least one film a week. "Especially on the weekend, the house'd have a twin bill," said Mel. "Maybe a crime film, then mystery. Between 'em they'd run a couple, three hours." The newsreel filled intermission: Hearst, Pathe, United Press, and largest, Twentieth Century-Fox. You would confuse baseball and bocce ball before "your Movietone reporter."

Twice weekly he wrote and spoke Fox newsreel script at its West Side Manhattan studio. "He does both," wrote Huston Horn, "after a quick look at the film." In one short, Yogi Berra tussled Dan Topping's hair in the clubhouse. In another, Allen bayed, "Northwestern beats California, 20 to 14, in Rose Bowl Classic." At Louisville, wearing goggles, he introduced 17 three-year-olds at the 1¼-mile course Kentucky Derby.

"One hundred thousand turf fans in historic Churchill Downs for the glamorous Derby. Ruby White ready to start 'em. This is Mel Allen saying, 'They're off!'" To many in the local Bijou, he was as familiar as the latest Roy Rogers flick.

Like the King of the Cowboys, baseball was in the saddle: two teams, not six divisions; fewer players to know; more worth knowing. For Mel, its 1949 began with Dewey—to his chagrin, still governor—deeming Allen again *TSN* A.L. Announcer of the Year. "Guess I got the honor a few times [10]," he said. Actually, he and another Voice retired it.

It might be! Baseball's Jackie Gleason.

It could be! Sarcasm, bombast, and cocksure brass.

It was! Harry Caray, tending America's then-southern and then-westernmost team.

From 1945 to 1969, "Holy Cow!" was a magical property in Webster, Iowa, and Cleveland, Tennessee, and Lawton, Oklahoma. "It's so apt that he and Mel won the award more than anyone," said Al Helfer. "They were so alike—volcanic, unpredictable, lightning quick on a play." Caray became a seven-time N.L. titlist. "Their dominance so overwhelmed that Taylor Spink said, 'Why the hell even vote?'"

The award died in 1958, Harry returning to sack probability, longevity, and cirrhosis of the liver. Mel retrieved an age that no sport had seen before, nor is likely to see again.

"Think of it," said Jack Buck. "Fourteen Yankees pennants in sixteen years [1949–64]. Baseball means the Yankees. They help Allen become baseball": seventeen straight Series and thirteen consecutive (1951–61) All-Star Games on Mutual Radio or NBC TV/wireless.

No Yankees player dominated. A gnarled ex-dentist, however, reigned. What a couplet: Casey Stengel spinning, and Mel Allen speaking. The Ol' Perfessor retired in 1965. Paid by the word, he could have retired the national debt.

In October 1948, the Bombers named Casey manager. Only twice in nine bigs years had he placed even fifth. "What are we getting: burlesque?" fumed a writer. The ex-National League skipper explained seeming a buffoon. "Clowning around is all right when you have a second division ball club," he told Allen. "But you don't have to always leave them laughing when you're up there—and I mean to be up there." Said Mel: "I don't know what I liked most, the strategist, philosopher, or historian who could make you laugh."

In 1992, Richard Nixon said, "If I had it to do over again, I'd name Casey secretary of state. The essence of diplomacy is to confuse the opposition. The opposition never knew what Stengel was talking about. He *always* knew."

George Kell recalled a CBS TV pregame show. "I had fifteen minutes and was going to ask Casey about his entire batting order."

"How'd it go?" Allen asked.

"Oh, fine," said Kell. "But in our fifteen minutes, Casey didn't get past the leadoff hitter."

Another day he opined that midgets are smart. "Smart, and as slick as eels. Know why?" Mel confessed puzzlement.

"It's because they're not able to do much with the short fingers they have," said Stengel. "You understand?" Mel deferred.

"Not being able to do much with their fingers, what do they do? They develop their brainpower. Short people need to be smarter all down the line."

Take bartenders. "A short one will outdo a tall one every time": no sore back. "He never has to bend over. You get it. He can work all night." Stengel's mouth could, and did.

"Casey's fifty-four years in baseball tied Tris Speaker and Tom Seaver," Nelson noted. The best were his Yanks record ten pennants and seven Series.

"He wouldn't have had to win anything to catch the fancy of America," said Allen. "He didn't obey periods at the end of sentences, just ran 'em together, like eras that he'd known." Ask a question. "He'd talk 'bout being a minor-leaguer in Montgomery and every club he played with and fans who gave him dinner before he'd answer the question which by now *you'd* forgot. Oh, yeah, 'How did you like playing under John McGraw?'"

Casey had been a minor-league player, manager, and president. "He didn't like it, and finally figured out what to do."

He quit as player.

As manager, he fired himself.

As president, he resigned.

St. Petersburg, Florida, March 1949. Stengel begins spring training by quizzing a geezer on the bench. "In reality," said Mel, "he did it so the man *next* to him, a rookie, could learn by indirection." Each life has a core: George Bush, *noblesse oblige*; Adlai Stevenson, language-made-literate; Huey Long, poverty. Casey's was that he would try anything. If it didn't work, he tried something else. Mostly, he tried platooning.

"He'd split right field between Hank Bauer and Gene Woodling," smiled Allen. "Gene'd get four hits, the other team'd put in a southpaw, and Stengel switched to [righty] Bauer." Woodling went bonkers. "Casey was a master psychologist," seldom chiding in defeat. "He knew you're more responsive to criticism when you win."

Rambling—i.e., Stengelese—hid a street-hard edge. Casey closed a bar at 3:00 A.M., grabbed the hotel operator, and offered a baseball. "I got to give this to a kid tomorrow. If guys come in, have 'em sign the ball and give it to me at breakfast." Next day the operator gave a ball signed by five Yanks after 3:00. Stengel fined each $50 for breaking curfew.

In 1922, Casey's .400 Series average beat a Bunyan acquired from A.L. Boston. On Opening Day 1949, the Stripes rookie skipper dedicated a Stadium monument to Babe Ruth. Better late than never: The Red Sox readied for revenge.

Eleven times since World War II the Sox have lost a pennant, League Championship Series, or Series on the next to last or final day. Save 1986, 1949 was worst. Ted Williams led the league in ten categories. The infield swanked Billy Goodman (.298), Bobby Doerr (.309), Vern Stephens (.290), and Johnny Pesky (.306). Mel Parnell won 25 games—a team lefty record. Ellis Kinder added 23. Said a mate: "Ellie could drink more bourbon and pitch more clutch baseball than anyone I knew." Boston even had McCarthy.

The Sox averaged .282. No Yankees regular topped .287. New York hit 115 homers *v.* 1936–39's average 174. In Ernest Hemingway's *The Old Man and the Sea*, Santiago says to Manolin, "Have faith in the Yankees, my son. Think of the great DiMaggio." On April 10, Joe limped off a Texas field after three innings of exhibition. The Great DiMaggio—"He had a heel spur," said Mel, "could barely walk"—missed the season's first sixty-five games.

On June 28, a Fenway night record 36,228 gathered. Listening in South Hadley, near Springfield, A. Bartlett Giamatti, eleven, thought Yanks-Sox "one of those great American events, like the coming of snow or the end of school." A year earlier his father, hand-in-hand, introduced him to the Back Bay cabash. "We went through the tunnel, and saw emerald grass and bases whiter than I'd ever seen"—also, sharp angles, asymmetrical alleys, scarce foul turf, and 37-foot leftfield wall topped by a 23-foot screen.

"I went there as a kid," once-Speaker of the House Thomas O. (Tip) O'Neill said. Like The Stadium, "You never knew what'd happen—pop-fly homers, a ball off the Wall, some guy missing an inside-the-parker." Center field stood 420 feet from home plate. Right-center required a deeper indrawing of breath: 380's built-for-Williams bull pen. Right and left—302 and 315, respectively—left a pitcher breathless. DiMag had not faced real pitching since September 1948.

Allen hoped for a "loud foul." Instead: "The incomparable DiMaggio hits the first pitch for a single!" Joe then crashed a third-inning homer. Stunned and moved, Mel shouted, "How about that!"—his JFK's "Vig-ah," FDR's "My friends," or Reagan's "Shining city on a hill." Next day DiMag twice went deep: 9–7, Stripes. "One of them went over the wall, screen, and everything," Pesky said. "It might have gone to the Hotel Kenmore, for all I know." Game 3: A three-run belt hit the leftfield tower. "How about that!" towered. The noise was insupportable.

"Sometimes, when the Yanks are flying," jibed the *Daily News*, "Mel shouts into the mike until he is barely intelligible. There is no doubt in the mind of anybody who heard that he thought Joe baseball's Superman." The Yanks swept the series: Joe had four dingers and nine RBI. A small plane trailed a banner: THE GREAT DIMAGGIO.

Number 5 made *Life* magazine's cover. Wrote David Halberstam: "It was the perfect combination, Joe DiMaggio's deeds, amplified by Mel Allen's voice"—an instrument the soloist was always pleased to play.

"I'm well aware that many persons say I'm too wordy," The Voice said at the time. "But I have heard tapes of other broadcasters and found that they actually talk as much as I do." Some wrote that "I don't talk enough. They want even more detailed explanation." An announcer should talk less on TV, "but still more than you imagine."

The dialectic—did he talk too much?—survived Mel's death. "Opinion to the contrary, during a baseball game the camera does not give the viewer a complete picture of the game." That meant giving the score, promptly and repeatedly. "Some may be annoyed. But there are thousands who tune in late and they have a right to know what's taken place before." At heart was the headliner's reluctance to shut up: also, self-doubt and insecurity.

"Somewhere there must be a middle ground: enough explanation for those who don't understand the game and not too much for those who do. If I don't qualify everything I say ["International Falls is the coldest spot in the U.S.—temperature-wise, that is"], here come the letters. I have lain awake nights wondering where that happy medium is."

By day, Mel drove to The Stadium, signed autographs, entered the clubhouse, rival dugout, and booth, "describing the first pitch even as he sits down," said Larry. "Sometimes Mel hasn't had time for breakfast. So he brings along four hot dogs and eats them as he works."

Talk was Allen's star, an Arcturus or Cassiopeia. One writer called "his voice a comfort, his handshake a benediction, his autograph an heirloom." Another said, "Mel Allen talks more than a mud pie—which isn't saying much." John Lardner transcribed his on one hand, or the other:

"By sending Mize to the bat rack," Mel began, "Stengel may have kept Boudreau from replacing Brown, because—you see, Collins is a left-handed hitter—well, we've got a right-handed pitcher in there now, but if Boudreau had called in a southpaw—of course, Collins is a left-handed hitter, too. But what this might mean—well, of course, it may mean nothing."

One reporter said, "Aren't you broadcasting the game tonight?"

"Naturally," Allen said, "I have got time to eat the chicken mother fried for me and wipe off every seat in The Stadium before— My God! The game's in *Philadelphia!*"

Mel now made an estimated $95,000: Yanks, $35; Movietone, $15; Mutual Saturday series, $20; football, hoops, and track and field, $15; and Series, All-Star Game, and other TV, $10. In person, said the *News*, "some of the Southern accent comes through." On air, "most of the Alabama has been trained out of him," leaving ad-lib, detail, and pun.

In 1947, MacPhail had summoned Hodges to The Stadium Club. "Tell Allen to stop ad-libbing. No more ad-libbing. Beginning right now."

"Yes, sir," said the ex-Marine, saluting. "And now may I have the script for the rest of the game."

MacPhail was unamused. "Before long Allen admirers began firing angry letters to the Yankee office," read the *Times*, "demanding to know why their hero wasn't rolling 'em in the aisles any more on a dull afternoon."

A year later Topping bought the Yankees. Mel's puns revived. "You just go on and fracture the listening audience," Russ told him, "I'm going out for a breath of fresh air."

One ball hit the facade, then ground near home plate. "From the facade to the sod," said Allen, "who's soddy now?"

A British umpire wouldn't work night games "because the sun never sets on the British umpire."

Later: "Are you thirsty? Well, glad to meet you, thirsty. I'm Mel Allen." New York's winter boat show bared cleavage. "The hull thing makes a fellow keel over from sheer delight."

The Gagwriters Association of America gave Mel an award for "humor." Four decades later he still worried it would recant.

Jiminy Cricket. Allen had used "How about that!" since the early 1940s. "For some reason," he said, "Joe's comeback was the catalyst. Folks discovered the phrase overnight," knitting the grandstand like a 1980s Wave. "People started screaming it even when a Yankee reached base," wrote Halberstam. Johnny Lindell ended a game J. Anthony Lukas heard at a friend's home in Scarsdale. "We rolled across the carpet shouting, 'How about that! How about that! How about that!'" Dick Rubin was Mel's long-time agent: "Visit the Yankee Stadium any summer afternoon and you'll hear Allen's catchphrase echoing through the seats." Added *Holiday*'s Peter Lyon: "It swiftly grew bigger than he was, and threatened to leave a permanent scar on American as she is spoke."

In 1940, Harwell met Mel's cousin, Elmo Ellis [Israel], later Cox Broadcasting Company vice-president and WSB Atlanta general manager. "I felt affinity with Mel's family—that Southern thing. We'd talk about his great descriptive power." In 1949, the Georgian heard it "go berserk." Down, 13–0, Cleveland's Larry Doby tried to steal home. "Mel started screaming 'How about that!'" Ernie said, "Had to be about forty times." A minute later the needle was still stuck. "It went on forever. Mel couldn't get over Doby's boner."

By coincidence, about this time Anna discovered baseball. "She hadn't been a fan," Mel allowed. "The only time she spanked me as a kid was when I'd play too much ball." Now, one 1949 morning, "mother was serving me coffee when she said, in an offhand way, 'I see where the Yankees lead has been cut down to 1½ games.'"

The Voice nearly dropped his saucer. "I was so amazed that I said, 'Now, just where have you been to hear that kind of talk?'"

Anna: "Oh, I get around," having discreetly gone with Julius to Yankee Stadium. Soon, said Allen, "Mom was the best second-guesser I ever had."

One day she was "ready to explode, she was so mad. 'That Casey Stengel! I love that man, but he sure did lose us that game last night!'" Boston surged from twelve games behind New York to within a game by Labor Day—before, as psychologists say, reverting.

"Back and forth," said Mel. "We'd grab a lead." Finally the Red Sox took a one-game edge. Ahead: at The Stadium, each team's final two. "Christ!" stormed Ted Williams. "I wanted to beat the Yankees!" Pinching himself, Allen's rookie aide still did not believe it.

"As long as I live I'll remember '49," Curt Gowdy said. "The volleys back and forth. Yankee fans roaring on every pitch. Down from New England, Sox fans answering." Born in Cheyenne, he would win four Emmy Awards, call thirteen Series and sixteen All-Star Games, and become the first sportscaster to win the George Foster Peabody Award for broadcast excellence. In 2004, Curt still gawked: "That weekend—I've never heard such noise."

Mel roused response to personality. Gowdy's style was home-style, educing courtesy, respectability, and pluck. By 1948, he did Oklahoma football, Oklahoma A&M basketball, and the Texas League Oklahoma Indians, the minors "putting the demands of the broadcast business—ads, production, play-by-play—into one." To most teams, business meant General Mills. Each year account executive Frank Slocum "looked for young talent to sell products"—Wheaties, above all.

"That fall," said Allen, "Russ told me he was leaving." Hearing Curt, Slocum asked for a brochure with tapes. The Rocky Mountaineer and Mel closeted. "I already knew him. He'd come to New York for basketball at the Garden, and had his biography with pictures. I'd say, 'You should have gone into Hollywood.'" Gowdy said that he would sign for nothing. "Fortunately, I didn't have to."

Next year the Wyoming Cowboy married. His best man made him better. "My other sports had come along. But Allen showed me how far from a baseball hot shot I was." He thought Mel, like wife Jerre, a perfectionist. "They can be a pain in the ass. If Mel wanted some statistics and Larry didn't have them, he'd blow a gasket. He had that attention to detail: timing, reading an ad, weaving it in, then done all the time."

A future peer felt Gowdy cowed. "He was intimidated because Mel wanted things precisely done," said Red Sox announcer Ned Martin. "For a while he thought he'd toss it." Not grinning, Curt bore it. "Mel could lose his temper in a game and ride you, but he was loyal and generous to the people who worked for him," including Hodges, Woods, and Desmond: "Alumni of Allen Tech," wrote Pete Coutros, "having shared hours of joy and anguished with him at the mike."

Gowdy conceded "a tense first year." Last weekend angst hung like cicadas on a screen. The penultimate game was Joe DiMaggio Day: Mel, Farley, Cardinal Spellman, and Ethel Merman lauding Santiago's hero. "I'd like to apologize to the people in the bleachers for having my back turned to them," No. 5 began. "I'd like to thank God for making me a Yankee." Brother Dominic was Red Sox centerfielder. Rosalie DiMaggio was asked, "Which team are you rooting for?" Son Tom said, "Mother is impartial"—unlike Saturday's 69,551. Boston built a 4–0 third-inning lead. New York rallied one run at a time. Lindell's drive broke a 4-all tie.

A year earlier the Sox lost a playoff to Cleveland. "Two straight seasons and one game settles it," said catcher Birdie Tebbetts. "When [general manager Joe] Cronin sends my contract for next year, I'm gonna' specify that I not show until October. It's better to play fresh than tired."

The final left you limp.

Allen lost ten pounds in the season's last two weeks. "His folks were actually afraid he was ill," wrote *Park East*'s Marty Abramson. Larry fessed: "If the Yankees had lost just one of those two games, well, he'd probably have wound up in a rest home."

Audiotape preserves The Voice. "Permit us, if you will," he starts, "to cast aside our partisan feelings." The outfield is "straightaway"; infield, "in at third, back at second"; Phil Rizzuto, picking up a pebble; Jerry Coleman, four strides to "the keystone's" right. "Big Cal Hubbard" calls balls and strikes. Vern Stephens becomes "Buster." Never forget the sugar daddy. "Enjoy the two Bs—baseball and Ballantine Beer. Look for the three rings!" The Yanks went looking for a run.

Rizzuto led off the first inning *v.* Ellis Kinder. "Swung on, lined down the leftfield line, and it is in there for a base hit!" cried Allen. "Bounces off into the corner! Phil goes for two! The ball gets away from Ted! Phil's going for three! Ted picks up the ball! The throw to third! Not in time! It's a three-base hit for the Scooter!" Henrich's grounder plated him: 1–0. The run soon loomed larger than Hubbard's 260 pounds.

Curt called the fifth inning, Mel sucking air. "This being the last day I wish to thank some people," he resumed: subway, sanitation, police, and fire workers. In the eighth, behind, 1–0, McCarthy pinch hit for Kinder. "If that bastard doesn't take me out, we win,"

Ellis said. Instead, Henrich "swings [*v.* reliever Tex Hughson] and sends a long drive to right field! I don't know if it's deep enough or not. It is going, going, it's gone!" The last word seemed trisyllabic.

New York led, 2–0. That same inning Coleman hit: two out, 3–2 count, bases full. "A little blooper into short right field. Zarilla comes fast and he can't get it! Here comes Bauer! Here comes Johnson! Here comes Mapes digging for the plate! . . . and Mapes scores! And there's the throw to third! And Coleman is out at third, but three runs score!"—5–0. The radio seemed to quiver.

The Sox, scoring thrice, would not be the Sox without a pre-2004 Lucy-steals-the-football tease. Boston's catcher was the ninth-inning tying run. "Birdie swings and pops it up in the air! Look out now! Look out now! He's got it! Tommy [Henrich] has [the foul ball]. The Yankees win the pennant!": to a writer, "Casey's greatest gag."

Training back to Boston, Kinder slugged McCarthy in the jaw. "When it was over," added Williams, "I just wanted to go and hide somewhere." Nirvana again hid from Flatbush.

"Where are the peanuts, the pop, the scorecards, hot dogs, and mustard pot?" *Times* reporter Orrin E. Dunlap Jr. said of the 1949 Series. "They don't come through on the [NBC Television] air." The *World-Telegram* likened the scene to "an infant in knee pants." The *Sun* rued: "None of the infield plays or outfield catches could be seen." The scoreless opener's last-inning climax could.

"Swung on, drilled out toward right field, going way back, back, that's the ball game [Stripes, 1–0], a home run for Tommy Henrich!" said Barber, with Mel manning Mutual. "Look at him grin! Big as a slice of watermelon." The belt would have hit Brooklyn's scoreboard. A Death Valley out might leave Ebbets Field. "In those days," wrote *Newsday*'s Stan Isaacs, "there was hardly a street corner analysis that wasn't replete with . . . how the day's particular battle might have gone had it been played in the other ballpark." The park made a difference, like Yankee Stadium's cachet.

Raised in Anderson, Indiana, pop. 55,000, Dodgers pitcher Carl Erskine visited The Stadium clubhouse recently vacated by the Stripes. Two lockers had uniforms: Ruth's and Gehrig's. "They were sending a message." That day he stepped off the rubber, fixed the grandstand, and mouthed, "Seventy thousand people. That's more than live in Anderson!"

Even Hoosiers hailed DiMag. Duke Snider robbed him in Game 5. The next up precluded theft. "Outfield swung on around toward left. Infield shaded well around toward third," said Mel. "Joe with that classic stance of his, bat cocked up off his right shoulder. The next pitch, he swings and sends a long drive! If it stays fair, it will go all the way! It is going! It is going! It is gone!": Yanks clinch, 10–6.

A record twenty-six of thirty-nine million homes with radios heard the Capulets and Montagues duel.

Man bites dog. "Joe Collins was slumping, Henrich hurt, so Casey put DiMaggio at first," Rizzuto said of 1950. On August 11, the Thames ran upstream: Joe was benched. A month later he became first to homer thrice in a game at Washington. "The Jolter missing a fourth homer," Mel said, "as Eddie Stevens makes a leaping catch against the leftfield wall!" The Yanks and Tigers hit eleven homers in a game. Rookie Whitey Ford went 9–1. Scooter roped 200 hits, 125 runs, and wizardry into MVP. "If I were a retired gentleman," said Stengel, "I would follow the Yankees around just to see Rizzuto work those miracles each day."

New York clinched September 29. Tailing .300, DiMag lined to shortstop. "He heads to center, mumbling to himself," said Jerry Coleman, "as Yogi fires the ball above second to start the next inning," striking Joe's heel.

"DiMaggio falls down, thinks it's my fault, yells 'Catch the ball,'" then one-hopped a throw that hit Jerry in the knee. Coleman fell, writhing. "We either won or lost, there was no second place."

Joe knew he was losing it. Pitcher Eddie Lopat kidded him: "You were like a young buck out there tonight." DiMag smiled. "It's the cool weather. A clean uniform, a shave, and haircut." CBS's Series coverage beamed them west to Omaha: thirty-eight million watched.

On Mutual, Mel and Philly's Gene Kelly saw New York run the table. The opener was again 1–0. Next day DiMag pricked Robin Roberts for a tenth-inning 2–1 blow. The Big Ballpark housed Game 3, its turn of sites confusing the three-error, 3–2 losing Phils. Ford crowned a 5–2 sweep—the Yanks first since 1939.

Jerry shook his head. "Winning in October was fun. Getting there wasn't."

What was: calling 1950's Kentucky-Santa Clara Orange Bowl, a 100-yard President's Cup runback by Texas A&M's Bob Smith; Michigan State's 36–33 lulu *v.* Notre Dame, and Ralph Kiner's All-Star Game dinger. "The first pitch," Mel preened, "after I'd predicted he would belt it out of the park and tie the score." Fun: Depending on the game, the Yanks Hooper radio rating blew warm (4.2) to hot (10). Afterward police led Allen to his steel-gray Buick convertible with red wheels and leather seats and the license BB (for baseball) 65.

Ultimately, Mel got: *Look* magazine's 1950 award for excellence; Radio-Television 1950–52 Academy of Arts and Sciences "Michael," later Emmy, best sportscaster; *Radio/TV Daily* 1950–63 poll, U.S. editors, "Number One Sports Announcer"; *Radio/TV Mirror* magazine 1950–63 best sportscaster; *TV Guide* 1951 Gold Medal football award; "Annual Most Wanted Name," 1957 Testimonial Advertising; *Who's Who in Television and Radio* 1959–60 best radio sportscaster; "Salesman of the Year," 1960 National Association of Direct Selling. Nelson laughed. "Superfluous voting. For whatever it was, you knew Mel'd win."

On August 27, 1950, he also got a day.

"The most unique tribute ever paid to a sportscaster sees a capacity crowd [*sic* 45,878] assembled at Yankee Stadium to honor baseball's first Voice," Fox chimed. "Movietone's own Mel Allen." Farley chaired. Gowdy emceed. Eddie Cantor popped eyes. Sixty-five gifts included a Cadillac, boat, TV set, and $9,000 in cash, used to start a Gehrig and Ruth scholarship fund at Columbia and Alabama, respectively.

A blonde unrolled a scroll: "Columbia Diamond Rings gift certificate presented to future Mrs. Mel Allen." Unlike the Yanks', its policy went unredeemed. "Some day, when I'm old," said The Voice, "perhaps have a grandchild, and have him sitting on my knee, maybe I'll point to some of these pictures in a scrapbook or other, I'll show him what a great day—the proudest day of my life that I've had. About all I'll be able to say to him is, 'How about that!'" Everywhere the phrase branded hats, coats, and signs.

Gowdy knew "Mel'd never leave on his own." Next spring the Red Sox job opened. "Part of me knew this was my chance to be Number One"—and stop being straight man.

"The rain's coming down helter skelter," Mel said. "Hi, helter." Curt, pained: "Hi, skelter."

Another part loved New York. "I'd done ads, Garden donkey basketball, trying to make my name," knowing that Allen's dwarfed it. "If I have to," said Mel, "I'll piggyback you to Fenway." Topping voided the Cowboy's contract. "Six states, great fans," Curt later mused. "I can't believe I was torn."

In April 1951, the Sox opened in New York. Botching Boston-area names like Worcester and Swampscott, Gowdy almost closed. Telegrams blared "Yankee-lover, go back home." Next day owner Tom Yawkey welcomed him: "A multimillionaire, but dressed in faded pants and shirt, looks like he doesn't have a dime." Not a whiff of Swampscott: Curt felt reborn.

"What kind of play-by-play do you want?" he said.

"They've had big-league baseball here since the 1876 Braves," said Yawkey. "No line drives made into pop-ups or excuses for errors, just give 'em the game." On September 28—Sox-Stripes, a Friday in The Bronx—the game was all they craved. Allie Reynolds had thrown a July no-hitter. "With two out in the ninth," Mel said, "now he had another." Williams popped a foul. The catcher dropped it. "Unbelievably, Ted then fouls to the *same* spot. Berra gets it—no-hitter."

MacPhail likened the Yankees 5-foot-7, 190-pounder to "the bottom man on an unemployed acrobatic team." Once Berra fielded a bunt and tagged a hitter and runner coming home. "I just tagged everybody, including the ump." Coach Bill Dickey helped: "He is learning me his experiences." Yogi's wed 358 homers, 1951 and 1954–55 MVP, and most Series played (14), won (10), games (75), and hits (71). Only Mantle tops his 39 RBI.

"Most seasons we made more money from Series cuts than we did our salary for the whole year," said Rizzuto. Phil knew how to field, hit behind the runner, win (nine flags in thirteen years), and bunt (to Joe D, "the greatest I ever saw"). On September 17, 1951, the Yanks, up by $\frac{1}{2}$ game, hosted Cleveland. "Boy, both teams would love to have this one," said Mel in the 1-all ninth inning. "They need first place and they need it badly and they want it badly and they're after it badly."

New York filled the bases. "Once again, Bob Lemon looks in, gets the sign. The three runners lead away . . . Here comes the pitch—and here comes Joe DiMaggio racing for the plate! He [Scooter] lays it down toward the first baseline. Bob Lemon races over, picks the ball up, has got nowhere to throw it as Joe DiMaggio crosses the plate with the running run as the Yankees win it, 2 to 1, on a squeeze play!"

That month Stengel knocked Tribe skipper Al Lopez for using just three pitchers. "Well, I always knew it couldn't be done, but somehow it don't always work."

The Yanks hoped to again work over Brooklyn. Instead, they remembered where they were for The Shot Heard 'Round the World. "It made him," Woods said of Hodges's call. "Say Russ, you think that day": October 3, 1951.

On August 11, the Giants trailed Brooklyn by $13\frac{1}{2}$ games. Each was 94–58 Friday, September 28, then won Saturday and Sunday to force a best-of-three playoff. "Think of it," said The Voice. "Three New York teams, one's in the Series, the other two tied." If ever "How about that!" applied, it did to The Miracle of Coogan's Bluff.

The series began in Flatbush: Jints, 3–1. Next day changed place and score: Dodgers, 10–0. A schoolboy knows Game 3's plot: Brooklyn, 4–2, ninth, one out, two on. "There's a long drive!" Hodges bayed on WMCA Radio. "It's going to be, I believe! The Giants win the pennant! The Giants win the pennant! The Giants win the pennant! The Giants win the pennant! Bobby Thomson hits into the lower deck of the leftfield stands! The Giants win the pennant! And they're going crazy! They are going crazy! Oh-ho!"

Confetti flew. The Bums staggered to their clubhouse. The Giants Eddie Stanky wrestled skipper Durocher to the ground. "I don't believe it! I don't believe it! I do not believe it!" Russ yelped, noise thick enough to chew. "Bobby Thomson hit a line drive into the lower deck of the leftfield stands, and the whole place is going crazy! The Giants—Horace Stoneham is now a winner—the Giants won it by a score of 5 to 4, and they're picking Bobby Thomson up and carrying him off the field!"

The Shot was clearly decreed by God. Thy will be done. Thy Series will was rain. The Nationals took a 2–1 game lead. "We had 'em," Hodges huffed, "till Game 4 was called." NBC TV had "slowly put together a network [sixty-four stations, including one in Mexico]," said The Voice, joining Jim Britt and Russ. The break let Stengel rest a tired staff: Stripes, 6–2 and 13–1. Next day the Giants scored twice in the ninth: Yanks, 4–3. Allen asked: "Is it going to happen again?"

Sal Yvars lined to right, where Bauer made a sliding catch, upon which Mel cried, "Three straight for The Perfessor!" A Jints rookie hit .182. Talullah Bankhead had not yet said: "There are two geniuses in the world—Willie Shakespeare and Willie Mays."

Like DiMaggio, Mays played center field. "You think you'll last forever," he said. Wiser, Joe, thirty-six, was often last to leave the park.

"He'll sit silently by his locker after a loss," said Coutros. "Many times, next to DiMaggio, is Mel." In 1951, a freshman played right to accommodate No. 5. Avoiding Joe on a fly, Mickey Mantle stepped on a drain cover, tore a knee, and fell. Said Coleman: "I thought he'd been shot, the way he went down." In the argot of the time, if you soon couldn't imagine being the Switcher, you were out of it, but good.

In 1952, the greenhorn, twenty, hit .311. Joe became a broadcaster, an Olympus stirring pity. "He never taught me how to hit," said Mel, "and I didn't teach him how to broadcast." In New Jersey, William F. Gavin, a Dodgers fan, perversely loved Joe's postgame show: "so bad it became a must for all the guys I knew, wooden, out of his element." Half a century later the ex-aide to U.S. House Minority Leader Robert Michel recalled Allen's "representing everything I despised."

Today more than 200 call bigs radio/video. About thirty-five to forty did then. As a boy, Nat Allbright broadcast to himself the Class B Bi-State League. In 1952, he launched the re-created Brooklyn Dodgers Radio Network. "Most Voices had an aide, a few two. All stayed until too old or dead. It was like the Round Table. Allen was our Arthur," his Excalibur crossing media, sport, and liege.

That fall Mel began NBC TV's *NCAA Game of the Week*, mooring *General Motors Scoreboard*. "Easy call," he said, comparing football with baseball. One was event, the greyhound you thrilled to: other, fact of life, a spaniel who held your heart. Football was show-biz: TV's future Bundys. Baseball was civic Beulahland, like the Depression Waltons, middlebrow and middleclass. "Different strokes, different folks," said The Voice in 1994.

In football, homework domineered. "I'd sit with officials a day or two before the game to discuss new rules." In 1949, Northwestern fullback Art Murakowski scored from the 4 yard line at Pasadena. Suddenly the ball dislodged. Mel eyed head linesman Jay Berwanger, "the first Heisman Trophy winner," who signaled possession at the goal. "Because of our meeting, I knew where to look."

Alabama coach Bear Bryant's look was a checkered hounds-tooth hat. Mel designed it in 1958. "He saw me wearing one and grabbed it off my head," said The Voice. Allen recouped it, asked, "What size's your hat?" and sent Bear another.

The Tide often led *Look* magazine's 1950s and early '60s annual "Mel Allen College Preview," "Bowl Preview," and "All-American Team." No one aired a more blue-chip consortium. A university photo shows "Mel and Larry in press box at the Army-Navy Game. President and Mrs. Eisenhower seated below NBC banner."

Nothing could replace The Game, nor Mel imagine anything he would rather air. In 1952, the average viewer showed that there was nothing he would rather watch.

NBC TV began a five-year, $7 million World Series contract, the event seen in all or part, said research firm J. A. Ward, by every other set. It was bigger than Ike, brassier than Milton Berle, more boffo than *Our Miss Brooks*. "Ask any kid," said Joe Garagiola, growing up in East St. Louis. "It wasn't October till we heard the Series."

As usual, the past assessed the present. "If you will it," said Theodore Herzl, "it is no dream." Brooklyn hadn't, losing its first five Series. Again the Faithful queued for standing room. Allen and Barber shared the booth—their last network link. Dodgers rookie Joe Black won the opener, 4–2. The Classic ricocheted through Game 5. Going home, up, 3–2, "We got 'em where we want 'em," crowed skipper Charlie Dressen. His Bums got the Bum's rush. The TV viewer got a rush.

"Here lies the summit," Edmund Burke defined a colleague. "He may live long. He may do much. But he can never exceed what he does this day." Game 6: Two Southern gentlemen climb a summit. "We acquainted you yesterday," said Allen. John Mize becomes "the storybook fella'." A "trickle ball [reaches] the right side." The Yanks are "down a game and down a run."

Mel glowingly presents Red, who dubs him "the pot calling the kettle black." Yogi parks one: "It's an even-up ballgame!"

Snider ripostes. "Boom!" Barber says. "Look out. Look out." The drive hit Bedford Avenue. "You needn't look any more." A park policeman snagged a foul. The crosswind blew at eight miles per hour. The Dodgers first baseman was 0 for 17. A priest closed his sermon: "Go home, keep the faith, obey the Ten Commandments, and pray for Gil Hodges." Yanks win, 3–2, a verisimilitude out *there*.

Eddie Gomez, who played bass with pianist Bill Evans, called jazz's aim "to make music that balanced passion and intellect." Balancing vibe and prose, The Voice and Redhead stayed at the summit next day.

The Gillette Safety Razor Company's "Cavalcade of Sports presentation" began with a voice that, like Ruth's, needed no introduction. "Good afternoon, baseball fans, this is Mel Allen, with Red Barber, greeting you. Welcome to the final game of the 1952 World Series." The whole country "stopped and paid attention," wrote Heywood Broun, to the "Blue Blades March" ("Da-*da*-da, da-da-da-da-da," sang Bob Costas), Sharpie the Parrot ("Mister, how ya' fixed for blades?"), and voice-over ("Look sharp. Feel sharp. Be sharp"). The Voice was not sufficient. He was, however, requisite. "I was always hopeful that [*v.* Barber] I held my own."

"How does this one look to you, Melrose?" Red commenced.

Seven seconds of dead air followed. "That pause," resumed Mel, "is meaningful." Each spoke into a large stationary microphone. "We're all set, the stage is set. Just sit back and watch it!" The day was dark and dank. "Topcoat weather," Allen said, "but you can be assured that as far as those men on the diamond are concerned, it's mighty hot."

Barber retired after 4½ innings. Robinson batted in Brooklyn's fifth. "There's a line drive!" said Allen. "Grabbed by [Rizzuto] for the out!" Turnabout came next inning. "There's a [Scooter] smash! Reese grabs it beautifully with a great backhander!" The "magnificent Mickey" Mantle then lofted to right field. "That ball is going,

going, it is gone! And the Yankees are back out in front, 3 to 2, in the Battle of the Home Runs!"

Relieving Black, Preacher Roe "is concerned about the situation. He's not afraid of it." Casey was "up and off that bench all day long." Reynolds's "got it where the heart is." With rest, "he's got it where the arm is." The boys "are moving around and about . . . shifting positions. Slapping hands together." The camera fixed each bench. "Tension is everywhere! No more baseball after today! This is it! Every pitch is it!"

Mel invoked the 1947 Series: "Remember that, Red?" Current strain was "further exemplified by our cameras." Bob Kuzava, "from Wyandotte, Michigan, a 6-foot-2, 200-pounder," relieved Vic Raschi in the seventh. "Pressure is past tense, even though we're in the present." New York, 4–2: two out, sacks full. "On third base is Furillo. On second base, Cox. On first base, Reese. Three runners ready to lead away."

Robinson swung. "It's a high pop-up! Who's going to get it? Here comes Billy Martin digging hard—and he makes the catch at the last second! How about that! . . . Man, it's been a great Series! It still is! We got two innings more at least to go!"

Allen's bass drum began the eighth—"Peak moment in World Series drama . . . Breaths are short! Hearts are beating rapidly! Pulses are racing!"—soon gentling to an oboe. "By the way," Mel nuanced, "a point I wish to make by way of distinction . . . without wishing to be patronizing . . . That is why, for example, among other reasons, Lopat once started in Brooklyn . . . If you wish to look ahead a bit." The Bombers did.

Next inning policemen manned each dugout, "anticipatory or not." Reese flew to left field. "Woodling getting under it. And the Yankees are champions! And look at Berra, piggybacking Bob Kuzava! Boy, the Yankees are happy! They had to do it the hard way again! They've always won the big game! And again they did it!"

The Voice went to break. A postgame Toni ad showed three belles shooting archery: "No one permanent is right for every type of hair. Have a lovelier wave than ever before!" To Mel, nothing was lovelier than the week before. "This has been one of the most terrific World Series of all time, and it's just a shame that one of these teams had to lose."

Both "covered themselves with glory." The camera panned baseball's Lourdes. The season ended with the "Blue Blades March." Winter would be a long time gone. ◆

# Fine and Dandy (1953–1954)

t began with the Salk vaccine, 3-D photography, and Marilyn Monroe's film *Niagara*. It ended in Dallas, on a sun-glint afternoon. Even now, something remains, if but a vague recollection, of circa 1953–63's sober poise. "Everyone has to have a place to go back to," Ronald Reagan said of another straight-arrow youth. "Dixon [Illinois] is that place for me."

Some wrongly call the age dull and pale. In particular, baseball mimed Reagan's later snapshot of America: "Hopeful, big-hearted, idealistic, daring, decent, and fair." In books and guides, as spring as bird chirps, and periodicals like the new *Sports Illustrated*, hailing "our national sport," it was *our* game, bub, and don't you forget it.

Let us return to the first Corvette and Davy Crockett caps and Fred Waring and the Pennsylvanians. Strangers talked ball. In pubs and restaurants, a cynosure was the Yanks. "I cannot now deny my recognition that the[se] years . . . ," wrote historian Theodore H. White, "were the most pleasant of our time."

For most, glad, like Dinah Shore, to see "the USA in your Chevrolet," it was a good time to be alive.

Shakespeare wrote in *Love's Labour's Lost* of "the heavenly rhetoric of thine eye." At best, baseball rhetoric can be heavenly, humane, and most often human. Before instant replay, fiber optics, and satellite telegraphy, the Voice functioned as writer, producer, cameraman, and star. "Don't much like TV," KDKA pioneer Harold Arlin said. "It leaves nothing to the imagination." Radio did.

"It's conversation. It's quirky. It's what did you do today," Bob Costas mused. "Tell me about the guy sitting down at the end of the dugout. Is he a character? Does he give guys the hot foot? Does he come from some tiny little town in Arkansas somewhere? How did he get here? It's a storyteller's game."

The story of the 1950s was an opiate and/or idiot box. By 1960, 88 percent of families—forty million homes—owned at least one TV set. "For the first time," White said, "it was possible to tell a foreigner what Americans do . . . They watch television." Ahead lay slow motion, stop-action, and the Telestrator. The screen got larger; picture, brighter; optical-turned-magnetic sound, clearer. At the time, TV's presence was enough.

In the late 1940s, New York's WPIX and WOR put baserunner and close-up cameras near each dugout and above first/third base. Color TV commenced August 11, 1951: Brooklyn at Boston. Next year the Series debuted NBC's split screen: left side, Raschi, pitching; right, Reese, off first. Later Charles P. Ginsburg of Ampex Corporation bred videotape, allowing replay. "Each year," said Allen, "things got a little more viewer-friendly."

WGN Chicago invented the centerfield camera shot. "A guy at a school prep game, seeing the scoreboard, thought, 'It'll focus the batter, pitcher, catcher, and ump,'" Cubs Voice Jack Brickhouse said. WPIX director Don Carney adopted it. The Peacock network (NBC's emblem, the bird) followed in the 1957 Series. At first George Weiss raged. "The other team'll steal our signs," the Yanks general manager told Mel. "Worse, you're showing too much. People'll stay at home."

Their '53ers drew 1,537,811, down half a million since 1950. One cause was TV's ubiquity. Another: the Stripes broadcast sheen. In 1948, Jim Woods replaced Harwell in Atlanta. Ernie's Dad was an invalid. One day Mom phoned. "Our son's broadcasts were our life," said Mrs. Harwell, thanking Jim. "You've made us forget our worries."

Next year's Crackers telecast a baseball-first entire schedule. In 1953, Mel phoned their Ponce de León Park. "He asks me to New

York," said Woods, "and as I walk into Allen's suite I know I'm in the big leagues. Mel's on the phone talking to Joe D about Marilyn Monroe."

A writer pondered, "Is this going to be good for DiMaggio?" Reply: "It's got to be better than rooming with [pitcher] Joe Page." That spring actor Joe E. Brown replaced DiMag on pregame/ postgame shows. "He was also supposed to do a couple innings," said The Voice. "Guess Brown should have stuck to film."

Jim quickly learned Mel's habit of snapping his fingers when something bothered him.

Mantle fouled a pitch "back on top," said Woods. Fingers snapped.

Poss: "What's wrong?"

Mel: "On top of what?"

"The roof."

"Then say the roof and complete your sentence!"

Jim never forgot the tutorial. "I learned to take nothing for granted and not to fear dead air, surprising for a guy recalled for talking." Possum recalled him differently: "the best announcer to cover this game—Melvin Allen Israel."

"Until Allen made his bow as a sportscaster, baseball and football were covered by the networks with a dry-as-dust objectivity more suited to a chess match than America's favorite sports," read Dick Rubin's press release. That changed, he said, "with Mel's informal, friendly appeal in which he used the quantity of information about sports that he had at his fingertips."

He had a lot, and many who wished to hear it. Raised in Brooklyn, Maury Allen spent his off-season eying a calendar. "You'd watch other sports, but you were counting till Opening Day," said the future *New York Post* columnist. "Your mind was baseball. In broadcasting, there was Mel—and everyone else."

By 1953, he was so familiar, wrote the *News*'s Ben Gross, that "on Broadway [and] Park Avenue, casual pedestrians, taxi drivers, and store owners treat him as an old friend." Said Abramson: "The hero worship bewilders him." Allen was "flattered to death, but I honestly can't figure it. After all, I never hit a home run for the Yanks—I'm just a side observer."

The *Journal-American* observed his stash: "[In 1946], he had $500 in the bank [*v.* now-$150,000 salary]. Money is secondary. Allen is in love with his job." To Coutros, the Yanks "Most Voluble Player" was "the man who came to broadcast and stayed to cheer." The MVP received about 1,000 weekly letters, more than any U.S. announcer, many addressed to "Mr. How About That." The few which "are anti-Semitic [stung], because of his deep feeling for his family."

Mel answered each—"I keep it high. Mom taught you don't descend to nasty people's level"—did scheduling, got train berths, and heard out cranks, yet for a long time nixed an office or secretary. Said Larry: "He just can't conceive himself as being important enough to rate these things."

Among things which did:

- Birthday cards, marriage proposals, and "intimate [mail] presents," wrote a columnist: also, as we will see, taunts meant for a bottom-dwelling slug.
- Releases from whatever network Allen buoyed at the moment: e.g., April 1953, Columbia, touting "color" for the 79th Kentucky Derby. "Tune in from 5:15–5:45 Eastern Time."
- CBS TV's 1951–54 *Mel Allen Sports Spot* between *Pabst Blue Ribbon Bouts* and 11:00 P.M. local news. "An interview show sponsored by White Owls," said his brother. "He'd talk with a sports celebrity." It ended when R. J. Reynolds Company, dumping White Owl, joined the Stripes.

"Money talks," mused Allen. "Here it homered."

On April 17, 1953, No. 7 did at Griffith Stadium. "Mantle swings [off Chuck Stobbs] . . . There's a tremendous drive going into deep left field!" said The Voice, re-creating. "It's going, going, it's going over the bleachers and over the sign atop the bleachers into the yards of houses across the street!"—Perry L. Cool's at 434 Oakdale Street. "It's got to be one of the longest home runs I've ever seen hit! How about that!"

Yanks publicist Arthur [Red] Patterson lacked a tape measure. On a hunch, he started walking off Mick's blast. Said Mel: "He's going to go out there to see how far that ball actually did go": 391 feet to the bleachers; another 69, outer wall; then, bonking the 60-foot-high National Bohemian Beer scoreboard, 105 across Fifth Street (565 feet total)—the first "tape measure" homer.

National Bohemian painted an "X" where the ball hit the board. Irked, Nats owner Clark Griffith erased the spot. Little could erase Brooklyn's 1953 assault. Campanella had an N.L.–best 142 RBI. Most years Snider's .336, 42, and 126 would have won the Triple Crown. Five regulars topped .300. With a 105–49 record, they led the National League in runs, home runs, and runs batted in, and slugging, fielding, and batting average.

In July, Dressen said, "The Giants is dead." Mel had a picnic. "Like that guy [Brooklyn Board of Education] said, 'You wouldn't say the United States *are* the best country in the world. So how can you say, "The Giants *are* dead"?'" Flatbush hoped that the Dodgers weren't. Said Reese: "Gotta' be some day we beat the Yankees."

McCarthy won four straight titles (1936–39). Stengel platooned New York to number five. Three players shared first base. Only Ford tossed more than 200 innings. Did fit and start miff the Stripes? "When you get that World Series check every November," said Hank Bauer, "you don't want to leave. There were no Yankees saying play me or trade me."

Brooklyn's sign read, BEAT ME. Up, three games to two, the Yanks led, 3–1, until Carl Furillo's ninth-inning tying homer. Martin then knocked a Classic-winning hit. "They'd seem human in the regular season," said Allen, televising his third straight Oktoberfest. "But with money on the line, they'd break the bank."

New York had broken Brooklyn in five straight Series. Soon only one club was still synonymic with its Voice.

◆ ◆ ◆

Since 1939, Gillette had owned the Classic. "It was growing an empire," said Barber, "but announcers only got a demeaning $200 a game." Most took it. By contrast, in September 1953, Red demanded "to negotiate my fee." Piqued, Gillette deemed him a disposable blade.

Naively, Barber phoned Walter O'Malley, unaware how the Dodgers owner and Topping had recently gotten gassed.

"I hate the son of a bitch [Barber]," O'Malley railed at Shor's.

Dan reciprocated: "I can't stand him [Mel]." Nearby, Woods watched "the bosses of baseball's two biggest teams ripping their own guys—at the time, broadcasting's two biggest names."

O'Malley raised his glass. "I'll trade you the son of a bitch."

Dan flushed. "I'll go you one more. I'll give you Allen."

Woods laughed. "Talk about a deal to shock the country—Allen for Barber, at the top of each career." Next day, "*sans* booze," they reneged.

O'Malley was less likely than A. Craig Smith to back Red's right to negotiate. "That is *your* problem," he sniffed. "I'll nominate [colleague Vin] Scully to take your place." Barber told himself, "Walter, the Dodgers are now *your* problem." Resigning, he was replaced by Scully, the son Red never had.

Next month Weiss said, "Mel, we've got a chance to get Barber. What do you think?"

"Jiminy Cricket, I would." In 1954, Brooklyn's archetype began Yanks TV/radio play-by-play and pregame/postgame video.

"New league," Red mused. "I don't know the players." Worse, offseason surgery sowed deafness in one ear. Hard on young players, one old gentleman might save another. "Stengel knew without my saying it that something was wrong. He'd brief me, take all the time in the world." Photos show him standing next to Barber's good ear.

NBC's Tom Gallery thought the lay preacher "a sanctimonious, Psalm-singing son of a bitch." Increasingly, that core turned public in The Bronx. "In Brooklyn, Red may have been the best ever," said

Costas, "but later he turned dry, somewhat bitter, almost interior, nowhere as good as Mel."

Perhaps, he simply missed being boss.

The boss defied easy judgment. Surely he grasped The Game. In 1952, Allen caught Mantle "pulling his bat back too far," said Rubin. "Neither the manager nor any of his coaches caught it so Mel sought out Mick and told him about it." Next day he doubled and went deep. Beyond that—what? It was hard to say we knew the man who said grace around baseball's table.

Now forty, Mel was a "happy-go-lucky punster" and interior "worrywart," would-be "shrewd practicing attorney" as "gullible as the most wide-eyed rube," and "man of the world" living with his parents in a new house—"like him," said *Post*man Leonard Shecter, "big and comfortable"—having moved to Bedford Village, 35 miles north of Yankee Stadium. "He is busy renovating it," yet could barely pound a nail. Allen "is not afraid to live in a style befitting his income," wrote Coutros, yet seemed almost otherworldly.

A *News* photo showed "Larry [with] the floor as the Allen boys get together with their parents . . . in breakfast nook." The Voice oozed *bonhomie*, yet had no home except his clan. The single guy was a joiner: to Saints and Sinners, a lifetime member; a Lambs Club sign read, MEL'S OUR [V]ALLENTINE; The Friars roasted him—Milton Berle, Phil Silvers, and Toots Shor, said Larry, "throwing hash." Mock serious, Jack Benny countered, "Hey! Let me add a little class."

Allen founded the ALS (Lou Gehrig Disease) Foundation. At one time or another he funded and even chaired the American Legion, Boy Scouts of America, Cancer Fund, Children to Palestine Drive, Fight for Sight, Greater New York Fund, Mickey Mantle Hodgkin's Foundation, Multiple Sclerosis, Muscular Dystrophy, Police Athletic League, St. Pascal's Catholic Church, United Cerebral Palsy, and United Jewish Appeal, yet raised hell over bric-a-brac.

Like a carpenter, The Voice measured his booth. "If it was too small [for Sports Broadcasters Association criteria]," said publicist

Jody Zierler, "he'd demand it be rebuilt." Another *idée fixe* cloaked Mel Allen Day, to which thousands had donated time or cash. "I'm the only one who can write to thank [them] and personalize it," Allen said. "They deserve that," but for a time didn't get it.

Months lapsed. Unacknowledged, givers fumed. "I begged Mel to let me help him out," Jody mused, "or have some of the Yankee office staff pitch in." Anna's son declined. Zierler kept telling him to "change his mind or a little thing would blow up into a real *cause célèbre.*"

Refusing, he finally finished, having learned at his mother's knee. "There are just certain things that were sensible and dignified." Southern Man could be a Stubborn Man.

There was always something about Allen from, not of, New York. "He has merrily made his way to the top of the field of limited opportunities without deceit and without cynicism," wrote *Sports Illustrated*, "and without it would seem half-trying, fate having stalked him more than the other way around." Arriving in Manhattan, he roomed with Edwards and Baruch. They would ring a bell, trick Mel into opening the door in pajamas, and lock him out. "If you told him the Queen of Sheba was standing at the men's bar at Cavanaugh's, drinking a zombie," said Andre, "chances are he'd run right down there and begin to wave!"

Allen waved at children in the upper deck, later befriending hard scrabblers near his car. "Out pops 50 cents to 'run home and wash your face,'" said Coutros, "with the side advice to the kid that ballplayers wash theirs." At home, he filibustered about Esther's young daughter Risa, "the apple of his eye. He likes talking about her as much as he does baseball."

Another writer saw the irony. "Allen's only hobby is children—his married sister's two children [Larry and wife Margie had two], his neighbors' children, and the children of all ages that he studies with rapt fascination along the narrow canyons of Manhattan on an afternoon when there is no game." In a photo, Mel holds a Little Leaguer. His T-shirt reads: "I'm a little Yankee."

A future team publicist invoked a rain relay. "Yankee Stadium was funny. We didn't have a real broadcast booth, just rows of seats," said Marty Appel. The Voice began interviewing. A fan parried by trying to snatch his hat. On air, Mel chided him. "He was so much like a father, lecturing his son."

Mel would make a great dad, even for a Yankee-hater. A parlor game became trying to tie him to the knot.

Tabloids of the time wrapped Mel in celluloid: "a strapping, magnetic fellow," said Ben Gross, "6-foot-1¼ inches tall, a 190-pounder with humorous hazel eyes and dark brown hair. He could double as a movie star." Sidney Fields added: "He is big, rather swarthy, with the flat nose of a prize fighter, and a quiet eagerness that always makes his deep, mellow voice deeper and mellower." A speech teacher might call it "rich and euphonious, with unusual depth and vibrancy," wrote Abramson, "but to the young ladies it is simply the voice of the boudoir." Singer Dorothy Sarnoff observed: "There is more socko sex appeal in Mel's simple 'Good afternoon, everyone' than in Charles Boyer's 'Come to the cas-baah.'"

The result was a chaser: pursuing, not drinking. Scribes cast stalkers on Park Avenue, behind posts at The Stadium, mailing socks and ties and cash "without return addresses," said Coutros, "so he can't send them back." Some sent "passionate letters, phone calls, telegrams, invitations to parties, dances, and weekend outings," misconstruing an off-air joke as a sonnet sung upon the heart. "They then write thanking him." Sensible and dignified, The Voice inevitably replied.

Archives show groupies as batty as a fungo stick. One woman wrote: "Here is pesty again with things on her mind . . . P.S. I'll bet your secretary thinks I'm a character." In Queens, Marge Kaiser was "pleased as a school girl on her first date [to get a letter]. Look for me," August 3, 1957, in lower section five, seat four. "I am tall, slim, red-headed, and shall wear a black dress." Two years later "I just want [again] to say I love you," black still her favorite color.

From Brooklyn, Aldo Tordo sent a pinup. "Hey, good lookin'. Tonight I'll kiss your picture." Flatbusher Rosane Dawn, at 160 Fenimore Street, Apt. 3D, mailed more than twenty letters and photos of her new car, glasses, and permanent. Helen (Wicks) Dodge of Upstate Frankfort shipped her high school ring, now rusty. Ann Rogers of Somerville, New Jersey, was going, going, gone. In 1956, she misheard Barber note "Mel's new wife." Crushed, the would-be Hammerstein tried verse. "'As if by a miracle the world was golden again'—a song for a musical comedy I am writing."

Five years later, unpublished, Ann penned: "Could I ever love another? No. You are the expression of all the beauty that God ever created." Mel's status became a cottage industry: especially, women's niche, threat, or lack.

"Men listen to him [and] women chase him, but no woman has quite caught him—yet," said the *News*. When would Allen get hitched? Depends on who you asked.

"Baching it," The Voice dated, Tom Meany wrote, "a stunning sequence of women." Of one knockout, he jibed, "Here comes Mel Allen with the future Miss Jones!" meaning Mel would never marry. "A bachelor by circumstances rather than design," Allen invoked the Army. "I was engaged [to college steady Miriam Rosenblum], but with my income cut off I let my head rule my heart. She got tired of waiting, I suppose. ["Mel called her up," Larry said, "and her Dad answered, 'Too late. She's married.'"] I want to marry more than anything in the world, marry and have children." In time, he tired of looking for love in all the wrong places.

Allen's "appearance, income, charm, and incalculable popularity with the female sex would seem to establish him as a gay blade, but he is the opposite," said Abramson. "He is so careful about being seen out socially with a female that people closest to him are convinced he is subconsciously afraid of the opposite gender." Mel treated women as flesh and blood, not catchphrase and caricature. "He hates to hurt people," an aide said. "If he'd just hang up on a groupie, just once." Instead, The Voice increasingly "shunned the saloon circuit," treating hearsay like poison ivy.

Once he guested on *The Queen of the Bust* [Dagmar's] TV show. She kissed him, stoking a rumored *affaire de coeur*. Allen "was beside himself," said a friend. "You'd think being mentioned in the same breath as Dagmar was a crime." Mail fueled his rage. "How dare you associate yourself with a woman who bares herself sinfully on the screen?" a letter read. Another: "You represent the highest standards of sport to my young sons and we expected better things." Mother's knee: He vowed to "never compromise all the shining ideals of the great American game."

Dagmar wed actor Danny Dayton. The Voice exhaled. Rumor then targeted film's Judy Lynn and singers Margaret Phelan and Dinah Shore. Finally, Mel found no business better than show business. "I don't want to sound like a preacher, but I just can't allow myself to get mixed up in loose notoriety." Otherwise, "before you know it, people say things about you which don't do you a bit of good. What's more, I wouldn't get any peace of mind in behaving like a wolf, keeping a woman, or running around town."

Later, Mel would loathe the mid- to late-sixties muck of "Do your own thing," "Don't trust anyone over thirty," and the self-congratulatory, "If it feels good, do it." Its simple-minded arrogance insulted his sense of right. On the other hand, some thought Allen Victorian, even for 1952. "He can go on for hours talking about the pure and simple in life, and even though he's sincere, he can get awfully tiresome," said a CBS secretary. "A lot of his ideas were old-fashioned even in grandmother's day."

It is worth noting that most found him loyal, polite, and virtuous. There are far worse ways to be recalled.

Barber recalls Mel as part of "what may have been the greatest threesome in baseball broadcast history": himself, Woods, and Allen. Brooklyn's Len Shapiro watched despite himself: "Ballantine! The

Yankees! Allen—so smooth and mellow!" milder, gentler, thus, more universal, than New York.

"I still picture being at home," said Shapiro, "breaking bread with Mel on TV," his voice a roller coaster. "'The big crowd is roaring on every pitch.'" Once 15,000 people specked Cleveland's 78,000-seat emporium. "There was no reaction, not even negative, no waves to push me up," said Allen. "I guess I didn't react the way Yankee fans wanted because they sent Weiss letters." The GM asked him what gave.

He was partisan, not prejudiced, The Voice explained. "Prejudiced you see only one side and dislike the other side. Partisan means you appreciate both sides, but favor one." Many felt that he crossed the line. "Undearest Mel. Those lousy Yanks are playing a great bunch of ball, good enough for sixth place," one wrote. "According to you, when a Yankee makes a [workaday] catch, it's the greatest play you've ever seen. If somebody on another team breaks his neck chasing a ball, it's just a routine play. I'll never stoop as low to be a Yankee fan."

Some stooped lower. "You're too damned hysterical when you're rooting for the home team and you're always hurting my ear drums," read a letter. Others termed Allen "overemotional. Let's just have the facts"; too "excited about a mere game. Man, don't you know there was just a war going on in Korea?"; and redolent of "hammed-up pro-Yankee [bias taking] the sportsmanship out of sports."

Mel "groans, writhes, grimaces and contorts himself in moral agony when his team falls behind," wrote Abramson, "then pours out huzzahs when 'that Yogi boy' or 'our little Scooter' sends the Yankees spurting to the fore." Jack Mann's eight papers included the *Herald Tribune.* "The tone of Mel Allen's voice was almost as indicative as a scoreboard."

Nelson likened him to "the drinking friend who takes home the town drunk. Since the anti-Yankees aren't able to change the team, they hit the nearest thing to a rolling pin—Mel." Partisan, not prejudiced: "You listen," said The Voice. "I call another team's home run the same as I call Mantle's. The guy who doesn't think so didn't want Mantle to hit that home run in the first place."

World Series Game 6, 1953: Furillo ties the Stripes. "Allen exploded with such frantic wonder," said Coutros, "that The Stadium switchboard lit up with calls from Yankee rooters who wanted him hanged," for once miming Yankee-haters. Said the *Times*: "To many, he is the connoisseur of the obvious on the cliché matinee."

Their *bete noire* bristled. "I never call first base the initial sack or home plate the dish. Or refer to the hot corner or keystone sack." The enemy set store by Mel's own missive: "You're a reporter, but a fan of the team."

Daily he got letters about bad seats at The Stadium. "Whether he likes it or not, Allen is Mr. Yankee," wrote Shecter. "And, as he might say, 'That's the way it goes.'" There is little to suggest he didn't like how it went.

To Ben Gross, Allen was "a truly happy man. For he is so enamored of his job that it has actually become his hobby." Baseball, Mel averred, "is my life"—October's, above all.

"I'll kid the [Yankees broadcast] team in the booth and sing 'Happy Birthday' to a player," he said. The Series was antipodean. "It has to be straight, impersonal, and completely factual. So during the last few games before the Classic, I prepare myself by eliminating personalities. Also, I try to get a lot of rest."

Allen woke at 10:00, had breakfast, read papers, made notes, and at 11:30 went "to the park to watch practice, visit the players, and tell stories to umpires." A favorite: Steamboat Johnson's call in a Southern Association game in Memphis.

Badgering, a woman howled, "If you were my husband, I'd give you poison in your coffee."

The umpire struck back: "Lady, if you were my wife, I'd take it."

Series game time was usually 1:00 P.M. Afterward Mel snacked— "a sandwich. I'm still so wound up, I can't eat more." Next: hotel, shower, nap, timing sponsor ads, and "collecting information" in the pressroom. "Then I go to bed, but it's a long time before sleep comes." Even the "slightest [on-air] error may cause the heavens to fall"—*uptight* over a decade before the term was coined.

The ex-high school jock unbent in the clubhouse. Ted Williams halted a monologue with Bobby Doerr to "thank me for being so nice to him." Allen laughed. "Hell, what else *could* you be to a lifetime .344 hitter?" Niceness wouldn't feed the bulldog. Ingenuity might.

Joe Page had been "The Fireman," rescuing a starter. Lopat was the "Junkman" or "Steady Eddie." Raschi became "The Springfield Rifle"; Woodling, "Old Faithful"; Bauer, "The Man of the Hour." Reynolds, aka "Super Chief," was an Oklahoman Indian and Nazarene minister's son. Bill Skowron segued into "Moose." The noise "you are hearing," said Allen, "is 'Moose'—not boos."

The Voice did not invent "When the sponsor writes your name / What he wants to hear / Is not who won or lost the game / But how you sold the beer." (Bob Wolff did with the 1947–60 sackcloth Senators.) He did grasp the umbilical cord between game and cult. "Puns, nicknames, come-ons, whatever you have to do, keep things fun. That's what the booth is for."

I liked baseball more before cross-licensing and consumer analysis. I liked how Chicago's Jack Brickhouse sold Hamm's Beer; Cleveland's Jimmy Dudley, Carling's "Mabel, Black Label"; and Philly's Byrum Saam, Phillies cigars. I liked it best when The Voice outpitched them all.

"The idea was to get in an extra plug for the sponsors," he observed, "so maybe they'd extend my contract." Each angel—Philip Morris, R. J. Reynolds, P. Ballantine and Sons—bought innings 1–3, 4–6, or 7–9. General Cigar sired the White Owl Wallop: "People don't smoke 'em now like today, but they were huge." As in a greasespot intellection, Atlantic Refining Company hyped "Red Ball Service," its aria, "Atlantic Keeps Your Car on the Go," as old-hat as "Old Cape Cod."

Thirty years later Mel still knew the song: "Atlantic keeps your car on the go / For business, for pleasure / in any kind of weather / Atlantic keeps your car on the go. When you want to go places and do things / What a pleasure your driving can be / With quality products and top-notch service / Your Atlantic dealer is the man to see. Atlantic keeps your car on the go, go, go / So keep on the go with Atlantic."

One night an eight-year-old heard Allen suggest "grab[bing] yourself a Ballantine."

Complying, I found the refrigerator blocked by my Baptist mother.

"We don't drink beer," she said.

Nodding, I receded. Ballantine's *real* blast was the Atlantic Seaboard, inhaling Mel on The Home of Champions Network.

In 1947, WABD TV Channel 5 replaced DuMont as the Yankees television home. WPIX Channel 11 succeeded it in 1952. "Each year we televised every home game. Come '53, we added road." The Stripes launched 140-game coverage upon the Bums and Jints 1958 Westward-Ho. By 1960, "The Yankees again are undisputed champions of the electronic circuit," wrote *The Sporting News*, "with a total of 124 games—all 77 at home and 47 on the road scheduled for telecasting": all weekend, most Tuesday and Friday nights, and others.

"Every year," Mel drawled, "our TV network got more attention," particularly in New Haven (1957), Wilkes-Barre and Waterbury (1958), and Albany, Binghamton, Scranton, and Utica (1962). By 1950, the Yanks' radio network tied Scranton, Springfield, and fourteen New York outlets. 1951: Add Norfolk and Williamsport. 1952: twenty-six stations included Binghamton; Buffalo; Rochester; Syracuse; Auburn, Harriet Tubman's hometown; and Jamestown, Lucille Ball's. 1957: thirty-eight knit Connecticut, Massachusetts, New Jersey, New York, Pennsylvania, and Vermont.

Most aides handled both: Hodges 1946–48, Bill Slater 1948 (TV only), Gowdy 1949–50, Albert (Dolly) Stark 1949 (TV), Dizzy Dean 1950–51, Art Gleeson 1951–52, DiMag and Bill Crowley 1952,

Brown 1953, Woods 1953–56, Barber 1954–64, Rizzuto 1957–64, and Coleman 1963–64.

Each year *TSN* listed slate and cast. A 1963 picture shows The Voice jowly, heavier, and without much hair. He lost most of it, Mel joked, in 1954.

Five times from 1951 to 1956 the Indians placed second to New York. "I think Cleveland had as much talent," said Allen. "The difference is that George Weiss'd buy or trade for a Johnny Mize or Country Slaughter in September." Dudley tried to forget. "The Yankees!" he gaped. "A reserve there, an injury there, and we'd have won—I counted it once—six pennants in a row."

Their *jihad* filled bars and salons and two places of address. "We'd have sixty thousand at The Stadium," said Allen. Unlike Dudley, the Tribe bowl shunned reserve. "They'd come in by train and bus from Buffalo and Erie and Wheeling, all sure this year to beat the Yankees. They'd go home with nothing, every time a heartache," 'till piercing Casey's impenetrable line.

Douglass Wallop wrote 1954's *The Year the Yankees Lost the Pennant.* The Ol' Perfessor taught a class. Cleveland led the A.L. in ERA (2.78) and dingers (156). Lemon, Feller, Mike Garcia, and Early Wynn went 78–29. An unwowed twenty-something Buckeye wrote Mel—"I would like to be a broadcaster, and am a big fan of yours"—requesting a signed picture. "My brother didn't know him," said Larry. Mel phoned, talked for an hour, and became the hero of a beefy shipbuilder's son.

"There's a sentimental streak, this loyalty to the underdog, to [1973– Yanks owner] George Steinbrenner," said Gannett News Service's Scott Pitoniak. "He coached on Lou Saban's [1955] football staff at Northwestern. Later Lou needs a job and George makes him Yankees president." Boss George helped revive Mel in the 1970s. In 1954, only the Stripes needed CPR.

On September 12, before 86,563, the Indians twice spanked Stengel. His train reached Manhattan via Pennsylvania and Upstate

New York. Casey was heckled. Drunks stained each station stop. Mel stared out his window. "Stengel never forgot it to the last day of his life."

Publicly, he kept calm. Yogi and Mantle played last-day third base and shortstop, respectively. "Welcome," said Casey, "to my power lineup." Allen's cool braved a summer phone call to Detroit's Cadillac Hotel. "At first I thought someone was ribbing me and I chatted along waiting for him to give himself away." The man then asked if Mel knew about local police raiding teenage gangs.

"Four hundred of us'll be at the game tonight," the stranger said, ostensibly to hurt Allen. Police screened the booth: New York beat Detroit, 4–3, closing a Stengel-best 103–51. On September 25, Cleveland flayed Detroit, 11–1, for symmetrical victory 111, topping Murderers Row's 110. "Too bad Mel died [in 1996]," said Gowdy. "He'd have enjoyed the Yankees 1998"—114–48.

Afterword: In 1954, one Stripes radio affiliate (Schenectady) played at another (Williamsport). "The Little League World Series final," Mel piped on Movietone. "There's a [Fulton, California] drive deep to left field, and it's in the leftfield seats for a mighty homer! Boy, are they happy! They've got a chance!"

Schenectady won, 5–1. The Yanks chance began next spring. ◆

# Legend in Your Own Time
## (1955–1959)

ay 1948. The Red Army occupies Poland, much of Germany, and the rest of Eastern Europe. Harry Truman hates it. "I'm tired," he writes, "of babying the Soviets." From Stettin to Trieste, "an Iron Curtain has descended across the continent," adds Winston Churchill. An Ozark encyclopedist gives a lecture: "Radio Announcing I Have Did." Dizzy Dean vows to "get me a bunch of bats and balls and sneak me a couple of empires and learn them kids behind the Iron Curtain how to bat and play baseball." Marshal Stalin—"Joe Stallion"—could run concessions. "[That way] he'd getta' outta' politics and get in a honest business."

Next year the ex-big-league righty jazzed the tone deaf Browns. "I slud along with them as long as I could [since 1947]," Diz said, "but I eventual made up my mind to quit." In 1950, he joined Allen at The Stadium, one night gracing TV's *What's My Line.*

"The guest could be Dizzy Dean," blindfolded panelist Arlene Francis said.

Dorothy Kilgallen: "Oh, no, this man is much too intelligent."

By now, Dean "had gotten to where he said, 'He slid, I mean, slud into third,'" mused Mel. A batter "swang"; pitcher, "throwed"; slugger, stood "confidentially." Diz gutted the language like no one had, or will. Convention expected him to own the Apple. Instead, he couldn't rent appeal. "Too rural," said The Voice. "It didn't work." In 1952, Dean rejoined the Browns, which had. "They got to be my words, 'cause no one else would have 'em."

No one would then have regular-season network TV baseball. "All local," Allen said. "Why would Omaha watch Red Sox-Browns?" In 1953, ABC began *Game of the Week*, crashing swanker CBS in 1955. Baseball banned it within 50 miles of a big-league city. Unvexed, *Game* wooed a giant fifteen rating (one point = 1 percent of TV homes). "One in three viewers were blacked out," puffed CBS sports head Bill MacPhail. "In the rest, four of five sets in use watched us!" To horsefeathers with New York. In Mayberry, Ol' Diz fused Ma Kettle, Billy Sunday, and Tennessee Ernie Ford.

At one time or another, Dean slept, ate a watermelon, and sang "Precious Memories" in the booth. He called everyone on the planet "pod-nuh," cracked Gallup's most admired list, and tied 300 pounds, a string tie, and Stetson—the whole rustic goods. "Stunning," mused MacPhail. "In Mid-America, watching him was a religion"; to Ron Powers, "a mythologizing presence," not courtly like Barber, or eastern like Husing, or a blast furnace like The Voice.

"By the mid-1950s," said Lindsey Nelson, "he passed Barber as baseball's next-to-Allen name"—Mel, kneading English; Diz, nuking it; each coming to mean the game. "In the Series, Mel showed how baseball could work each fall. Diz was first to show how it could work each week." Later Gowdy became a network paradigm; Tony Kubek, analyst's analyst; Vin Scully, homer's Homer. "Maybe none of this happens but for Mel and Diz."

Today Tim McCarver wiles eggheads and workingmen. Costas melds David Letterman and Tom Lasorda. To ESPN's Jon Miller, "Baseball means company. It comforts you and you enjoy it."

There was much to enjoy about 1955.

Streaking would gain a 1970s out-of-body tilt. Unsure of a culprit's sex, Yogi Berra said, "He had a bag over his head." The 1950s differed: Streaking meant the Stripes. The '55ers won the first of another four straight flags. Ford threw two one-hitters. Mantle led the league in walks, on-base, slugging, and going deep. New York would naturally win the Series—playing, as it did, Brooklyn. The Voice liked a story from 1949. Games 1-2 at The Stadium split. "Poi-fect! We got 'ya!" a fan told him outside the park. The Yankees won the next three—at Ebbets Field.

"You just expected it," said Allen, despite, as Leonard Koppett wrote, "no other team generat[ing] a richer collection of memories, more closely held by so many people," than the Bums. Gil Hodges spelled respect. Roy Campanella resembled a sumo wrestler. Billy Cox turned doubles into slumps. Surnames seemed *de trop*. Oisk, Big Newk, and Preach replaced Carl Erskine, Don Newcombe, and Preacher Roe. Other sports became something to take or leave.

In 1946, John Updike, fourteen, listened to Game 7 in his father's car in a Shillington, Pennsylvania, high school parking lot. Red Sox lose, 4–3. "I don't know if I cried, sitting alone in that old car" 400 miles from Boston, "but I might have." Updike emerged "dazed and with something lost forever." Brooklyn nodded, cross-hatching victory and misery: six postwar pennants, but with a thing about losing a final-day flag or Series (1946–47 and 1949–53).

After Thomson's 1951 homer beat them, Pee Wee Reese returned to the training room. "You know what I really don't understand?" he said.

"What?" said Jackie Robinson.

"How after all these years playing baseball I haven't gone insane."

The 1955 Stripes won Games 1-2. Brooklyn took the next three at Ebbets, inverting 1949. Ford took Game 6. The borough braced, having lost seven straight Series. "Don't worry," said Johnny Podres, twenty-three, too young to grasp history. "I'll shut 'em out tomorrow": October 4, in The Bronx.

Role reversal. Madonna becomes Mary Poppins; Dick Cheney, Errol Flynn; Bums, Yanks. Allen did the final's first 4½ innings. Succeeding him: Scully, twenty-seven. In the sixth inning, Brooklyn led, 2–0. Martin walked, leading off. Gil McDougald bunted safely. "Yogi

Berra the batter," said Mel, re-creating. "The outfield swung way around toward right. Sandy Amoros is playing way into left-center. Berra is basically a pull hitter," except now.

"Berra swings and he does hit one to the opposite field, down the leftfield line." Left-handed Amoros bolted toward the pole. Said Reese: "If he'd been right-handed the ball probably would have dropped to tie the score. Berra'd been at second with no outs." Instead, "he makes a sensational, running, one-handed catch!" said Mel. "He turns, whirls, fires to Pee Wee Reese. Reese fires to Gil Hodges at first base in time to double up Gil McDougald! And the Yankees rally is stymied!"

Ninth inning: Jupiter aligns with Mars. With two away, Elston Howard grounded out, aptly, Reese to Hodges: Captain to Quiet Man. "Ladies and gentlemen," said Scully, "the Brooklyn Dodgers are the champions of the world." All winter people asked how he stayed calm. "The truth is I was so emotionally overwhelmed that if I had said another word I would have cried."

Erskine found the clubhouse he first visited in 1949. "There was a quietness when we first walked in, almost a spiritual feeling. Then someone opened champagne, and the lid blew off." It already had in Flatbush. "We dood it! We beat 'em! We beat them Yankees! We spot 'em th' foist two games . . . an' we beat 'em! That Podres! Woil Cham-peens! Me!" screeched the *Daily News*'s Brooklyn Bum.

In the *Times*, John Drebinger wrote, "Brooklyn at long last has won the World Series and now let someone suggest moving the Dodgers elsewhere."

Two years later, someone did.

"Trying to put a dateline into a story about Curt Gowdy's life," said a writer, "is like trying to establish residency for a migratory duck." Allen's, too. All-Star Game 1954: The Voice opens a bottle of soda, which explodes, leaving his right hand, wrote Melvin Durslag, "a bleeding, lacerated mess." At a train stop the doctor orders Mel to a hospital. He refuses. The medic binds him up. Fall 1955: The

Bombers tour Japan, "even there," said HBO, "instantly recognizable." Fall Classic: Pick a year. Entire year: Pick 1956.

*Sports Illustrated* dedicated its April 12 issue to "The Great American Game." "You feel this more in the North than you do in the sun country, but one day late in the winter you hear a voice over the radio," wrote Robert Creamer. "You may be driving a car through slush, with bags of groceries on the floor in front and a bunch of kids in mufflers and galoshes on the back seat. You don't mind. You're used to your lot. Slush and muddy galoshes are a way of life. Then the car radio, which you have turned on haphazardly, warms up and a familiar voice says, 'Two away now. Musial down off third. Cards lead, 2–0. The pitch. It's in there! Strike one.'

"It is the somewhat droning, somewhat nasal voice of your favorite baseball announcer, broadcasting a spring training game from Florida. Last summer you cursed him out when he failed for an inning and a half to mention the score of a game you had tuned in on late. But now, in the slush, you love him. His voice is the promised kiss of springtime." Retrieve the Song of Solomon. "It is the voice of the turtle, heralding the return of baseball to the land."

At that moment, *SI* said, "the baseball fan, like the crocus, pokes his head up, through the snow and starts to live again. It is hard to explain, to those who do not understand, how large a role baseball plays in the warm-weather life of the average American male. They know about Eating Hot dogs in the Bleachers, or Getting Out the Old Mitt and Throwing a Few. But they do not know that this, like the flag raising at Iwo Jima, is only a small part of the whole. Actually, most baseball fans attend only a handful of games each season and the get-out-the-old-mitt school is limited in practice to a small, if vigorous, few."

Baseball's lure, Creamer wrote, was greater: "To your average, balding, loose-bellied, sedentary American male, something to read about, to talk about, to listen to on radio, to watch on television. It occupies an extraordinarily large part of his time. He listens to baseball over the radio while he works in the garden or lolls on the beach. He reads about it in the morning paper the next day. He talks about it at the office. He reads about it in the afternoon newspaper. He talks more about it that night. It does not interfere with his business or with his relations with his family or with his bowling or his church-going or his duties as a citizen. But it is always with him.

"Why? Because baseball is a game of limitless dramatic possibility, an incredible melodrama, a constant theater of delight, the great American *divertissement*, a flamboyant and continuing drama bound by certain hard unities: nine innings, three outs, one pennant. Within these unities baseball presents a variety as endless as the waves of the ocean, as intricate as a fugue by Bach."

The Senators would win the pennant before The Pastime's music died.

Pollster George Gallup says we would rather relive the 1950s than any decade of the century. Its apogee, wrote William Manchester, "extended from the Korean Armistice of 1953 to the autumn of 1957. To those who had cherished it, the 1953–57 breather would come to be remembered as an uncomplicated, golden time, mourned as lost childhoods are mourned and remembered, in nostalgia, as cloudless." Baseball's peak was 1956. The Yanks were its *lingua franca*.

"Local play-by-play, TV's *Game*, and, above all, papers sold the big leagues," mused Allen. "The Commissioner's Office and the teams did little in film or PR. Didn't have to, why bother?" An anomaly was Coca-Cola's thirty-minute *Winning with the Yankees*—produced by Condor Films; writer, Jack Brady; illustrator, Willard Mullin; narrator, The Voice: in then-rare "living color"—rousing "an infinite feeling for the spirit of the past," said novelist Ellen Glasgow, "and the lingering poetry of time and place."

"What makes the Yankees tick?" Mel begins. Personae fuse: Martin steals home, The Perfessor tutors rookies, his Palace Guard stars coaches Crosetti, Dickey, and Ralph Houk. "The scout's a nice guy, and tries to put you all at ease," staffing eight farm clubs below

Triple-A Denver and Richmond. At their St. Petersburg training site, "Nifty and shifty makes a first baseman"; Weiss, Webb, and Topping gather; "newsreel and TV cameras record the action." Ahead: The Stadium, "a monument to clean, hard, fair competition."

It starts Opening Day. Stengel raises the 1955 pennant flag: "an extra thrill," Allen puns, "except that no Yanks are extras." Bauer pricks Early Wynn. Joe Collins pierces Dick Donovan. Bob Turley faces Kansas City: "a thrill, a spill, but a daily doing." The Voice introduces DiMaggio, Gabby Hartnett, Dazzy Vance, Ty Cobb, Tris Speaker, and McCarthy on Old-Timers Day. Afterward "Another Yankees win [is] flashed to the world" by the "press-radio contingent."

Mantle slud, Dean would say, into second. "Watch the extra burst of speed. How about that!" Mel beamed. He might have taped the moniker for whenever No. 7 hit, caught, or ran.

Teresa Brewer's song, *I Love Mickey*, spoke to and for a generation: the Baby Boomer, born 1946–64. Costas put a dog-eared 1958 All-Star card in his wallet: "I believe you should carry a religious artifact with you at all times." No one could run faster, hit farther, or was hurt more often. "Healthy, Mantle was the best I ever saw," said Mel. "Who else could drag a bunt, or hit a 600-foot homer?"

The Switcher's father and grandfather had osteomyelitis, a degenerative bone disease. Thomas Wolfe thought he would never die. Mantle thought he might die by forty. "So arose the yarn that because of this Mickey stayed out every night with Whitey and Billy," Allen mused. The Switcher caroused and pushed the clock. "But that's not what broke him down. It came from the field and Mantle pushing himself so hard."

Mick could reach first base in 3.1 seconds, but swung to go yard: 536 homers, 20 All-Star teams, and 12 Series: leading in taters (18), runs (42) and RBI (40). "I wish I was half the player he is," Al Kaline said of 1956's .353, 52 dingers, and 130 RBI Triple Crown. "Mantle," ogled the normally been-there, done-that Stengel, "is better on one leg than anybody else on two."

Mike Garcia disclosed how to pitch him in a close game. "Easy. You don't." Mostly, you had to. On May 18, 1956, Mick homered a record third time left- and right-handed. Twelve days later he almost hit the first fair ball out of Yankee Stadium. "The ball is rising when it hit rightfield's copper frieze," gaped Bob Wolff. Said pitcher Pedro Ramos: "If it hadn't hit the roof, it would have been in Brooklyn."

Later, Washington's Chuck Stobbs flung baseball's longest wild pitch. "It bounced into the concession stand," said Wolff. "Add '53's tape measure shot, and no one called more record plays than me": mostly, New York's. Bob was Mel's antithesis. "His teams kept you glued. Mine kept you crazed." To survive, he headed the Knothole Gang, interviewed scouts and vendors, and midwived a magic ray: "sadly, not magic enough to hit the first division."

Washington began one ninth inning seven runs behind. "I haven't resorted to this," said Bob, "but if we focus on a fielder, our camera ray will so mesmerize him that the ball will go through, by, or over. This demands a concentrated thought process. If even one of you isn't thinking 'hit,' our rays can malfunction." A camera fixed the shortstop: The batter singled. Next shot: hit to left. A blur of Nats reached: "each after the camera predicted where the baseball'd go."

D.C. trails, 10–9, bases full, two out. Mickey Vernon lines toward right. Leaping, the first sacker snags the game. Dazed, Wolff spun viewers in self-congratulation. "They'd almost wrought a miracle until a viewer had to leave the TV at the critical moment," breaking the spell. Bob went to break, hoping to spawn one.

In 1956, Gillette was still baseball's exclusive network sponsor. "How about national work?" Wolff pled.

"If your name gets big enough," it said, "we'll put you on."

"Put me on tonight, and my name will be big enough tomorrow."

The Bombers clinched, 3–2, September 18 at Comiskey Park. Brooklyn waved a final flag. Worn out, Gillette put Wolff on the fifty-third Series. Like Allen, once cleansed by Ivory Soap, he soon found how a tyro could run into luck.

♦ ♦ ♦

"For nearly a decade the Subway Series raged between the Yankees and the Dodgers," said ESPN. "The whole world watched. It was a rivalry that was embodied by hotly disputed matchups. The Duke of Flatbush versus Number 7. Sal the Barber Maglie and The Springfield Rifle, Vic Raschi. The Captain, Harold (Pee Wee) Reese, and the Scooter, Phil Rizzuto. But ultimately, the argument came down to the announcers"—except that by 1956 the rivalry seemed to be a rout.

For the third time in four years NBC TV named Mel and Brooklyn's born-in-The-Bronx Voice to a silk salesman and an "Irish, redhaired, and like me, at times unemotional" mother. Their radio became Scully's temple: "a four-legged monster so high off the ground that I was able to crawl up under it—actually *under* it." Broadcasting was neither an acquired nor belated taste.

In 1950, Vin, twenty-two, began radio/TV's longest same-team skein. For the rookie, still living with his parents, humility, not history, was in the air. "Barber taught to avoid hearing other Voices. 'Don't copy. You will water your own wine.' Instead, bring to the booth an ingredient no one else could—me, and whatever qualities made me a human being." The newcomer's intuitions were in tune.

Ultimately, he became sport's Olivier. Twilight bared "little footsteps of sunshine." A shortstop "catches the ball gingerly, like a baby chick falling from the tree." That, as they say, was in another country—California. "It took the Dodgers move," Harold Rosenthal said, "to make Scully a star. In Brooklyn, he was dwarfed by Allen, who dominated everybody." Vin owned Malibu, once liberated from Mel.

"Pulses quicken!" said The Voice in *Winning with the Yankees*. America "stops for a few [Series] hours each day." Credits rolled: 1949, "Henrich 1, Dodgers 0"; 1950, DiMaggio homers; 1951, No. 5's last blast; 1952, the sweet swing of Big Jawn Mize; 1953, Martin's record-tying dozenth hit. 'Fifty-six's forged a feel-good shrine: Ike enters through Ebbets Field's leftfield door; Adlai Stevenson wears both a Bums and Yankees cap; Joe D throws out the first ball at The Stadium. By then, Brooklyn had a 2–0 game lead.

Enos Slaughter—to Mel, "the old campaigner"—ripped Game 3's decider: Yanks, 5–3. Next day the Switcher drove twelve rows above the 407 sign. "It wouldn't have gone over the fence [in Brooklyn]," said Campanella. "Might have gone *through* it, though." Bill Millsaps, later a Richmond columnist, was the child of a Tennessee schoolmaster. Next afternoon—October 8—Dad led his son from the classroom to the hall.

"Come with me, Billy," he said.

"What'd I do?"

"Just come."

Bill panicked. What had he done? Passing several secretaries, they finally neared dad's office.

"What is it? What's wrong?"

"Close the door. You won't believe what Don Larsen is doing to the Dodgers."

In Game 2, Larsen, twenty-seven, in his fourth bigs year, still a drinker and curfew-breaker, had been knocked out, 13–8. Skipping a windup, "a fine pitcher," said Mel, "when his head's on straight," faced Maglie in Game 5.

With two out in the fourth inning, Snider fixed the rightfield pole. "There's a drive, but it is goiiiing foul!" Allen brayed. "That ball was mighty close!" That inning Mantle broke a scoreless tie: "There's one if it stays fair! It is going, going, gone! Mickey Mantle achieves his third home run of the Series, his eighth in World Series play, two behind Snider and Gehrig and seven behind Babe Ruth!" In the fifth, Hodges hit to left-center. "Mantle on the run! Going, going! He makes the catch! How about that!"

Methodically, Larsen twirled the bigs first perfect game since 1922. Only Reese went to a 3–2 count. Just three Dodgers neared a hit: Robinson, caroming to McDougald; Hodges; and Amoros, hooking foul. "Can he do what no one in [Series] history has ever done?" The Voice later asked on film. Scully did NBC's last 4½ innings.

"I was just a fan in the second half," said Allen. "It was the first time I can recall becoming emotionally involved in a sports event. I was rooting so hard I broke a blood vessel in my throat." Mel could barely talk that night on his new ABC Radio daily *Sports Report*—worth it, he added. To Wolff, it was worth even more. "The Series made me," Bob said: a gut-wrenching, palm-sweating can you believe it day?

New York led, 2–0. Haze and sunlight meshed. Ribbon fell from the rightfield stands. Larsen got Furillo and Campy to start the ninth. Veteran Dale Mitchell pinch-hit. In the dugout, Stengel said, everyone became a manager. Even to Casey—"I have been around so long, I can get along with anybody"—the day lacked frame of reference. How could you compare?

"Two strikes, ball one, on Dale Mitchell. Listen to this crowd. I'll guarantee that nobody—but nobody—has left this ball park," gulped Wolff. "And if somebody did manage to leave early—man, he's missing the greatest! Two strikes and a ball! . . . Mitchell waiting, stands deep, feet close together. Larsen is ready, gets the sign. Two strikes, ball one. Here comes the pitch. Strike three!" on the outside corner. "A no-hitter! A perfect game for Don Larsen!"

Umpire Babe Pinelli's call has been replayed more than Reagan's "There you go again." Berra leapt into Larsen's arms. That March, Don had plowed his car into a St. Petersburg telephone pole at 5:30 A.M. Del Webb grasped reality. "This will set spring training back ten years."

A clubhouse writer said: "Casey, do you think this was the best game he ever pitched?" Ignored, Yogi spotted publicity director Jackie Farrell. "Hi," said No. 8. "What's new?"

How do you top the topper? In Brooklyn, the home team forged its last Series run and victory. "Here comes the [Game 6] pitch—and there goes a line drive to left field!" said Wolff. "Slaughter's after it, he leaps! It's over his head against the wall! Here comes Gilliam scoring! Brooklyn wins! [1–0, in the tenth] Jackie Robinson is being pummeled!"

Like Larsen, Don Newcombe flunked Game 2. The home crowd taunted him: Newk socked a lout in the mouth. "I want to beat them more than anything else in my life," he said before the final. Instead, Berra hit two two-run shots: "just owned him," said Allen. The ace left with a 21.21 ERA. Later Skowron homered. "Look at that!" crowed Mel. "Moose's tremendous grand slam!" It was a brutal (9–0) note on which to end.

Since 1941, Stan Isaacs wrote, the Bums and Yanks "had played each other so often, it seemed safe to assume that everything possible had already happened." Only The Voice called, coached in, or played each game—forty-four. "What more could happen? Larsen had an answer. He strolled to the mound and retired twenty-seven straight Dodgers. That effort must have destroyed the scriptmaker. There was nothing else to say. So the Yankees and . . . Brooklyn never played another World Series after 1956, at least for the price of a subway ride."

Allen, with boom mike, in white shirt, gray suit and sweater, and blue hat and tie, flanked Webb and O'Malley in the clubhouse. "Yes, it's great to be a Yankee," he later said, "and great to keep on winning with the Yankees."

Umpire Larry Goetz understood their wizardry. "Stengel must talk to God."

Stranger than fiction. The sole Yankee to play every pre-1956 Series v. Brooklyn was born there. By 1954, Rizzuto hit .195. 1955: The Yanks held his Day. 1956: They hung his noose.

"We've got a chance to get Enos Slaughter. What do you think?" said Weiss that August.

"Boy, getting him would be a help," said the Scooter, taking cyanide. Country replaced him on the roster: Released on Old-Timer's Day, Phil, thirty-nine, was unemployed. "From a damn good living, suddenly I didn't have anything." Mel had him call a half-inning here or there. The Orioles made an offer. He was torn, not wanting to leave New York.

As Richard Reeves writes of politics, broadcasting magnifies charm and institutionalizes seduction. By late 1956, Rizzuto had charmed Ballantine head Carl Badenhausen, who told Weiss to hire him. Jim Woods entered the GM's office to find George staring at the floor. "Jim," he said, groping, "I have to do something I hate doing, something I've never done—fire someone without cause."

Stunned, Poss joined Russ Hodges with the Giants. Scooter, wrote Peter Lyon, "became the junior member of the team that broadcasts all of the Yankees games with Mel Allen and Red Barber, the country's best-known sports announcers." To his credit, Phil knew the score. "Can you picture a thorn between two roses? I wouldn't have hired myself!" The joke was on them: Stomaching each other, they resented him.

"Mel and Red were pros," said Woods. "Rizzuto'd write down stories in the dugout, go on the air, and hide the paper." Interrupting, he stole the sign—"Oh, my God! He's going to steal home!"—as Allen called a pitch. One day they left the neophyte. Said Scooter: "They were outside the booth if I messed up, but I was alone," forced not to butcher or brook dead air.

"Kansas City Ath-a-letics," he would say.

"No, it's Athletics," The Voice corrected him. Phil accepted it. His mother detested it. Gradually, the two roses warmed. In 1957, the thorn caught a petal—CBS Radio's thrice-weekly five-minute *Phil Rizzuto on Sports*—and Mel's hell for saying only ex-jocks knew the game. "For twenty years I've been talking to players, reading the rule book, watching games," already 2,300, Allen said. "Believe me, you don't have to have been a player to know the game well enough to call it."

In March, he and Scooter met for a session of dos and don'ts. "I wanted to talk about pace and style," said The Voice. "All that intrigued Phil was having an expression—he started to use 'Holy Cow!'" Having sired it, Harry Caray asked Mel to tell him to stop. "I said no, but I'd be glad to pass on a note. It was amazing. To Phil, saying 'Holy Cow!' was the most important thing."

Appropriating, he was compensating.

◆ ◆ ◆

At first Rizzuto did two innings daily. "He'd finish after the seventh or eighth," said Allen. "Red and I'd complete the game." One went overtime. Mel: "And now to take you into the tenth, here is . . . here is." Phil was on the George Washington Bridge. "He became famed for leaving early. Even when he stayed, you'd hear him hook the mike into the stand announcing the final score."

The performer more than play-by-playman had a wife, four children, and extended family. Mel had work. "He was just so much more dedicated," said Woods. "Also, unlike Rizzuto, he had little to fall back on"—no life beyond the booth. On the other hand, "Like me, Phil was intimidated. At this time there wasn't much Mel did upon which you could improve."

Scooter envied his "picking up the baseball as it left the bat. The good broadcaster reacts before the sound, not always right, but the crowd doesn't lead him." Allen "built up the drama of a play before he sensed the play would be playable. The Yankees grabbed anything in sight. He was anticipating great plays." In turn, anticipation made The Voice "a very superstitious guy."

He and Larry often swapped pencils to change team luck. If it worked, Mel used them the next day. He wore the same shoes, suit, hat, and tie in a winning streak: also, said the *News*, "drove the same route to the ballpark each day. When they lose, he will go miles out of his way to help them break the jinx."

Mantle might have three hits. Allen would avoid noting his perfect day. "That would be jinxing him," said Phil. "Mel rooted in a way that could only be classified as 'reverse English.' He would build up the opposition before the fact, the Yankees only afterward." There was no need to build up the time.

A typical day—the *Post*'s May 2, 1957—suggests a place worth returning to: "Sports on the Air: Giants *v.* Redlegs, Ch. 11, WMCA, 1:25 P.M.; Dodgers *v.* Cards, Ch. 9, WMGM, 7:55 P.M.; Yanks *v.* Athletics, WINS, 9:55 P.M." Bill Schulz would like to retrieve it still.

The Antioch College freshman interned with the *Times*: hours, odd (4:00 P.M. to midnight); pay, cheap ($35 a week); niche, low (copy boy). Later, the *Reader's Digest* editor interviewed eight U.S. presidents; profiled Yasser Arafat, Sam Ervin, and Ross Perot; and ran the world's largest circulation (eighteen million) magazine. "Yet there never was anything like the summer of '57."

Daily, Schulz got paid to eat free food and drink free beer, "write captions for Pulitzer-Prize winning photographers," and sit in the press box at The Stadium, Polo Grounds, and Ebbets Field. "You'd hear the broadcasters and form impressions. Scully was with the Dodgers, but strangely underappreciated. Red's memory clung." Thomson's still clung to Hodges. "Except for that, I wouldn't even remember him." Schulz's parents, from Chicago, despised the Bombers—but not Mel. "He brought more excitement to the game than anyone then, or ever."

To his credit, Allen could not imagine the Jints or Bums unabiding on New York's behalf. "New York is fully capable of supporting three clubs," he said that August. "The loss of either of these damages the sports atmosphere of our city. Neither can be truly themselves outside New York. New York won't be New York without them."

Why would either leave? The Giants needed only a new park. Flatbush revered the Dodgers, drawing a million people a league-record thirteen straight years. How could you trade Brooklyn for Los Angeles, a place Fred Allen called "great, if you're an orange"? More easily than Mel supposed.

"Man, we'd put a man on the moon before the National League left New York," he said. Happy in his home town, Scully agreed. "Everything I cherished was here. It's like the wife whose husband is transferred. She may not want to go, but she goes." The Dodgers last home game was September 22. A month earlier the *World-Telegram* bannered: IT'S OFFICIAL: GIANTS TO FRISCO. For baseball, moving day had truly come.

"You have to understand the shock," said Rosenthal: the Apple's twin tiaras, "now, of a sudden, gone." Many went underground. Others foreswore the game for a while, or life. Few saw the effect on a sport once akin to wrestling—expect that wrestling had a niche. "Pro football has been a sad cousin," wrote Ken Smith. "Now, with only one baseball team, the media needs something to write about." The future Rozelles raised their hand.

The irony of baseball midwifing the NFL's rise is unappreciated, even now. Promptly grasped was Stripes monopoly. "New York is where sports things happened," said Nelson. "Overnight all the great baseball broadcasters were gone": Harwell, to Baltimore; Woods, Pittsburgh; Hodges, San Francisco; Scully, Los Angeles. Even Barber was The Voice's aide. "Allen stood alone."

A secretary, Elsie Kurrus, split mail into pro and con. "I always answer critical letters first," Mel said. "I'd say 75 percent of the time I get a nice response. In person or mail, they can see I'm not an ogre."

On April 19, 1957, at 10:30 P.M. Eastern Standard Time, they saw his life on CBS Television.


Primetime's *Person to Person* had never profiled a sportscaster. "Mel grew up in Birmingham, Alabama, went to college when he was only fifteen," host Edward R. Murrow began. "He graduated from law school, but he deserted the law to become a sports announcer. He has done other special events, and done them very well."

The program bared Allen, in suit and tie, rowing a boat, near Bedford Village. "I've known [Mel] for a long while," Murrow said in studio, "and the only time we have any disagreement is when his Yankees are playing in the World Series against my Dodgers."

Thirty years later TV's *This Week In Baseball* replayed the show. "I got a big kick out of it," Allen said. "For the most part, they were world-wide-known people." Mel ended by reading an anonymous sportsman's prayer:

"Dear God, help me to be a sport in this game of life. I don't ask for any easy place. I only ask for the stuff to give 100 percent of what

I've got. Help me to take the bad breaks as part of the game. Help me to understand that the game is full of knocks and trouble. Help me to play on the square. And, finally, if I'm laid on the shelf in sickness or old age, help me to take that as part of the game, too. Help me not to whimper or squeal that I had a raw deal. And at the end, I ask for no lying compliments. I'd only like to know that I've been a game guy": proper, sentimental, and contrary to hip, camp, and pop.

CBS got thousands of calls. Mail swamped The Stadium, P.O. Box 51, The Bronx, New York. "There's nothing phony about it," wrote the *Post*. "It's corn, but also Mel Allen. He wants, even needs, to be liked," delaying an appointment to answer a street stranger's question. "This doesn't come hard. He likes to talk. He talks on radio, he talks on television, he talks at restaurants. He'll talk to anybody who will listen."

To Murrow, Anna confessed having seen the speaking on the wall. "I've seldom known Mel to be at a loss for words. As a matter of fact, by one he could almost talk to us, you know. He'd talk phrases." Next year "my husband took him to a ball game, against my wishes. Ever since then I knew I was going to live with baseball all my life."

Harder to live with would ordinarily have been a first-since-1948 non-Apple World Series–winning team. "Given the move west," Allen noted, "losing to Milwaukee seemed just another blow." In a month, Ernie Kovacs had shaved his mustache, Jackie Gleason become a teetotaler, and Lucille Ball's hair turned blond.

On March 18, 1953, Wisconsin's largest city acquired the Braves of Boston since 1876. "It was a holiday when we heard they were coming," said Bud Selig, then eighteen. Milwaukee nearly killed its new team with love. A parade snaked to downtown's Schroeder Hotel. "People put up a Christmas tree!" said pitcher Ernie Johnson. "Said that since we'd missed Christmas, let's celebrate it now. There were hundreds of presents under the tree—shaving kits, radios, appliances. Ga-ga from day one."

Through 1959, the Braves won two flags, barely missed two more, and built an All-Star team. Del Crandall caught. Henry Aaron, Bill Bruton, and Wes Covington outfielded. The infield wed Joe Adcock, Red Schoendienst, Johnny Logan, and Eddie Mathews. Burghers gave players free gas, milk, and beer. Tidy streets ringed the park. Tailgating evoked Wisconsin *v.* Purdue.

Allen meant The Big Ballpark. Barber caught a borough. Caray packed the Church of Cardinals Baseball. "None had what we did," said Earl Gillespie, his river running through Wisconsin, Michigan, and parts of Minnesota, Illinois, and Iowa. Four times Milwaukee hit two million in attendance. "Baseball's smallest town became its hub."

The Braves were the first franchise to change cities in half a century. Gazing green-eyed—"We can't compete with this," O'Malley said as early as 1954. "Something's got to change"—the Dodgers and Giants ensured it would not be the last.

The 1956 Braves lost a pennant race decided the last weekend. The '57 variety clinched September 23. "I wasn't well-known yet," said Gillespie, doing NBC Radio's Series. "They figured I wasn't in Allen's [doing TV with Al Helfer] league." Bob Allen was Braves then-publicist. "We were Bushville, the Series our chance to get respect." It pivoted in Game 4. Down, two games to one, Milwaukee soldered a tenth-inning hit batsman, Logan double, and Mathews homer: 7–5. "Cinderella stuff," said Mel. "They're on the ropes, and the Classic's tied."

Game 7 lagged. "Only 61,207 saw it," said Rosenthal. "A day before the Dodgers announced their exit. There was a bitterness at The Stadium." The Braves led, 5–0, in the ninth. "Hank Aaron is pulled around in left-center field," said NBC's Bob Neal. "A breeze is blowing across from left to right. [Lew] Burdette's [sacks-full] pitch. Swung on, lined, grabbed by Mathews who steps on third—and the World Series is over and the Milwaukee Braves are the new world champions of baseball!"

Mel at home in Alabama
Age 2

13th birthday

Sgt. Allen. 1944-1945

Mel in his first New York apartment with roommate. Ralph Edwards

"Give me a child until he is seven," said Saint Francis of Assisi, "and you may have him afterward." Mel Allen, clockwise from upper left: at 2; in high school, 13; with "This Is Your Life" roommate Ralph Edwards, 20s; as U.S. Army sergeant, broadcasting in World War II, 31. (*Larry Allen and Esther Kaufman aka Mel Allen Estate*)

Born in 1913, Allen used sentences at a year, read box scores at 5, and entered the University of Alabama at 15. He joined Kappa Nu fraternity (back row, second left). (*Mel Allen Estate*)

In 1936, Mel began a New York vacation, instead joined CBS Radio, and aired a 1938 parade feting Howard Hughes's flight around the world. (*W.S. Hoole Special Collections Library, University of Alabama*)

At CBS, Allen (shown at right) understudied Robert Trout and Ted Husing, broadcast big band music and the *Hindenburg* crash, and clowned at this network announcers' party. (*W.S. Hoole Special Collections Library, University of Alabama*)

In 1939, he began baseball play-by-play. Next year: Mel, 27, shown at Yankee Stadium, was named the Yankees Voice. (*Mel Allen Estate*)

On September 3, 1943, his third day in the Army, Allen introduced Joe Louis at a boxing exhibition. (*W. S. Hoole Special Collections Library, University of Alabama*)

With Dodgers' Voice Red Barber, he meant baseball at mid-century. Red was white wine, crepes suzette, and bluegrass music. Mel was hot dogs, beer, and the U.S. Marine Band. (*W.S. Hoole Special Collections Library, University of Alabama*)

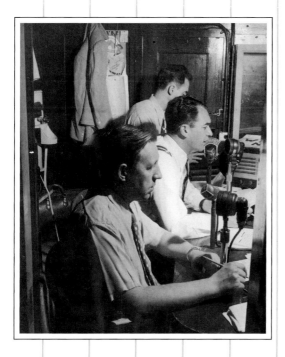

Unmarried, Mel's love was his career — and kin. In 1948, Allen got the key to his native Birmingham. L to R: Father Julius, mother Anna, unknown, and Mel. (*Mel Allen Estate*)

Allen was named *The Sporting News* Announcer of the Year a record ten times. New York governor Thomas E. Dewey (left) presents the award. Baseball commissioner Albert B. (Happy) Chandler looks on. (*Mel Allen Estate*)

The Big Ballpark in the Bronx. Mel, at home plate, emceed 1950's Connie Mack Day at Yankee Stadium. (*W.S. Hoole Special Collections Library, University of Alabama*)

A fine athlete, Allen excelled in the annual New York Baseball Writers game, using his arm and bat, not the voice that a florist must have decorated. (*Mel Allen Estate*)

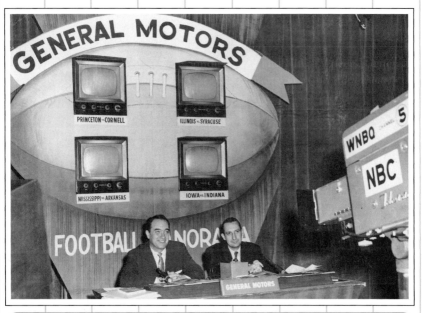

Allen and Lindsey Nelson were Southern pals and NBC TV peers. General Motors sponsored their 1950s "Football Panorama." (*Mel Allen Estate*)

A generation identified Mel with football's then-Everest event, the Rose Bowl. He emceed the yearly Tournament of Roses dinner. In 1957, Iowa beat Oregon State, 35-19. (*W.S. Hoole Special Collections Library, University of Alabama*)

By the '50s, Mel was sport's five-star mouthpiece: to *Variety* Magazine, one of the world's "25 most recognizable voices." Deep, full, and riveting, it fused Alexander Scourby and James Earl Jones. Once, in Omaha, Allen hailed a taxi, saying, "Sheraton, please." The cabbie's head jerked around like a swivel. (*Mel Allen Estate*)

The Voice holds a Little Leaguer, T-shirt reading, "I'm a little Yankee." Mel's irony — perhaps tragedy — is that the man with no children would have been a wondrous dad. One writer said: "Allen's only hobby is children . . . that he studies with rapt fascination." (*Mel Allen Estate*)

The Voice greets kids outside Yankee Stadium in the late 1950s. (*Mel Allen Estate*)

To many Boomers, Mel was as large as a U.S. president. In 1962, he met with John F. Kennedy before Washington's (and Allen's last) All-Star Game. (*Mel Allen Estate*)

The 1963-64 Yankees broadcast team included Jerry Coleman, Barber, and Phil Rizzuto (L to R). Shockingly, each outlasted sportscasting's ultimate celebrity. (*Mel Allen Estate*)

I n 1950, ex-Postmaster General James Farley chaired Mel Allen Day.
In 1964, above, Mel flanked him (center, with glasses). (*National Baseball
Hall of Fame and Museum*).

T hat fall the Yanks axed Allen: sportscasting's still most mysterious
dismissal. It especially stunned Florida's Mel Allen Little League team.
The Voice mended, but never healed. (*Mel Allen Estate*)

F ired after 21 World Series, 24 All-Star Games, 14 Rose Bowls, and
nearly 3,000 Movietone newsreels, Mel began a decade of private hell.
Overnight sportscasting's Valentino vanished, a nonperson. Myth deemed
him gay, a drunk, drug addict, and/or "breakdown victim." Said *Sports
Illustrated*: "It was as if he had leprosy." (*Mel Allen Estate*)

Mel made "How about that!" a national institution. It described his 1970s re-emergence. Allen flanks Mickey Mantle, Billy Martin, and Joe DiMaggio (L to R). (*National Baseball Hall of Fame and Museum*)

In 1978, he and Barber became the first Voices to make Cooperstown. Mel said his LLB degree meant "Long Live Baseball." (*National Baseball Hall of Fame and Museum*)

Threads part, then coalesce. Allen, speaking, and Mantle, swinging, defined the Yanks. They reminisce in 1985. A decade later Mick died as Mel lay in a hospital. (*Mel Allen Estate*)

Another thread: the Presidency. In 1941, Allen aired FDR's third Inaugural. In 1986, he saw old friends Ronald Reagan and George Bush at the White House. (*Mel Allen Estate*)

No broadcast life matches Mel's rise, ruin, and recovery. TV's 1977–96 *This Week In Baseball* made him The Grand Old Man of Broadcasting. Wrote *SI*: "For years he was a forgotten man, but it has all come back to him in abundance. The taste must be sweet . . ."—and it was. Allen died a kind and shy, stoic and heroic, solitary but, at last, not unhappy man. (*National Baseball Hall of Fame and Museum*)

Brewtown led it in 1953–58 attendance, including 1957's league record 2,215,404. The bloom then began to wilt, though few realized at the time. Next year totaled 1,971,101. Again Gillespie did Series wireless. "In 1959 we lost the flag by a game. I almost called four Series in a row. Maybe they'd a' let me talk with Allen."

In 1958, Mel on occasion must have felt he was talking to himself. Exclusivity, shmivity: The Yanks drew a worst-since-1945 1,428,438.

In June, the Bombers checked into Washington's Shoreham Hotel after a Saturday night game. Stengel liked a postgame drink, said Allen, "or four or six or eight. He could go to bed at three o'clock and be up fresh as a daisy at 6:30."

At 12:30 A.M., The Voice saw him frowning near the elevator. "What's the matter, skipper?"

"It's [now] Sunday," said Casey. "They didn't tell me this was a blue town."

Not to worry. "I carry a fifth of scotch with me in case of an emergency and *this* is an emergency," Mel observed. "Have a drink if you don't mind coming up."

The Perfessor brightened. Luis Aparicio never moved so fast.

In his room, Mel phones for ice and soda. Stengel replays the game, then stops. "We don't have to wait on ice, do we?"

"No, skipper."

Casey swills two drinks. Ice and soda arrive. Finally Allen eyes his watch. "Skip, don't we have a doubleheader this afternoon?"

"Yep," he says, gulping a last round.

In the doorway, Casey expounds for half an hour. "Wish I'd patented Stengelese," said Mel. "He befuddled. He clarified. He mystified. He taught."

Winking, The Perfessor left. The door closed at 3:45.

That afternoon Stengel asked a large, loping, and blind as a bat reliever to close Washington's. (Ryne Duren did, ending 1958 with a 2.02 ERA, league-high 20 saves, and 87 Ks in seventy-five innings.)

Entering a game, Casey told him to vault the bull pen barrier. "He figured the batter'd say," said Allen, "'Man, the guy can't wait to get at me.'" Huge glasses freighted fear. Stengel had Duren throw the first warm-up on the screen, then bounce the next wildly. "By now the hitter wished he were in the clubhouse. Casey loved all these little tricks." It was no trick to see their logic.

A Yankees batter didn't bunt in a bunting situation: "He can't bunt," explained Stengel. Slaughter pinch-hit *v.* a fellow lefty: "Shoot, he played enough with that fella over in St. Louis [Stan Musial] to know a left-handed hitter can hit a left-handed pitcher."

A starting pitcher insisted he wasn't tired. "Well, I'm tired of you," Casey said, relieving him.

Second baseman Jerry Lumpe hit one liner after another in batting practice. "He looks like the greatest hitter in the world 'till he plays."

Bob Turley brooked a slump. "Look at him. He don't smoke, he don't drink, he don't chase women—and he don't win."

Once Stengel sat next to Bob Cerv on the bench. "Nobody knows this," he said, cupping a hand, "but one of us has just been traded to Kansas City."

Casey mused that he managed strength against weakness, weakness against strength. "I learned that under John McGraw, who is dead at the present time."

On July 9, 1958, the Perfessor testified before a U.S. Senate committee on baseball's antitrust exemption. For an hour Stengelese scratched heads, opened mouths, and careened around the Cannon Office Building. "No one had the slightest idea what he was talking about," Mel laughed. The next witness famously abstained. "I don't got much to say," said Mantle. "My views are just about the same as Casey's."

He clinched a ninth A.L. flag, tying McCarthy, September 14, in Kansas City. "Celebration?" wrote Jack Mann. "The Yankees [inured to victory] don't even shake hands." Vainly, The Voice tried to get Bobby Shantz, Andy Carey, Crosetti, and Slaughter, among others, to "commertate" (Dizzy Dean). Stengel finally rescued him, filibustering for ten minutes. The soliloquy ended: "I could'na done it without the players."

Their Classic convened at County Stadium. Movietone headlined: MEL ALLEN RELIVES SERIES THRILLS. Skowron "homers off Spahn," Crandall "cracks a single," "Milwaukee wins the opening game, 4 to 3," on Bruton's single. Mel's Peacock partner was a pal. "Allen a professional but too obviously so, talking too much for TV," said one critic. "Gowdy is our type of announcer. Just enough chatter, newsy, interesting, restrained"—and how.

"I wore a steel back brace with a painkiller in my pocket with a prescription for my injured back," Curt moaned. Maids found him sleeping on the floor. NBC's sports head often found Mel a blabbermouth. In Game 2, Tom Gallery bayed, "Enough damned statistics! Just do the game!" Unbowed, Allen read a sourcebook. Tom then cracked a headset on his head. "I *told* you to leave statistics alone!" The Voice straightaway grew still.

Behind, three games to one, Stengel summoned Turley, who blanked Burdette, 7–0, saved Game 6, 4–3, and next day relieved Larsen. "Nobody will ever forget the old man standing out on top of the dugout steps pumping his arms like a boxer," said Mel, "yelling at everybody all at once, the men on the field and the men on the bench, insistent as a fire engine, demanding that they go get them." Skowron did, in the final.

"A right-handed batter," Allen mused. "Lew Burdette, a right-handed pitcher, is on the mound. Two runners on base. Burdette looks in, gets the sign, is all set to go. Takes the stretch. Here's the pitch. Moose swings. There's a long drive going out into deep left field! It's going, it's going, it is gone! A [three-run eighth-inning] home run. And the Yankees lead, 6 to 2!"

Pleased, Casey was proud in a to hell-with-being-sixty-eight sort of way. "I guess," he said, "this shows we could play in the National League."

◆ ◆ ◆

The Voice won *Look* magazine's 1958 "Best Sports Series" for the Oktoberfest. On New Year's Day 1959, he aired the Iowa-California Rose Bowl, hailing "former heroes of the Classic," including 1925's Stanford fullback Ernie Nevers and Notre Dame's Four Horsemen and Seven Mules. "Things come full circle. You're talking the first Rose Bowl I remember."

In February, Allen flew to Binghamton, New York, for a Hot Stove dinner, visiting hospital patient Danny Hill, leg severed by a railroad accident. "Do you think I'll be able to play baseball again?" asked the ten-year-old. Mel evoked Monty Stratton, Bert Shepard, and Lou Brissie, who lost or maimed a leg. Danny's face brightened. "I could see that he had that instinctive yearning to achieve something he held most dear," Allen wrote. "Sometimes we call that intangible quality heart."

Released in April 1959, his first book, with Frank Graham Jr., by Harper & Brothers, put Danny in the preface. *It Takes Heart* cast fifteen athletes against the odds. Among them: 1949's DiMag; boxer Jim Braddock, beating Max Baer for the 1935 title; tennis's Helen Wills, fighting pain and the field; and Doak Walker, "the littlest man in pro football": 5-foot-10 and 170 pounds. By 1924, Walter Johnson had hurled eighteen years without a Series. In Game 7, skipper Bucky Harris summoned him from the pen. "That's pretty far gone," Walter said of his age, thirty-six, "to be walking into [a Classic]." A fire having burned his left foot and shriveled the right leg at age eight, Kansas miler Glenn Cunningham eventually set a national high school record.

By 1938, the Cubs Dizzy Dean had hurt an arm, changed his motion, and lost the fastball. Said Mel on CBS: "He's got nothing left but his 'nothin' ball.'" It nearly swung the Series.

Diz led Game 2, 3–2: eighth inning, one on. Yanks shortstop Frank Crosetti homered. "You'd never 'a' done that if I'd had my fastball!" Dean screamed.

Said Crosetti: "Damn if you ain't right!"

Ben Hogan lost more in a car accident that fractured his pelvis, broke the left collarbone and ankle, chipped a rib, and clotted blood, nearly killing him. "There's nothing about death that'll frighten me now," Mel quoted the 1950 U.S. Open champion. A 1958 car crash broke Roy Campanella's neck and left both arms and legs paralyzed. On May 3, 1959, baseball's largest-ever crowd, 93,103 at Memorial Coliseum, cheered No. 39, wheeled by Pee Wee Reese near the mound.

Lights dimmed, like the ex-catcher's body. Each person lit a candle, like Campy's vaulting heart. Heart, Allen wrote, "is a mosaic of man's reaction to the opportunities and obstacles that confront him along the way to winning a reputation, with the lesson learned that its athletic event is only the beginning of endeavor, not the finish." One day that lesson would confront Mel, too.

On April 12, 1959, The Stadium hoisted Allen's ninth World Series flag. A listener noted Ballantine's new scoreboard atop right-center field. "It's a wonder," mooed Barber. Moveable type read: "Welcome to the 1958 world champion Yankees." Below and to each side horizontal ads tied "New Mobil Gas . . . Coca-Cola . . . Yoo-Hoo . . . Philip Morris . . . Seagram's Seven Crown."

The twice-delayed opener, Red said, was "like Alaska," the new forty-ninth State. "Miss Lucy Monroe" sang the Anthem. The lineup listed Bauer RF; Norm Siebern LF; Mantle CF; Berra C; McDougald 2B; Marv Throneberry 1B; Carey 3B; Bobby Richardson SS; and Turley, pitching. New York led Boston, 2–0. In the seventh, The Voice switched to radio. "Hello, there, everybody," he began, slow and syrupy. "Despite the cold, the crowd is warming with every pitch."

Turley had a no-hitter going. Superstition made it unmentionable: thus, a late tuner-in missed the first safety's niche: "Swung on [by Pete Runnels] and looped down the leftfield line. It is in there for a base hit! And twists into the stands for a ground-rule double."

Next inning Stengel changed his order. "Speaking of order, hope you remember to order some Ballantine Beer, the largest-selling beer in the East." Siebern broke a 2-all tie: "There's a high drive to deep right-center field. That ball is going, going, gone into the bleachers for a home run!"

A Richardson to McDougald force-out ended things: Yanks, 3–2. They should have quit while ahead.

Berra once described Allen: "Too many woids." The round man used his own that year on Yogi Berra Day: "No one ever hit a baseball with his face." Mel, arms folded, a broad smile, emceed. On July 17, Ralph Terry no-hit Chicago through eight innings. Jim McAnany singled to start the ninth. Videotape now let Red show postgame TV highlights. On a whim, Allen asked director Jack Murphy—"on the air! We were family"—if he could reshow the hit. "Wasn't exactly instant," The Voice laughed. "But it was the first-ever replay. A couple minutes later you saw Siebern not quite get to the ball."

The Yanks were not quite the Yanks, brooking a third-place, 79–75, worst post-1925 record. Mel aired his 3,000th bigs game September 13. "Friends asked, 'Did you change your style? You didn't sound as excited as usual this year.'

"I said, 'There wasn't that much to get excited about.'"

The 1959 Series matched the White Sox and Dodgers. "Mel'd done its TV since Abraham," said Nelson, "but since the Yankees weren't in this year Allen was out." In Del Mar, California, a future *Los Angeles Times* writer gloomed. "I'd only known him on the Series," said Larry Stewart, then nine. "To me, his voice wasn't as great as Harry Kalas or Charlie Jones. He was more like an institution: He had heft."

A South Sider would do network video. "The problem was," said Lindsey, "Tom Gallery didn't think the White Sox [1929–70 radio] guy was in Allen's league." Growing up on the same block, Bob Elson and Gallery had "rubbed each other wrong. Tom shouted, 'That bastard will not do the World Series!'" Nelson turned to baseball's first daily telecaster. "Jack Brickhouse does Sox TV," he smiled. "You could always pick him."

NBC's Series audience topped a composite 120 million. Shunted to WCFL Chicago, Elson "reached ten people," he said, still bitter, in 1975. "Not doing it was the biggest hurt of my career." Mel did Peacocks radio. "And so the [opener's] scene is set," he said, sharp and taut. Chicago forged a seven-run third inning. "This is quite surprising in view of the fact that the White Sox have been known as a team that beat you with a base hit or a walk, a bunt or sacrifice, a stolen base. Suddenly, they have broken loose with tremendous power."

After 4½ innings, Byrum Saam introduced Mel as "tops in our business."

"What a workout you had in your World Series debut," said The Voice.

By replied, prophetically: "Maybe the Sox [ahead, 9–0] should have saved some runs."

Next day Los Angeles nipped an eighth-inning Hose rally: 4–3. The convention moved west: Allen's briefcase held a *New Yorker* cartoon of a man crying at Ebbets Field. "Somewhere the sun is shining," read William Thayer's text, "somewhere hearts are light." Flatbush waited fifty-five years for a title. The Dodgers could win a Series in L.A. Year II.

Chicago lost Game 3, 3–1. Next day Norm Larker "lines out over second into center for a [Dodgers] base hit . . . [Wally] Moon rounding second, on to third," said Mel. The throw evaded third baseman Billy Goodman. "Here comes Moon to the plate, and he scores!" Gil Hodges then "lofted over short. There's Aparicio out, and it drops for a base hit!": 2–0, ex-Bums. In the eighth, breaking a 4-all tie, Gil cleared the screen. A tear grew in Brooklyn.

Memorial Coliseum had a 93,000 capacity, 251-foot leftfield pole, and bleachers in Orange County. Loud pants and coolie hats jammed the cave. Mel's simple presence fit its din, size, and trumpet blare, "C-H-A-R-G-E!" It also sold the "remarkable new Gillette adjustable razor. Your beard may be light or heavy, skin tender or tough. This razor handles them all with speed and comfort!"

A micrometer dial, with nine numbered settings, and "dispenser of blue blades and a modern travel case," cost $1.95. Inflation had not yet flown the cage. Gillette wanted a seven-game Series. Less would cost cash. "So the question is," Allen said before Game 5, "will the Series be ended right here today, or will we move back to Comiskey Park?"

To find out, he gave "the Gillette microphone with a great deal of pleasure to amiable, affable, able Byrum Saam."

Flustered, By misheard him.

"Right you are, Mel," he said.

The first run scored on a Dodgers double play. In the seventh, L.A. still trailed, 1–0: two out and on. "And it's swung on [by Charlie Neal]. There's a drive to deep right-center!" barked Mel. "Jim Landis digging hard! And the ball is caught by Rivera! A tremendous catch by Jim Rivera as he raced over to right field! An electrifying catch by Jim Rivera!"

Next inning Moon arced to center field. "Landis moves in—and he loses the ball in the sun!" L.A. filled the bases. Two relievers replaced Bob Shaw. A third straight record crowd, 92,706, howled like reprobates. Carl Furillo and Don Zimmer made out. Given Hose desperation, "The last half of the eighth inning was certainly one of the most dramatic in World Series history."

It merely postponed the reckoning. At Comiskey, before a still-record ninety million viewers, the Sox Early Wynn was shelled, 9–3. Chicago would not recover until 2005. The Yanks revived next year. ◆

# Up on the Roof (1960–1962)

**M**y political baptism was Dwight Eisenhower at the 1960 Republican Convention—his smile ahead of him, like Wilma Rudolph fleeing the field. The year's headline density wows in retrospect: Ike, globe-trotting; Nikita Khrushchev, banging his shoe at the United Nations; Nixon and Kennedy, still lore, myth, and truth.

Allen's decade had been as full: Joe D, the Switcher, and 1949–53 fiesta; Podres, Amoros, and Brooklyn's Millennium in the Morn; Mick's 1956, Larsen's perfect game, and as we shall see, Bill Mazeroski. Ahead: M for Murder, The Greatest Team, and tearful welcome to collapse.

"Some people's lives change incrementally," The Voice said later. "Man, I'd hoped my life would be interesting, but not change in a flash." It was, and would, in a way he had not expected, or hoped.

Ask any seven-year-old to choose a baseball nicety. He will spurn the pitchout, squeeze, and hit-and-run. He likes the soul-crushing blast—the homer. The early 1960s Yankees made children of us all.

As Mel said, the 1959 White Sox fused pitching, defense, and speed. Next year owner Bill Veeck installed an "exploding" scoreboard of fireworks, aerial bombs, rockets, and pinwheels: "shrieks, crashes, howls," wrote a critic, "that rivaled a train wreck, diving planes, and circus." The board mocked precedent. "Man, I thought I'd gone to Disneyland!" Allen huffed of one South Side poke. Twitting excess, the '60 Yanks hailed a homer by lighting sparklers in the dugout.

That June, Chicago visited The Stadium. The Voice arrived after Jim Landis, leading off, made out. "Over the years," Barber echoed Larry, "Mel had begun cutting it close, coming into the booth at the very last minute." Ego or entrance? Who could tell? "He'd done it all," Red guessed. "Routine became tiring." Unroutine: Ford-Billy Pierce. "Many a wonderful duel," Allen spieled, "through the years."

Minnie Minoso, "the ageless wonder, as it were," flew 400 feet to left-center field. Mantle, hitting .237, was jeered for grounding out. A Brooklynite could boo at June 27's "annual [Stripes-Dodgers] charity exhibition." To attend, write "Yankee Ticket Director, Yankee Stadium, The Bronx": box seats $3.50, reserved $2.50, "add 25 cents for mailing charges" by check or money order, the credit card then as still-born as the Amazin' Mets.

The Yanks led baseball in radio/TV rights. At break, Mel paid bills. "To be crisp, a beer must be icily light, with true lager flavor precisely right." Next inning bred halting ad-lib. "One and one makes two. You have to start with that, don't you? Unless you want, you know, to get into fractions. But when it comes to, uh, you know, full things, good round numbers, you have to have one plus one. Now, that's a generalization. I know this, though": It took two things to make a great beer. "Lightness is fine, but lightness alone can't do it." Adrift, could Allen?

About this time, said Nelson, "you began to see a duality": grand in October; iffy, before. Mel's delivery could ooze disinterest. Then, like a switch: "Little Foxxie's [Nelson Fox] worked hard to make himself a top ballplayer." Hector Lopez blooped a hit. "I'll tell you what he did! He'd already started his swing! He stopped," seeing a change, "then pushed the ball over second." Mantle's next up peaked form. "There's a smash! A great stop—Aparicio throws to second, and they get him at second base on a great play by Aparicio!"

The Sox palatine—to Mel, Loo-*ees* Ap-ar-*eech*-i-o—"went way into the hole, made an acrobatic diving backhanded grab of a hard-hit ball, raised up, and then fired to Fox to get Skowron, taking a base hit away from Mantle and a run from the Yankees! A spectacular play by a great shortstop!" Later: "You know, he actually flung himself at that ball headlong, glove outstretched, just great!"

Mel went to station identification. At 9:00 P.M., past bedtime, mesmerized by force, not fumbling, I grudgingly went to bed.

"Those damn Yankees," Joe Hardy chimed in the 1958 movie. "Why can't we beat 'em?" On July 5, 1960, Washington did. Behind, 3–1, Reno Bertoia "sends a drive to deep center! Mantle going back toward the wall, and what?" Allen said. "The ball's off the wall! Whisenant scores. Here comes Bertoia around second, on to third!": 3–2. Later Faye Throneberry singled to score the Nats Billy Gardner. Holiday fireworks lit the sky above the capitol.

At break Mel again added one plus one into two. A marathon swimmer in Mexico quit a 26-mile race, having swallowed a jellyfish. Pause. "They've been doing that at Harvard for a long while."

A doctor got two hits in a semipro game despite treating a sick spectator and birthing two babies. "Never did find out whether they were twins."

In the tenth inning, Bob Allison found one Art Ditmar sufficient. "Swings and lines it deep to center field! It is going, going, it is gone, and the ball game is over." Senators, 4–3. It did not become a habit.

Next week The Voice aired the first 1960 All-Star Game at Kansas City—to many Stripes, a second home. Baseball is relative. Early Wynn vowed to knock down his grandmother. Depending on your view, he was a son of a bitch, mother of competitors, or made hitters cry uncle. The Athletics were the Yankees cousins.

"[In 1955, owner Arnold] Johnson got 'em because Topping convinced baseball to leave Philadelphia," said Allen. "Arnold thought he owed the Yankees." The A's shipped Ditmar, Lopez, Shantz, and Terry, among others, to New York. In 1959, Johnson dealt Roger Maris for Siebern, Larsen, Bauer, and Marv

Throneberry. One night in 1956 K.C. bit the Apple for twenty-six hits. "For once *they* felt like the powerhouse." Mel brightened: "'Course, that feeling didn't last long."

Maris led 1960 A.L.ers in RBI (112) and slugging (.581). Mantle topped in runs (119), homers (40), and total bases (294). The Yanks 193 taters led the league. My favorite player, second baseman Bobby Richardson, had one. Dad found him "a fine family man and Christian gentleman." Germane to me was Bobby's smooth sailing at the double play.

The Pirates ship had listed since their last pennant in 1927. In 1960, western Pennsylvania, eastern Ohio, and West Virginia brayed "Beat 'em Bucs" and "The Bucs Are Going All the Way" and set an all-time Pittsburgh attendance record. Cy Younger Vernon Law ended 20–9. Roberto Clemente patrolled right field. MVP shortstop Dick Groat hit a bigs-high .325. Mazeroski surpassed even Richardson at two for the price of one.

Wrote Les Biederman: "The 1960 Pirates were something special," clinching September 25. Beating Boston, 4–3, New York clinched the same afternoon.

On October 2, Mel etched baseball's remembered or reinvented past. "Of course, this is a purely personal choice," he qualified, "and many may disagree with me." His team of the century tied catcher, Bill Dickey; left field to right field, Ty Cobb, Joe DiMaggio, and Babe Ruth; pitcher, Walter Johnson or Christy Mathewson; right infield side, Lou Gehrig and Charlie Gehringer; shortstop and third base, Bucs Honus Wagner and Pie Traynor, respectively. "Bowling is number one as individual participation is concerned. But baseball is still the great national pastime."

Its Classic began three days later: a Boomer's touchstone, even now. That summer John Costas, a Greek electrical engineer, left New York for California. "In Ohio, we'd pick up Waite Hoyt on our radio," said son Bob, eight. "Later, Earl Gillespie, Buck and Caray." Nevada spawned Scully. "Dad said, 'That's the Dodgers. We're almost there.'" The Yanks in the Series made L.A. seem like home. Bob told pop he would watch each game. "You can send me to school, but you'll never see me again because I'll run away."

Ron Howard, five, already had, to Mayberry. "I was a kid actor when I joined *The Andy Griffith Show*," filmed at Hollywood's Desilu Studios. Work dawned at 6:00 A.M. Pacific time. Bucs-Yanks started four hours later. Transistors on the set ferried baseball. At break the cast played, too. "I'd catch, Andy'd pitch, and Don Knotts would be hitting. That's how magic the World Series was. Even Barney Fife played Mickey Mantle."

Mel was content to play himself: to the banal and great, shy and strutting, self-assured and unself-confident people that is the people of the United States, more synonymous with the Series than Sharpie, Stengel, or the "Blue Blades March." His 1960 partner was a baseball Original. To Bob Prince, a crack play sired "How sweet it is!"; dingers, "Kiss it good-bye!"; a Pirates triumph, "We had 'em allll the way!"

In one inning Prince could segue from U.S. Steel stock via Dizzy Gillespie to golf with Bing Crosby. "Oh, by the way," he would say, "Groat grounded out, Clemente flied out, and the Bucs are retired." Bob's moniker was The Gunner. (Once he made a joke to a woman in a bar. Her husband then pointed a gun.) Some thought Prince a maniac. Surely he was maniacally riveting.

The Series broke mild and bright at a place of haze and horizon, with pews so close to players that you could sense what they were like. A brick wall enclosed the outfield. Bleachers lay beyond third base. Forbes Field strutted a rightfield pavilion, in-play batting cage, and vast stretch of acreage grown heavy with base hits. "This was my first Series," said Prince. "Mike fright didn't bother Mel, but even at home I was terrified." At 12:58, a director in the production truck said in Prince's earpiece, "All right, let's get 'em. We've got sixty million people watching." Bob whitened. Two minutes—a TV eternity—passed without a word.

Thirty seconds to air time. Vainly, Mel tried to calm him. "Bob," he finally said, "you know who in our broadcasting team is the most nervous of all right now?" Affecting a lisp, Allen pointed to the NBC emblem. "Can you imagine how long that dad-gum peacock has been waiting to spread his feathers?" Prince laughed. "It saved me. Otherwise, I'd have fallen apart on the air. From then on it was the old Gunner at work": like The Voice, airing shock and awe.

The Pirates won Games 1, 4, and 5, outscoring New York, 14–8. The Bombers swaggered, 10–0, 16–3, and 12–0. A .252 season hitter, Richardson set a Series mark for most RBI in a game (six, Game 3) and Series (12). Ford threw two shutouts. Nova merge: diving stops by Don Hoak and Mazeroski; Mantle, clearing Forbes's 436 right-center mark; centerfielder Bill Virdon's leaping catch off Berra.

At The Stadium, Herbert Hoover and Indian prime minister Jawaharlal Nehru were introduced before Game 4. The next day boyhood bud Joe Garagiola said, "You amaze me, Yog. You've now become such a world figure that you drew more applause than either a prime minister or former president. Can you explain it?"

"Certainly," said Yogi. "I'm a better hitter." His team outhit (.338–.256), outhomered (10–4), and outscored (55–27) Pittsburgh. Pee Wee Reese saw one rout, having recently joined CBS's *Game of the Week*. All winter he used a tape recorder, watching "stuff on the monitor Mel'd done—he was the gold standard—and I *still* had problems." In Game 4, Maz hit long and foul. Allen's problem was malapropism: "That brought the crowd to its collective feet." The Yanks' was tangible, not oratorical: They couldn't shake the Pirates.

"If you've never been to Yankee Stadium, you've never been in the big leagues," A's pitcher Bill Fischer later said. October 13, at Forbes, was big enough. "We have been blessed again with summer weather," Mel commenced. Prince was asked if he wanted a drink. "Don't worry," he passed. "I'm just as crazy sober."

Game 7 left you feeling like a morning-after binge.

Tide: Rocky Nelson, first inning. "There's a drive!" said Gunner. "Deep into right field! Back she goes! You can kiss that one good-bye!" Pirates, 2–0. Riptide: Yanks rally. Down, 4–2, Berra batted in the sixth. "There's a drive hit deep to right field! It is going to go . . . foul! Out of play . . . And it is all the way, excuse me!" Mel revised. "All the way for a home run! Clemente never moved over, and we thought the ball was curving foul! And it is a [5–4] home run for Yogi Berra!"

*Sports Illustrated* mocked "[the] greatest Classic miscue since Clem McCarthy's historic miscall of the 1947 Kentucky Derby [*sic* Preakness: the error was contagious]." Strangely, Allen didn't mind: The Yanks soon led, 7–4. "This World Series is being brought to you in color, exclusively on NBC TV," he began Pittsburgh's eighth. Leading off, Gino Cimoli singled. Next, Virdon lanced a 1–1 pitch. "There's a ground ball to short, and all hands safe!"

Kubek later said, "The ball hit something"—pebble, divot, or Forbes rough spot, no one knows—"and hit me [in the larynx]." Tony fell, grabbed his throat, and started to cough blood. "Give him room," rasped Stengel, bolting the dugout. The Voice empathized: "He wants to stay in, but Casey is saying, 'This is no time to be a hero.'" An ambulance carted Kubek to the hospital.

Dick Groat singled, Cimoli scoring. Bob Skinner's bunt advanced the runners. Nelson popped to Maris. Clemente topped a "soft dribbler toward Skowron. And nobody's going to get over! Bases loaded [actually, Virdon scored: 7–6]." An ex-Yanks catcher then worked a 2–2 count. "Hal Smith hits a drive to deep left field!" Allen said. "That ball is way back out there! Going, going, gone!": 9–7, Bucs. "And pandemonium breaks loose at Forbes Field! The fans go wild in Pittsburgh!"

Richardson and Dale Long reached in the ninth. After Mick plated a run, Yogi hacked at a 2–0 pitch. "And there's a shot, grabbed by Nelson, steps on first, and Mantle gets back!" Mel whooped. "He's safe, and [pinch-runner Gil] McDougald scores the tying run on an amazing turn of events! On a hard shot by Berra, Nelson grabbed the ball, stepped on first, and Mantle, with quick thinking, stopped in his tracks, slid underneath the tag, got back to first, as McDougald scored the tying run! How about that!" his sketch quick, precise, and true.

"Sudden death now," Mel said as fourth reliever Terry threw a last-of-the-ninth slider. The left-center field Timex clock read 3:36 P.M. "There's a drive deep into left field!" Berra receded to the 406 sign. "Look out now! That ball is going . . . going, gone! And the World Series is over! Mazeroski hits it over the leftfield fence for a home run! And the Pirates win it, 10 to 9, and win the World Series!"

Thirty years later The Voice smiled, wryly. "Great baseball. I got excited. Yankees fans still get mad at me." In Upstate New York, I began crying at a Cub Scout meeting. In Los Angeles, Maz retired Costas to his room. "I'm sitting there, eyes welling with tears as I take a vow of silence. My plan was not to speak until opening day of the '61 season." Reality soon broke. "But I kept mute for twenty-four hours—protesting this cosmic curse."

In suburban Pittsburgh, Larry Lucchino, thirteen, was walking home from school. "I was a Pirates fan, and had a radio. When Maz homered, I threw it toward the sky." Alight, the future president of the Orioles, Padres, and Red Sox raced home: "Really, I was walking on air."

David Eisenhower was on a nearby "Nixon for President" campaign bus, Pennsylvania dangling between the Republican and JFK. "It was like the universe had ended," said the then-vice president's future son-in-law. Unlike Prince, at least he knew how the Buccos won.

"We're up in the ninth," said Gunner. "A guy says, 'Do the clubhouse celebration.' I get there, find a tie," and refind the booth, a din shaking the yard. "You win!" an NBCer yelled. "Get back downstairs!"

Breathless, Prince interviewed manager Danny Murtaugh, N.L. head Warren Giles, and Pittsburgh mayor Joe Barr. "Everyone," Mel laughed, "except the one guy we hoped Bob'd get."

Maz was finally maneuvered to the mike. "How does it feel," Gunner asked, "to be a member of the world champions?"

"Great."

"Congratulations." End of interview. The hero is led away. "By the way, how *did* we win?" Bob asked at dinner.

Wife Betty stared. "You must be kidding. Maz hit a homer."

Prince felt less hungry than Roseanne Barr after lunch.

Even a Yankees fan remembers 1960's top-this Series week of climax and capital. Baseball's primo linguist never forgot, but tried.

On October 18, the Stripes fired the Old Perfessor. "The main reason is that . . . as Mr. Topping explained, that there is a program going on with the Yankees, and it has an annuity program," said Stengel, "and the annuity program means that after a certain length of time some people think you should retire." He breathed. "Now he's of the opinion that you should retire. And his other partner, Mr. Webb, is of the same opinion. [George Weiss was axed, too.] I'll never make the mistake of being seventy again."

Casey had nursed the son of a Queens saloonkeeper. "He'd spot-start me. I never got more than thirty-three," said Ford. "Pretty hard to win twenty." New skipper Ralph Houk vowed to pitch him each fourth day, then phoned Stengel's 1958 shortstop, third baseman, and entire outfield. "I'd played them all," said Kubek, "and that was just in a Series game. Casey liked to be cute"—also cruel— with colts like Tony and Richardson. "[He] and I have talked," said Houk, "and Kubek will play shortstop, period."

Name a season. Nineteen thirty-four means the Gas House Gang; 1955, Brooklyn; 1968, The Year of the Tiger. Could anyone be worse than the barely more wins (67) than Sammy Sosa homers (63) 1999 Cubs? Which was better—1976 Big Red Machine, or 1984's 104–58 Detroit? Neither, said Allen: "Five straight world titles, all those pennants, but nothing can touch it"—it being the '61 Yanks.

"I just want 'em to play hard, which I'm sure the boys will do," said their once-catcher, bull pen coach, and Battle of the Bulge hero. Harder was Houk's dropping Mick to cleanup: "Batting third, I thought he'd [Maris] get better pitches," not walked intentionally all year. Mantle had 9 homers in the first eighteen games. Not dinging till April 26, Roger hit 10 in May. The Yanks broke 13–6, then broke down (17–15).

Dial M for mediocrity: On May 24, New York trailed Detroit by a half-dozen games.

John F. Kennedy called a group of Nobel Prize laureates "the most extraordinary collection of talent . . . that has ever been gathered in the White House—with the possible exception of when Thomas Jefferson dined alone." On May 30, a day after his forty-fourth birthday, the Yanks, in JFK's home city, finally bared the most extraordinary collection of baseball talent ever gathered—with the possible exception of Murderers' Row. "A good mixture of Red Sox and Yankees fans," Allen said, including Governor Paul Dever and Democratic National Chairman John Bailey, had converged on the Hub. "They just wanted to talk baseball," having soon much to talk about.

Mantle smacked a three-run jumbo. Gene Conley then ceded solos to Maris, Moose, and the Yog. "Three balls, one strike," Mel began the eighth. "There's a drive hit deep to right field! That ball is going, going, it is gone! Maris hits his second homer of the day. The Yankees sixth homer of the ball game is two short of the record of eight in one game." No. 7 hit number seven. "There's a drive to deep right-center field. And that ball is going, going, gone, into the bleachers for Mickey Mantle!" By now Boston was talking politics: Stripes, 12–3.

New York convened June by winning twelve of fifteen. Ford started and finished the month 8–0. Kubek hit in nineteen straight games. Bob Turley left the rotation. Terry (16–3) and Bill Stafford (second-best league ERA) joined it. Howard hit .369 at the All-Star break. Maris (27 homers) and Mantle (25) led Ruth's 1927 pace. The snag was the expanded ten-team A.L.'s new 162-game schedule. "Any record," said Commissioner Ford Frick, Babe's ex-ghostwriter, "must be set in his old 154."

On July 25, Maris had four of New York's eight twin-bill blasts. M & M had ninety by August 13. "My greatest thrill was [not dinging twice *v.* 1957 hometown Milwaukee but] batting second in the order behind Mantle and Maris," Kubek said. Allen agreed. Bars, stores, and schools—"You couldn't go anywhere and not hear about it"—echoed baseball's then-hold on America's sensibility.

The Yanks began August 11–1 to pass first-place Detroit. Late that month, again laboring, Mel misstated a future airtime and Yanks and Indians record. "I can see, you know, Old Glory, occasion to, uh." Jim Perry "throws in and out, uh, changes speeds." The Voice's sped as "Mantle rocks it in the rightfield stands for his forty-sixth home run of the year. Thousands who came here today have seen part of what they've come for." Even Tribesmen "would like to see one of the two guys homer. It has been a tremendously exciting thing over the United States."

Of a play, Mel mused, "Oh, say, [it's like] a fellow like Jim Landis would have made." Weather evoked the football Browns. "Think I'll buy me some winter clothes and just store 'em. Case something happens, I'll have 'em here." Springtime happened in the third. "Maris pounds one to right field! How about that! Number 49! Thunder and lightning have struck in Cleveland." Pause and pun. "[Yankee Bobby] Hale's on the bench." At break Mel asked listeners to vote. "All in favor [of Ballantine], say aye. Aye! Well, everyone's got to make a living."

Behind by 1½ games, the Tigers crashed New York for a September 1–3 series. "The Lions that first night had a preseason game," said Ernie Harwell. "But interest was so high they postponed it so Detroit could watch baseball": Yanks, 1–0. A day later Maris hit in the 2-all sixth. "There it is! A long drive to deep right field! Number 52!" yelped Allen. Once was not enough. "There's a high drive to deep right! Kaline going back! And the ball is going, going, gone!" On the screen, WPIX blinked "53," as quaint now as a cherry fizzy.

Next day Detroit led, 5–4. "There's a high [ninth-inning Mantle] drive to deep right field. Look out now! Kaline—he is not going to get it! A [5-all] home run! Number 50!" Howard hit with two on and out. The more marathoner than sprinter once slid into second base: "I made it! I made it!" Umpire Jim Honochick called him out. "You sure did, Ellie. But what detained you?" Now: "Swung on . . . high drive to left! Colavito going back! And the ball is going, going, gone! And the ball game's over! Elston Howard belted it into the leftfield stands for a three-run home run and the ball game"—also pennant race—"is over!"

The 1960 season ended with a fifteen-game Stripes winning streak. The '61ers now forged an eleven game lead. "Will Maris do it?" signs appeared away and at The Stadium. Abruptly, no one asked that about the Mick.

Mantle homered September 10: Number 53. That week he caught a virus. Trying to help, Allen touted his Upper East Side doctor, Max Jacobson, an Eastern European emigrant who treated actors, singers, and the president of the United States. "I know a great doctor," he told the Switcher, "who can give you a penicillin shot, it'll work almost instantly, you'll get well in a day."

On September 19, Mantle left the lineup too ill to play a double-header. In Jacobson's office, the doctor, in a bloodstained smock, gave a shot. His needle struck Mick's hip bone. The patient grew dizzy. On September 24, he hit Number 54. Two days later No. 7 left a game. "It's nothing serious," said Houk. "Mostly, he's suffering from the . . . effect of the medication he received for his cold."

The effect was Jacobson's. Mick's temperature hit 104 degrees. He entered the hospital, where infection began. The abscess was lanced, then drained. "My God," said Kubek, "you could put your hand into it." Blood gushed from the open sore. Houk blamed the Good Samaritan. "Jacobson was a quack," said team publicist Bob Fishel. The Major—"a combat soldier in the Ninth Armored Division reconnaissance group," wrote Allen, "with a Silver Star and a whole lot of dead Germans to his credit"—never forgot who suggested him.

Like Mel, Houk forced a smile. "'Sixty-one had such a ferment," said The Voice. "The team was 109–53. Six guys belt twenty or more homers—Maris and Mantle, Moose's 28, and each catcher—John

Blanchard, Elston Howard, and Yogi—with at least 21." The Yanks 240 set a record. M & M's 115 goosed Ruth and Gehrig's 107 (1927). Ford was a Cy Young 25–4. "Every day seemed like Luis Arroyo came out of the bullpen [15–5 and 29 saves in sixty-five games]."

Churchill coined "The Terrible Ifs." Stripes defense became a rival's. "Yogi'd scare you in left field, but caught what he got near," said Mel. In center, "Mantle outran everything." The encore A.L. MVP was "vastly underrated. Maris had a fine arm, covered ground in right." The infield made most of the Bombers league-high 180 double plays. "Moose was steady, Kubek and Richardson, a magician [Cletis Boyer] at third. Ft. Knox had more holes."

The Yanks drew a most-since-1951 1,747,725. In 1987, Kubek, now a fine NBC analyst, wrote *Sixty-One: The Team, The Record, The Men.* "Nothing like it for pure excitement day in and out," said The Voice. It peaked as a summer fled impossible to forget.

The way it was: Allen, forty-eight, "[with] heavy features, translucent eyes, handsome in an aging way," wrote Huston Horn, "like his father and brother, balding, but unlike them [recently] disguising the truth with a hairpiece," hosting his WPIX guest, in a studio chair, hands clasped on an arm. "When did this pressure start building up on you, Roger?" he said. "I wish some day, and I'm sure that after this is all over, somebody's going to really write the story of this severe pressure." It stopped baseball's world. Only Maris wanted to get off.

Game 154 (*sic* 155, including a tie) was at Baltimore. "There's one! It is going! It is going! Number 59!" Mel vamped. Next up, Maris faced reliever Dick Hall, "[here] well-nigh invincible . . . There's a high fly ball out to right field! Deep! But it's gonna' be caught by Robinson." Baseball tests endurance. No. 9's ended with a ninth-inning tap, not bang. "Out comes Roger Maris . . . A roller down the line on a half-swing and Wilhelm tagged him out," a checked swing checking Number 60.

Consolation: a pennant, clinched, 4–2. In the clubhouse, cliche gulped champagne. "Come on over, boys," Allen told Howard, Blanchard, and Earl Torgeson. *Déjà vu* was all over again: "Yog, how many pennants?" Arroyo became "The Grand Master of Relief." Pitcher Jim Coates's relief was corked: "Put that bottle down, you come here a minute." Coach Wally Moses got "the [same] treatment"—Great Western.

Finally: Maris, replacing Bauer as The Man of the Hour.

"Hey, Rog. I'm sorry you didn't get number 60."

"That's alright, Mel."

"I know you've been under severe pressure."

"Friend, you're right on that."

Allen noted Number 59's wire service photo. "They all promised you copies?"

"I think I've got enough pictures to wallpaper my house."

*The* House hosted Game 159. "Two outs, nobody on. There it is! There it is! If it stays fair, there it is! Number 60!" Mel piped. The ball rebounded on the field. WPIX flashed "60" as Maris neared home. "A standing ovation for Roger Maris . . . And they're calling him out of the dugout! This is *most* unusual! They are asking him to come out of the dugout! Now this is something! They are standing and asking Roger to come out! Come on out! How about that! Come on out of there!

"There he is!"—and was, October 1.

Mantle watched the Yanks 163rd and final game from a hospital bed. "That week that son of a bitch Jacobson had the nerve to send me a bill," he groused. "I never did pay it. I wanted to sue." On Boston's pregame show, starter Tracy Stallard vowed not to walk the healthy M & Mer. "I'll throw Maris the fastball. More power to him if he hits it."

In the fourth, Roger worked a 2–0 count. "Here's the windup," said Rizzuto. "Fastball, hit deep to right! This could be it! Way back there! Holy Cow, he did it! Sixty-one for Maris! Look at 'em fight for that ball out there! Holy Cow! What a shot! And they're still fighting for that ball out there! People are climbing over each other's backs. One of the greatest sights I've seen here at Yankee Stadium!"

Maris had expunged a ghost. "If I never hit another home run, this is one they can never take away from me." He hit 117 more. They never did. Allen readied to call his nineteenth Series. Scooter called on aspirin. "I screamed so loud on Maris' call I had a headache for a week!" It is safe to say the memory lasted longer.

That morning a future American Revolutionary scholar, Princeton University baseball team advisor, and member of Richard Nixon's "enemies list," left Flatbush for The Bronx. "I pleaded with my mother after church," said Sean Wilentz, "despite her never wanting me to go to another game." He and Bobby Kritzer, each ten, took the A train to 59th Street, changed trains, and paid 75 cents for a right-centerfield bleacher seat. "Wisdom told us to sit nearer the pole, since Maris liked to pull, but it's all we could afford."

Historian, meet history. "You-know-who [Maris] hit you-know-what [number 61], though not you-know-where [Wilentz]." The Brooklynite rued Scooter's airing it. "Mel's call of number 60 was classic, graceful, such a strong barrel-chested presence in his voice, that great signature call, not just 'How about that!' but 'Going, going, gone!'"

Trudging home, Sean sat in subway seats "woven out of rattan-like laces, not molded out of plastic like today": his radio, a transistor: its music, Dixie's. "Baseball was one of the few places that a Southerner didn't have to talk Yankee. Barber had a detached, painterly style. Nelson was mellow. New Yorkers talk different anyway. Allen was different personally": to Catholic Wilentz, in background, above all.

"A Southern Jew from Alabama becomes the Yankees! No wonder he was dramatic": to Sean, notable for "setting the moment," deranging Stripeaphobes, and "skills getting erratic in the end." Mel "helped change my life—and life's work forever": the 1961 Series being work for The Voice, not his team.

◆ ◆ ◆

"By now, you'd think he would approach the impending October Classic as just another assignment," said the *Journal-American*. "Nothing could be further from the truth. 'Well, heck,' he said, 'it's the greatest sports event of the year.' And Mel Allen is an integral part of it, year-in and year-out."

Cincinnati hadn't been since 1940. Two years later ex-Yanks pitcher and vaudevillian Waite Hoyt began play-by-play. The ordinary mike-man says, "Ground ball. The shortstop catches it, throws to first. Safe!" Whatever else he was, the minstrel's son was not ordinary: "He hit a ground ball. The shortstop caught it and threw to first. The runner beat the throw." Why: "*accuracy*!" Waite rasped. "As I speak to you, what happened a moment ago is gone"—often, like the Reds.

Allen, he said, was "a *good* news broadcaster." Agreeing, Mel minimized making *Who's Who in America*: "If the Yankees had been an eighth-place team, I'd be an eighth-place announcer." Waite was a "*bad* news broadcaster," missing the 1944–55 first division. Then, in 1961, Vada Pinson hit .343. Frank Robinson was MVP. The Reds clinched a tie September 26: Carolers packed Cincy's Fountain Square. Speakers blared Dodgers-Bucs play-by-play. At 11:26 P.M., L.A. was eliminated, buoying Lynchburg and Loudonville and Springdale and Sardinia.

Hoyt should have telecast the Series. Instead, NBC's Tom Gallery busted him to radio: "like Gillespie," said Nelson. "Didn't measure up to Mel." Coca-Cola produced the highlight film. "Autumn in New York," said Allen, "and even at the United Nations Building there will be time out for baseball." Ford and Jim O'Toole parleyed before the opener. Howard homered: outfielder Wally Post "a little too late and a little too short." Dick Gernert smashed to third. "Boyer makes a miraculous diving catch!" Stripes, 2–0.

Next day Gordy Coleman dinged. Yogi's twelfth Series tater followed: "Watch!" Mel urged. "There's a drive to deep right field!" Ellie muffed a fifth-inning curve. "[Elio] Chacon suddenly storms home, and he's safe!" Boyer robbed F. Robby: "The Yankee Gibraltar again!" Suits garbed The Stadium: Joey Jay dressed New York down, 6–2. The Classic moved to "Cincinnati, the very cradle of professional baseball." The Series would soon be put to sleep.

Crosley Field led the bigs in smallest size (27,603) and turf (387 feet to center) and most lemonade. TV/radio filled its open rooftop box. "We're thankful for good weather," said Gallery, "'cause when it rains, it floods." By Game 3, the Switcher was thankful to junk the hospital. "You'd see him in the clubhouse," said Kubek, "with tape like a football player."

Blood stained Mick's uniform. The Yanks' seemed merely tired. In the seventh, Robinson doubled off the scoreboard: 2–1, Cincy. Tying, Blanchard homered an inning later. Mantle knelt on deck in the ninth. "If ever it was pitch-measuring time, it's right now, Joe [Garagiola]," Mel mused on NBC.

"You'd better measure right," said the analyst.

Maris did. "There's one. It is deep to right field! And that ball is going, going, it is gone!" said Allen. "Roger Maris gets his first hit of the Series—and you could tell when it left the bat that it was gone! And the Yankees lead, 3 to 2!"

Technology now bares *Star Wars* via *Captain Video*. In 1961, opaque script flashing "ROGER MARIS" seemed futuristic as the Rajah rounded third. "Coverage was primitive," Mel mused. On the other hand, home plate's camera was far lower—thus, bird's-eye—than today's perched in the upper deck. One change lasted. Allen and Barber seldom interrupted the other's play-by-play. Garagiola did. "[Yankees] nits and gnats precede their big guns." Arroyo, Mel followed, "toyed around [v. Robinson]—I don't mean by that in a playful way."

Next afternoon Mick barely played. "Pure moxie," Allen said. "He just can't go at top speed." Singling, he left. "Joe, he's had an opening in the side so big that you could put a baseball into." In left, Berra robbed Pinson: "Racing over hard, he makes the catch beautifully!" Ford, "the little lefty with the big heart," broke Ruth's Series streak of 29⅔ scoreless innings. Kubek punched "a [run-scoring] looper into right-center field—a Texas leaguer among Pinson, Robinson, and Chacon." Child's play blanked the Reds, 7–0.

A day later "blue skies and balmy weather" lit the Queen City of the West. Jay "has the weight of the world, baseballwise, on his shoulders." The Bombers crushed them. "There goes Robinson back to the fence," seeking Blanchard's two-run blast. Too little, late: "Post ties into one and sends it soaring!" Cincy was sent packing, 13–5. "The Yankees again are world champions!"

Allen emceed a City Hall ceremony. Nine years earlier a woman said of Dwight Eisenhower's election, "It's like America has come home again." The title had come back to New York, for the first time since 1958. To Mel, it seemed as natural as a Pig Chase in Johns.

"Before I ever felt the pull of the pigskin, I was a baseball fan," said Emmy-winning NFL Films producer David Plaut. Then eight, the Rhinelander whiled Christmas 1961 trying to reverse the Series. His vehicle: "Mel Allen's Baseball Game," complete with scorecard, rules, and 33⅓ rpm "RCA Victor high-fidelity recording." For $1.98, "Mel calls the plays. You play the game."

On his household floor, Plaut held an album cover of The Stadium, Mel in hat, and "all-purpose Yankee sliding into third." The game board was spartan: diamond, outfield, and bases. "We used pennies for runners. On the stereo, you'd start dropping the needle on the 33⅓ record to hear Mel's call."

The Voice must have spent, he laughed, a dog's age in studio. "He had 1,000 calls for any situation." Some were obvious. "There's a fly ball," Allen droned. "It's going! It's going! It's gone!" Others: "Strike three!" "single to left," or "double play!" Some braved disconnect: "6–4–3!" *sans* runner. "If a call made no sense, we'd keep dropping the needle on the record until one applied."

Baseball broadcasting is regional. In Pittsburgh, if cleanliness trailed only Godliness, Prince topped both. "If Cincinnati, you'd hear Hoyt," David said. "In St. Louis, Caray." Mel meant baseball generically: "the guy who embodied the golden age of baseball."

"The Yankees! The Series! Mel Allen's Baseball Game!" still coming to an eBay auction near you.

Change came to the presidency January 20, 1961. Marian Anderson began the inaugural by singing "The Star-Spangled Banner." Robert Frost prepared a preface to his poem, "The Gift Outright." JFK outdid each: "Let the word go forth to friend and foe alike, that the torch has been passed to a new generation of Americans."

In Bedford Village, Mel warmed to time and tone. "Next to New York, more things happened to me in Washington than anywhere else. I almost replace Arch, then spend part of the war there. Mantle hits his tape measure. I do Larsen's game with Bob Wolff." The torch passed to a new president and generation of ballparks, which Allen grasped—and his last All-Star Game and pro football, which he didn't.

The Voice at least casually knew each president from FDR through George H. W. Bush. Truman's eyesight precluded baseball. Ike played it at West Point. "[As a boy] I wanted to be a real major league baseball player, a genuine professional like Honus Wagner," he said. "My friend said he'd like to be president of the United States." Neither got his wish.

A 1966 photo shows Mel, with Lyndon Johnson, in the Oval Office after he, Hank Aaron, Harmon Killebrew, Stan Musial, Brooks Robinson, and Joe Torre visited U.S. soldiers in Vietnam. Successor Richard Nixon loved baseball in an unslick Walter Mitty way. "I have always enjoyed our meetings in such places as the Heisman Trophy Dinner," Allen penned in 1970. "Congratulations on your election to the pinnacle of world leadership."

Nixon's bobbed-cork life eerily resembled Mel's: "He had taken punishment, there was an attentiveness in his eyes which gave offer of some knowledge of the abyss, even the gentleness which ex-drunkards attain after years in AA," wrote Norman Mailer, as easily etching Allen. "If I had it to do over again," said Nixon later, "I'd have been a sports announcer." A future president who was left baseball for Hollywood.

In 1935, four Des Moines, Iowa, outlets aired the Cubs. "Thanks to re-creations," said WHO Radio's Ronald Reagan, "I could do them from hundreds of miles away." Once the wire stopped. Reagan considered returning to the station. "Then I thought, no, if we put music on, people'll turn to another station doing it in person." What to do? Make a big *to*-do.

"Fouls don't make the box score, so for seven minutes I had Billy Jurges set a record." Pitcher Dizzy Dean used the resin bag, mopped his brow, tied a shoe. Rain neared. A fight began. "None of this happened, but at home it seemed real." Finally the wire reawoke. "Jurges popped out on first ball pitched."

Two years later Warner Brothers signed the Gipper. In 1940, then-agent Sonny Werblin petitioned Allen. "He wanted him for movies," said brother Larry. "Mel said, 'No it's too insecure.'" In 1986, one small-town Voice met another, like frames in Capra celluloid. Aide Patrick Buchanan sent a telegram inviting Mel to the White House. "It was for the off-day between Games 2 and 3 of the Series," said Allen. "Other writers and announcers were there, but I wound up sitting across from the president, whom I'd met years earlier in Pasadena."

Reagan did late-1950s Rose Bowl parade TV. "Why don't you help here," he said to Mel one New Year's Day, "and then you can go out and do the football?"

Allen rode an ambulance to the famed empyrean. "But I remember," he now told the president, "that you used to do some sports announcing of your own." Lunch was to take an hour. Ninety minutes later Billy Jurges was still fouling balls off.

In 1989, Reagan handed off to his protégé, a friend of Mel's since the '50s. "His family'd lived in Greenwich, near me, and gone to Yale." That year George Bush, sixty-five, read *The Baseball Encyclopedia* to Little Leaguers on the South Lawn. "Wanna' know about

Yaz [Carl Yastrzemski]?' Ya' gotta' have this book." He seemed al-most as young as Kennedy at Griffith Stadium's last opener: April 10, 1961.

JFK liked the ancient Greeks definition of happiness—"the full use of your powers along lines of excellence"—hating the second-rate, in others and himself. Rehearsing his first pitch in the Rose Garden, he became the first U.S. president interviewed on TV at a game.

WGN's Vince Lloyd: "Mr. President, have you had an opportu-nity to do any warming up for this, sir?"

JFK: "Well, we've just been getting ready here today."

"Throwing nothing but strikes? Very good."

"I feel it important that we get, uh, not be a nation of just spec-tators, even though that's what we are today, but also a nation of participants—particularly to make it possible for young men and women to participate actively in physical effort."

Leaving, Lloyd asked about Mrs. Kennedy.

"Well, it's Monday. She's home doing the wash."


Next year District of Columbia Stadium opened: the first multisport cookie-cutter. "It had great football sightlines," said *Washington Post* columnist Shirley Povich, "and was formal, pretentious, and cold." In July 1962, Allen aired his twenty-fourth and last All-Star Game from the symmetrical, lights affixed to a dipping roof—to Povich, "like a wet straw hat"—antiseptic oval.

In 1960, Kennedy, forty-two, had met Stan Musial, forty. "They say you're too old to play baseball and I'm too young to be presi-dent," said JFK, "but maybe we'll fool them."

"Guess we fooled 'em," recalled The Man.

A previous-night picture showed Mel and Kennedy, each in black tie, at a White House reception. The Boston Brahmin now threw out another ball.

"I just was thinking," Allen said on NBC, "this is the first time I have followed Joe Garagiola, who followed the president of the

United States." The Game became "The Mid-Summer's Day Dream." Mantle's "beautiful throw" trying to nab Roberto Clemente "was [actually far] off the bag." Mel eyed Orlando Cepeda's feet: "Look at that wide stance." Two months later, returning to D.C. Stadium, he fixed another game.

In 1920, Rock Island and St. Paul staged football's first pay-for-play: professional teams staking matches on the air. Mel did the "football Giants," distinguished from posher baseball's, as early as 1939. In 1951, the entire NFL made $50,000 in TV profit: screen, black and white; sound, uneven; money, as small-timey as the pros. Sunday we read, heard radio, or took a trip: anything but watch the tube.

In 1953, DuMont launched *Saturday Night Football*. Its diva later exteriorized the NFL. "When Ray Scott intoned, slowly, profoundly, 'First down, Green Bay,'" wrote *TV Guide*, "10 million spines would quiver." By 1956, CBS Sunday coverage tied the viewer to Marion Motley, Norm Van Brocklin, and Bobby Layne. Football became appointment television.

By luck, the first *America's* Team rose contemporaneously in the den of TV, finance, and big-city ad men: the Giants Kyle Rote, Alex Webster, and Frank Gifford—glamour, even pretty, boys—taking six conference titles from 1956 to 1963. "I saw it coming," Allen said of football less college guys than ex-dead-end kids. "Making it in New York was bigger than, say, Detroit." Shor's and 21 toasted our team, here, on top.

Chris Schenkel joined them in 1952. "Marty Glickman and I did radio, except that no one knew. Everything was baseball." Next year he aired local, then CBS, TV. "Mel said, 'Some day when the Giants are good, you're going to know what it's been like to be the Yankees announcer.'" Soon Chris "couldn't walk anywhere without being stopped in Manhattan—especially when they won."

On September 25, 1960, the Stripes played at Boston. Allen was "on assignment," said Barber: Giants-49ers radio. That past winter Redskins owner George Preston Marshall had cornered him in Washington.

"How'd you like to do our games?"

"You already have somebody, don't you?" said Mel.

"Yeah, but he's leaving."

"What do you mean, leaving?"

"Harry [Wismer] doesn't know I know," Marshall said, "but he's bought the [American Football League] Titans and is leaving."

In 1945, honor bound The Voice to Stoneham. Now it made him protect a peer. "Until Harry says he's leaving there's no job. If and when he does, I hope you would ask me again." Mel's Jints pact ended in 1960: Marshall did.

Geography was dicier. Each Saturday Allen did Joe College. "I don't know if I can get to wherever the Redskins are Sunday."

"Hell, we've got airplanes," said Papa Redskin. "Let's try."

Once Mel aired USC-UCLA, got to D.C. at 3:00 A.M., and woke to find a blizzard, the tarpaulin covered, and game delayed for forty-five minutes "hoping for a miracle." Finally, the 'Skins put wooden stubs as markers in each 10 yards of snow. "You only knew the goal lines because they were a different color."

Allen's 1961–62ers dredged a 6–19–3 record. "There wasn't much to cheer about, but that one day made it worthwhile." Back in New York, he faced a task starker than the storm: How could baseball seem as worthwhile as '61?

"Even a casual fan," The Voice said, "knew 1962 might be a downer." On May 26, Al Kaline broke his shoulder blade making a game-saving catch. "What a play!" roared Allen. "Is he getting up?" Mr. Tiger didn't. Fast and glib, Mel did. "Curve, is swung on, a little dribbler hit by the mound, coming in is [Jake] Wood, up with it, throws to first, in time, on a great play!" He sounded like 1952.

Bob Turley makes a last Stripes start; Marshall Bridges becomes the new Arroyo; a freak runs on the field. "He'll spend the night in the jug," says the counselor, "according to the law." The Yanks spent June 24 at Detroit. Gorged by 35,638: 32,000 hot dogs and 41,000 and 34,500 bottles of beer and pop, respectively, over 600 pitches, three seventh-inning stretches, and baseball's longest game (7 hours: New York, 9–7, on Jack Reed's twenty-second-inning homer).

"I've got to leave," an Ontario writer said two innings earlier.

"Where are you going?" said a colleague.

"My visa just expired."

You gotta' be kiddin'! What a huckleberry! Smaller than the game, Rizzuto already made baseball larger than it was. Phil left in the seventh, flew to LaGuardia, and began driving to Jersey. Time: 7:00 P.M. The 1:30 game should have ended three hours earlier.

"I turn on the radio and drop my jaw," said Scooter. "Red's starting the nineteenth": Allen has TV; neither can take a leak. "Phil gets on the bridge and says, 'Holy Cow!'" mused Mel. "Should he turn around and fly back to Detroit? Jiminy Cricket, no." Home, Rizzuto turns on 'PIX. The Voice's warm-voweled vent never seemed so cold.

Next week the Angels, like New York ½ game behind Cleveland, winged to The Stadium. Mel hailed a father and child reunion—Tom Tresh, dinging Don Lee: "Both their fathers had formed a battery [Thornton Lee and Mike Tresh]"—segueing to Earl Averill, whose dad also played the bigs. Closing Day he critiqued runs batted in. "Mel used RBI, and starts saying how others use RBIs," said Jon Miller, hearing the tape in 1993. It amused, then abashed. "He forgot what he was trying to say."

In 2004, Pedro Martínez said, "The Yankees are my daddy." Mantle, 1962's, became a three-time MVP. Richardson got 209 hits and second of five straight Gold Gloves. Terry led the league in wins (23), starts (39), and innings (298⅔). Nothing dimmed a team— the first-year Metropolitans; the Amazin' Mets—that unexpectedly greased Mel's fall.

"After the Dodgers and Giants left New York, you could see soccer, hoops, midget auto racing, and boxing," wrote Dick Young. "Even the AFL Titans. Just no baseball." To regain a team, Mayor Robert Wagner formed a five-man committee chaired by lawyer William A. Shea.

Ill wind: The Reds, Pirates, and Phillies spurned relocation. Whirlwind: In 1959, Shea named the eight cities, including New York, of a proposed new major circuit—the Continental League. "Branch Rickey was its president," said official baseball historian Jerome Holtzman. The threat made the National League expand.

Casey unretired, Weiss became GM, and the New York State Senate OK'd $55 million for a new stadium in Queens. Meanwhile, work began on gussying up the Polo Grounds. A child learns baseball by falling in love with a team. To me, the Senators meant the cellar; Red Sox, Dead Sox; Amazins, something to tune to when the Yanks were rained out. By contrast, in New York the Mets gripped the ephemera capital of the world.

One whyfore was broadcaster Ralph Kiner. Marv Throneberry became Marv Strawberry; Howard Johnson, Walter Johnson; Gary Carter, Gary Cooper; and Milt May, Mel Ott. "We'll be right back," he said, "after this word for Manufacturers Hangover." Another: The Okie whose voice rose an octave, bred "The Happy Recap," and became "the first sign of spring," Jay Greenberg wrote of Bob Murphy, "as big a part of your twilights as a golden sun."

The Greek poet Sophocles said, "One must wait until the evening to see how splendid the day has been." Stengel's main radio/TV phonetist made the Mets dawn splendid. At eight, Lindsey Nelson heard Graham McNamee call a fight so near that he could "reach out and touch the canvas." The rectangular box speaker—an Arbiphone—"looked like a question mark." Lindsey's answer was radio: by 1952, also video, meeting Mel. Allen meant *Events*: Nelson, *events*, as NBC *nonesuch*. "One overwhelmed you," said Gallery. "The other was perfect for week in and out."

In 1959, *Radio/Television Daily* named Lindsey best wireless/TV sportscaster. In turn, NBC's assistant sports director named The

Voice to fourteen All-Star Games and eleven Series. "Ours was a unique relationship," said Nelson. "We were colleagues and competitors. I was Mel's boss. I was also his friend."

At one point or another he aired *Major League Baseball,* the All-Star Game and Series, NBA and NCAA *Game of the Week,* Army-Navy Game, Bob Hope-Desert Classic, and Cotton, Rose, Gator, Sugar, Sun, Liberty, and Poinsettia Bowl.

Who would trade this for The Metropolitan Baseball Club of New York, Inc.? Lindsey Nelson would.

Like Mel, he thought daily baseball broadcasting's king of the hill. "The game is theater. It has drama, tragedy, comedy." NBC's 1957–61 weekly series was blacked out in New York. "Many people, not knowing that, said, 'Why are the Mets hiring a *football* guy?'" If this were Broadway, Nelson said, the tryout had run five years.

Like the Arbiphone, the Amazins were a question mark. Moving to Ft. Lauderdale in '61, the Yanks left St. Pete to Stengel, who hoped to "work on the little finesses," as if still managing General Motors. "Runners at first and second, and the first baseman breaks in and back to take a pickoff throw," he drilled. The Mets lost, 17–1. Casey saw the light, not liking what he saw. "The little finesses ain't gonna' be our problem."

Their first game was Metsian: St. Louis, 11–4. Things went downhill from there. New York ended 40–120. Next year: 51–111. "Don't cut my throat," The Perfessor told a barber, "I'm saving that for myself." Hobie Landrith was his first expansion pick. "If you ain't got no catcher," Casey said, "you get all passed balls."

The puzzle was if New York would pass. The 1962–63 Metropolitans drew 2,002,638. "We'd look over, see how bad they were," said Allen, "and were stunned." Yarns still stitch them. "I tell them myself," added Nelson. "Thank heavens for Stengel. He spread more happiness than anyone I've ever known—because he was doing exactly what he wanted."

One night Casey surveyed the house. "We are frauds—frauds for this attendance. But if we can make losing popular, I'm for it." Their WOR TV/WABC Radio audience even beat the Yankees! It was akin, said Murphy, to a mule lapping Man O' War.

"My [weekly Saturday three-hour] job with [NBC's] *Monitor*," Mel said at the time, "is pleasant and it pays well, but it is not the sort of thing that keeps me in this business." Play-by-play did. "Dadgummit, it's creative. The players on the field are the actors, and I, in a sense, do the narrative." Murphy doubted he could match it. "Here we are against Mel, Red, and Yankee Stadium. People thought we'd be run out of town." In 1962, radio/TV editors named Allen "America's best sportscaster" for the thirteenth straight year. That May Nelson stopped at a men's clothing store at 49th and Broadway.

"Show me jackets that you can't sell," he told the owner, buying seven "gaudy, showy, awful" coats. "We were competing with *Mel Allen*. I needed attention."

Next month a cabby said, "You're the guy who wears all those wild jackets!"

Lindsey smiled. "See, he doesn't know my name, but he knows what I do. Against Mel, it pays to advertise." In 1963, they both aired New York's Mayor's Trophy Game: Stengel's return to The Stadium after his 1960 firing.

"The Yanks were champions," Nelson began. "Casey *despised* them, like our fans." Lindsey's wife and two daughters brought horns and bells. "The Yankees confiscated it, took away all noisemakers. Fifty thousand people there, and forty-nine backed the Mets."

Sixth inning: Mets lead; Casey calls the bullpen. "[Vapid Ken] MacKenzie?" said a coach.

"No!" Stengel boiled: his best pitcher, Carl Willey, to save an *exhibition*.

Amazins: 6–2. The Bronx aped Picadilly Circus. The Mets, Nelson said, were a last age of innocence. "They played for fun. They

weren't capable of playing for anything else." In 1962, their prede-
cessor at Coogan's Bluff was.

Each early century baseball site had individuality: none more glo-
riously absurd than the oblong cafe's at 157 and 159th Streets and
Eighth Avenue, across the Harlem River from Yankee Stadium,
flowing gently to the sea. "I loved the Polo Grounds," said Russ
Hodges, whose next home, not glorious, was certifiably absurd.
Built on a point, Candlestick Park inherited the wind.

In 1961, the Stick hosted the All-Star Game: N.L., 5–4, on tenth-
inning hits by Hank Aaron, Mays, and Roberto Clemente. "Great
names," said Mel, manning NBC with Russ, "but what people remember is reliever Stu Miller, balking in the ninth." Papers blared:
MILLER BLOWN OFF MOUND! The Giants blew off L.A. in a 1962 playoff. Ahead: a Transcontinental (nee Subway) Series.

"How ya' doing, everybody?" Hodges began Game 1.

Almost everybody's duds did finer than his. "A clothing store
asked him to take the labels out of his clothes," Jints partner Lon
Simmons laughed. "Said he was ruining their image."

Russ's favorite label was Dewars. "Here's what we'll do," he
counseled Lon.

"If we win the game we'll drink because we're happy.

"If we lose we'll drink because we're sad.

"The only way we won't drink is if we tie."

Landrith's extra-inning muff tied a game. Curfew extended it.
Said Hodges: "We're just gonna' break a rule."

The 1962 Series conjured Wellington at Waterloo: "A close-run
thing." Again Allen narrated its highlight film. Ford won the
opener, 6–2. Frisco countered, 2–0. The camera brandished Fisher-
man's Wharf, cable cars, and Candlestick, already a belly laugh. At
The Stadium, 71,434 paid "a [Game 3] testimonial," said Mel, "to
baseball's tremendous appeal." In left field, "Up he [Giants Felipe]
Alou goes for a leaping, one-handed stab of the ball." Despite it:
Yanks, 3–2.

Next day now-Jint Larsen won, 7–3, on the sixth date of his Perfect Game. "And there it goes [by Chuck Hiller]!" pealed The Voice. "Maris won't reach this one! It's gone!"—the first N.L. Series slam. Game 5 hinged on another blast: "[Rookie leftfielder Tom] Tresh swings—look out now!"—a three-run homer: Bombers, 5–3. Billy Pierce then retied the Classic, 5–2. Game 7 became Terry's chance to turn history on its head.

"I came into the Series with a bad record [0–3, including Mazeroski]," he said. "You rarely get a second opportunity." New York led, 1–0, as Mays hit in the seventh inning. "Tresh races over!" Allen said. "Makes a spectacular one-handed running catch!" In the ninth, Matty Alou pinch-singled, Felipe Alou and Hiller K'd, and Mays doubled to the rightfield corner. "The grass was wet," he said, "or it would have got past Maris." Instead, Matty stopped at third.

Chemistry/memory: Russ and Mel shared a final batter. "My heart was in my throat," Terry said, almost swallowing a 1–1 pitch. Willie McCovey lined to Richardson. "A foot either way," rued Willie, "we win."

The California Giants have never won a Series. Mel's favorite partner never broadcast another network game.

"What people remember is rain," Mays observed. Game 6 was thrice postponed, the Series lasting a longest-since-1911 thirteen days. NBC pregame show host BobWolff remembers queuing to buy a paper.

Recognizing Allen, the vendor said, "I think we're going to beat the Yankees."

"What?" Mel barked. "What do you mean? You trying to taunt me?" Onlookers locked eyes.

A year earlier Wolff's Senators moved to Minnesota. Weiss phoned that fall. "We got talking about the '62 Mets, and George said, 'If you move back East, how you gonna' cope with Allen?'"

Bob had known him since 1946. "You can't beat his voice, or presence. If I come, I'll generate stories, do homework, what he doesn't": Mel becoming, he felt, too slow. "You'd be so mesmerized by the round, full sound that you missed how it took longer to say things, ironically covering dead air."

In December 1961 the *Daily News* bayed, WOLFF COMING TO METS, who still lacked a station/sponsor. Time passed. The re-named Twins made Wolff choose. "I went to Weiss, and he couldn't make a commitment." Bob rejoined Minnesota, then replaced Nelson on NBC's *Major League Baseball*, often seeing Mel in Boston or New York.

In 1969, named Atlantic Collegiate Baseball League commissioner, he launched a cable TV series. "I signed Mel for $500 a game, all I could afford. Great headlines." Nineteen sixty-three's evoked The Shot, pitching's Caesar and Pompey, and a Voice and team in late bloom. ◆

# Stormy Weather (1963–1964)

n January 1, 1963, Allen aired his twenty-first and last bowl game, though it would have seemed lunatic to suggest so. "It's dusk at the Rose Bowl, Wisconsin storms back [from a 28-point deficit, losing to USC, 42–37], the crowd's ballistic, and that voice overwhelms it all," said Curt Gowdy. Watching: Bob Costas, awash in dad betting up to $10,000 daily. "A great storyteller. My father'd meet his bookie on a dark street, under a lamp," having left California for Long Island in 1961.

"The Granddaddy of Them All" was a yearly meeting place. Bob got other scores, in pop's car, by nightly turning the dial. Phils-Braves could lose their home; Cubs-Cards, reclaim it. "If his teams were losing, I didn't want to tell him. Winning, I'd race inside to tell Dad what was happening." Happening, was love.

"Listening to these announcers, they became the game," said Costas. "Its mythology drew me in. I fell asleep with a transistor under the pillow." Caray wooed. Saam and Prince seemed voice pals. The Voice spellbound: "So much warmth to relate to. The moment you heard him, he put you in a baseball frame of mind." Like Mel, Bob could have given an hour lecture on every member of the Stripes. His idol was No. 7. His company was the world.

In 1991, Costas entered a restaurant to find Mantle and Billy Crystal. "Billy was a little older than me, had grown up on Long Island, idolized Mick." For four hours they rehashed his life. "He *did* it. Billy and I *remembered* it. The whole time Mickey's saying, 'I don't remember that, damn, did that happen?'"

Happening: a 1963 game in Baltimore. "Mantle hurt his knee, ran into a fence," said Allen, "tore the other, was out a month, and returned by homering." Another: any twin bill, the trainer changing bandages and massaging Mick's legs. "As circulation returned, he'd amaze just by playing."

May 22, 1963, towered like an obelisk. "Mickey Mantle batting left-handed against right-hand pitching. Around comes the right arm, in comes the pitch," Mel began. "There goes a long drive going to deep right field! It's soaring up high! It's going, it's going, it is gone! . . . Mickey Mantle, for the second time in his career, has come within a few feet of becoming the first man to ever hit a ball clear out of Yankee Stadium!"

It hit the facade. Otherwise, said a Harvard professor, the ball would have gone 620 feet. "Of course," he noted, "I wasn't at the game." Having thrown the pitch, Kansas City pitcher Bill Fischer was. "Six feet over and it would have killed somebody waiting at the subway."

Mick mispronounced *facade*—"fah-KAD"—on Allen's postgame show. Mel replied by chasing him around the clubhouse with a towel. "We were having fun," he said. "You know, goofing around with players, you got to know 'em, what they'd take, what they wouldn't."

What The Voice couldn't take was saying no.

"The road'll make a bum of the best of 'em," Dan Daniel wrote of baseball travel. "And, kid," he told a colleague, "you ain't the best." A bigs broadcaster leaves the plane, finds his hotel, then migrates to the park. Dugout talk precedes the game. Tedium succeeds it. Ernie Harwell visited friends in every city. Caray never met a bar he didn't like. Wolff culled celebrities, phoning Truman, in Kansas City, near Independence. Mel busied an already bustling life.

"Allen is a tireless worker," *Sports Illustrated* said, "driving himself to accept as many obligations, commitments, and duties as daylight and dark will allow." Mail archives a son in school, daughter's wedding, or crop just planted; asks a photo, autograph, or cash; notes a long-ago meeting, sure that Mel will recall. Replying, he addressed radio/TV promotion; taste in literature; tryouts and tickets; general thank-you for advice. A compliment bred, "A million thanks"; birthday card, "I am indebted"; lost letter, "I am disturbed to discover a question of yours has inadvertently gone unanswered."

Mail swelled after network coverage: e.g., 1958's. Benjamin Mount, of Princeton, was a most happy fella. "I caught you making a [Series] boo-boo. Please send a box of White Owls." Mel: "Better make it Gillette Blue Blades." Cleveland's Clarence Popelka suggested the box score show "exceptional [All-Star] plays." Allen: Write the Commissioner. In Norwich, Connecticut, John Riley asked about office pools. The Voice: "You might wish to ask someone better informed."

Even correspondence fell to a warp-speed schedule. One day Mel met "a yard full of inmates," he wrote, "at Indiana State Prison"; another, "a bunch of kids outside Yankee Stadium"; finally, "a bunch of adults outside Freehold Raceway [New Jersey, for Ballantine]." He saw U.S. Navy officers and men "at our big base on Guantanamo Bay in Cuba"; Ted Williams at St. Petersburg; fellow members of the President's Citizens Advisory Committee on Physical Fitness at the White House; and John F. Kennedy at the National Football Hall of Fame dinner, handing a phone to JFK, who lauded the 1961 Tide title team, huddled in Tuscaloosa.

In one month, Allen addressed the Bethlehem, Pennsylvania, interfaith luncheon; Brooklyn Berriman Junior High assembly; University of Notre Dame football banquet; Flushing, New York, Holy Name Society; Winstead, Connecticut, Kiwanis Sports Night; New York Salvation Army meeting; Columbus, Ohio, Touchdown Club; Teaneck, New Jersey, Knights of Columbus; and sports dinner of B'nai B'rith Lodge of New York, Greenwich Old Timers Athletic Association, Norwalk Jewish Center, St. John the Evangelist Church of New Haven, and University of Miami Gridiron Club.

"He'd just run to engagements," said Barber. Few sensed time running out. On May 22, 1963, Mel earned the second Dr. Raphael M. Dansker Humanitarian Award for Retarded Children (first, Attorney General Robert Kennedy). Following: Hoboken American Legion; National Law Enforcement Associates; New York fire department, making him honorary deputy chief, and Commonwealth of Kentucky, a Colonel; The Wisdom Society, awarding a certificate, and Marco Island, Florida, his own Little League team and field. At Alabama, kudos fill more than twenty-five large boxes. "Amazing what he got," said Larry Allen, "and people that he knew."

In June 1961, The Voice took Anna and Julius to Israel for their forty-ninth wedding anniversary, returning via The Vatican. At St. Peter's Cathedral, "Archbishop [Martin] O'Connor arranged seats for us, right in the area where they brought in the Pope."

Mom told O'Connor, "Monsignor, I want to thank you for those wonderful seats. They were right behind home plate." Back home, Mel taped ads unblue and -wiseacre, like their Fred MacMurray age.

In the clubhouse, he watches Ford prepare to shave. "Show 'em, Whitey. Wash. Lather. A Gillette Super Speed razor that matches the face."

Near home plate, Howard hails his "great shave." Allen notes: "That's what they all say, Ellie. Quick, easy clean. And those super blue blades are double-edged for economy."

Shedding it, the '63ers added a fourth announcer. "Red was traveling less," explained Jerry Coleman. "The Yanks needed a warm body [his]." Later, the 1949–57 infielder "worried about malapropisms. Before then I figured, 'They add to my sex appeal.'"

Jesus Alou is "in the on-deck circus." Randy Jones was "the left-hander with the Karl Marx hairdo." Dave "Winfield [was] going back . . . back . . . he hits his head against the wall. It's rolling toward second base!" Sit back, "put a star on that baby," and hail evolution, going yard. "Sometimes big trees grow out of acorns. I think I heard that from a squirrel."

In 1960, Coleman joined CBS's [pre-] *Game of the Week*. He was interviewing Cookie Lavagetto when "The Star-Spangled Banner" started.

"Better keep talking," thought the tyro, who did through the Anthem.

"Believe me," Jerry, scolded, later said. "When the Anthem starts, I stop, whether I'm taping, talking, or eating a banana."

A 1963 photo shows him, Mel, Red, and Rizzuto. "In the mid-fifties we had no jocks. Now we had two," said Allen, the augury plain. "Some can do the job, but most don't know English, can't set the stage, and cheat their audience."

Having never kept score, Jerry was assigned an inning his first game in Florida. Instead, twelve men hit in the top half alone. "I think you've had enough for today," said Mel. Coleman agreed. "I went over to the corner, got into a fetal position, curled up," and slept.

That summer Tribe lefties Sam McDowell and Jack Kralick were to hurl a doubleheader. The opening pitcher blanked New York inning after inning. "McDowell had erratic control," said Jerry, "but his control this day was astounding." In the sixth inning, he learned why.

WPIX telephoned the booth. "Is that McDowell?" Coleman turned to Indians Voice Bob Neal: "Who's pitching?" Bob lip-synchs: "Kralick." Four decades later Jerry's face fell. "They were similar in build, but even that doesn't explain why we had the wrong guy pitching."

The immediate problem was Mel. "I was just a busher," said the World War II and Korea veteran. "Allen was the virtuoso." Who would tell him? An engineer. "Mel's on radio in the next booth, and as he found out his head literally drops to the table."

The Voice forgave, perhaps having other things on his mind.

In *The Making of the President 1960*, Theodore H. White wrote: "Nixon had persisted as a puzzle to my mind and understanding from my first glimpse and sound of him. Now I decided that . . . he was above all a friend seeker, almost pathetic in his eagerness to be liked. He wanted to identify with people and have a connection with them. And this effort to communicate, to evoke warmth and sympathy, was his greatest problem."

For those recalling his fifties magic, Mel unable to communicate seems cosmically antithetical. Increasingly, however, he began to struggle on air. One night Allen froze on a WNBC New York newscast. "His face assumed a stricken expression, like that of a speaker who has forgotten his lines," wrote Ron Powers. "He was unable to finish the show." J. Anthony Lukas added: "He belabored the obvious and qualified explanations to death." People had liked working with him. "A regular guy," mused Scooter, "always a word for a technician, the cameraman." Now, Powers said, he could become cold, even surly, chiding members of the crew.

"His exultant yell, 'How About That!' became a national catchword," a *Cleveland Plain Dealer* columnist later wrote. "He was Howard Cosell, Brent Musburger, and Curt Gowdy rolled into one." Bob Dolgan enjoyed Mel's "friendly loquaciousness. But something began to happen to him around 1963. He began to look bad." In June, Allen spoke at a Wahoo Club luncheon. "He began a rambling discourse, droning on and on, with no focus to the speech." People began walking out. The Voice kept talking. An hour later the audience was half gone. Mel didn't see, or care.

That night Dolgan saw Ralph Houk. "I hear Mel did it again today," the manager laughed.

"What do you mean? Has he done this before?"

"It happens lately in every town we go in."

Next month the Yanks played at Baltimore. In a rain delay, said Larry, Ballantine had Mel leave TV for radio. "He'd tell great stories like nobody. When it rained, like that night, he was told to fill." Coleman was doing wireless. "You could tell when Mel wanted to get on. He'd sit by the mike, not saying a thing," vaunting posture and comity. "But I knew he couldn't wait to speak."

Jerry asked a question. For two hours, not paid by the word, Allen acted like he was. "It kept raining. He kept talking and talking.

I couldn't interrupt. He was wild"—a word rarely used, in another sense, for pitching's Chairman of the Board.

"If you got Whitey into bases loaded and no out, you were in trouble," John Blanchard said. Allen thought Ford "a professor of pitching. Nobody did more with the ability they had."

Once Ford called Blanchard to the mound.

"What's wrong?" asked the catcher.

"Nothing," said Whitey.

"Then why bring me out here?"

"Because I figured you could use the break."

Ford's 236–106 record forged a century-best .690 winning percentage. He got better, older: 66–19 under Houk, including 24–7 in 1963. Elston Howard became the A.L.'s first black MVP. Meanwhile, in Los Angeles the team of baseball's first black player hit only .251, had a 2.85 ERA, and "was the opposite of how we were in Brooklyn," said Vin Scully. "Those Dodgers clubbed you. Here it's a hit, steal, grounder, score on a fly." October 1963 matched two Boswells of the pitching condition.

"For years," said Mantle, "Whitey'd been the Series"—record 10 wins, 8 losses, 22 starts, 8 opening-game starts, 146 innings, 94 strikeouts, 34 walks, and 33⅔ straight scoreless innings—till Sandy Koufax K'd a record 15 Game 1 Yanks. A day later Johnny Podres won, 4–1. The third set packed Chavez Ravine: L.A., 1–0. The dynasty was breaking up, though few grasped it at the time.

Next day baseball's largest TV audience, 25.6 million homes, saw "Sandy throw that hellacious curve that dropped out of the sky," said Dodgers catcher John Roseboro. "Then he nailed Mantle with a fastball around the letters." Mick "stood there," NBC Radio's Harwell gawked, "like a house by the side of the road." Roseboro heard him mutter: "How in the hell are you supposed to hit that shit?"

Game 4 was scoreless till Frank Howard's fifth-inning blast. "How about that!" caroled the Peacocked Allen. "The first man to hit it [second deck] at Dodger Stadium!" The sky was blue; weather, warm; Mel's outlook, fitful. In 1960, he yelped "Look out now!" of Maz's belt. The warning now applied most directly to himself.

Out of the blue, "Allen began to emit strange noises in his throat during the late innings . . . a series of croaking, almost choking sounds," wrote Powers. In the seventh, Mick homered to tie the game. "The crowd roared," The Voice said. "I started to roar, too. Then suddenly I lost my voice": He tried to talk, but couldn't.

"Vin saw I was in terrible trouble, so he took over as I ran out of the booth." Inhaling coffee and lemon juice, Mel eventually returned.

"In the first half of the ninth inning," he rasped over NBC, "the Dodgers out in front, 2 to 1. Bobby Richardson the batter. Struck out, doubled to center, and grounded to short." Allen could barely speak. "The Dodgers on the verge!" he croaked. "Ball 1, low and inside. Good fastball. A 1 and 1 count."

"That's enough," whispered NBC's hulking Tom Gallery.

"Wait a minute," Mel said. "One ball, one strike," he resumed, hoarsely. Gallery seized Allen with both hands, lifting him from the booth.

"Two and one the count to Bobby Richardson," Scully said. "And, Mel, we all understand . . . just hang in there."

In shock—the *Series!* his signature—Allen retrieved post-game. "And that's the way it went today at Dodger Stadium, as the Dodgers are now the world champions."

The guesswork then began.

"If you have a television set, you know of the emotional crackup that knocked him off the air in the fourth game," Dick Young wrote. "They said he had laryngitis, but if it was, it was psychosomatic laryngitis. Mel Allen couldn't believe his beloved Yankees were losing four straight to the Dodgers. His voice refused to believe it, and therefore he could not repeat it."

Poppycock, said Mel. "If that were true, how could I have broadcast games the Yankees lost: 1960, or Game 7 in '55?" Truth was tamer. "A nasal condition I'd had earlier that year flared up. I'd had it treated by Frank Sinatra's throat doctor, and we thought it was cleared up." Instead, "something dropped down on my vocal cords," like a hand over Allen's mouth.

Barber shook his head. "I'd get to the park, and Mel'd be jabbering to fans. His voice was tired, but he wouldn't stop." Another Allen met The Voice in 1959. "Groupies'd phone our hotel, and get routed to the wrong M. Allen—*me*," said Maury. "The next day Mel'd joke, 'Did any of my girl friends call?' A terrific guy." Slowly the past settled on his consciousness. "'Ruffing, DiMaggio, Henrich.' You sensed that the game was passing him by."

Stan Isaacs recalled "a sweetheart who lost perspective": baseball, as be- and end-all. "He got defensive, worried about second-guessing." Habit could turn harangue. "Allen had trouble not talking" on or off air. "Many people were kind and hung in there." Others—he named Mantle—"would just walk away from him with a smirk while still in midsentence."

Steve Jacobson played against Allen in press/radio baseball. "Mel was MVP in the [New York Baseball Writers annual] game. He'd have a beer and was fun to be around—before he changed." As a boy, George Vecsey screamed, "Shut up, Allen," at the radio. "He seemed a cock-a-doodle do—a blowhard, like his team." In person, the *Times*man found Mel "almost Garrison Keillor-like in his quietude, just hiding out, who found his niche in baseball."

Another polarity intrigued Nelson. "No matter how he'd do in the regular season, he was great on a Rose Bowl. A big event focused him. Not now. Something was happening." Allen's last All-Star Game was in 1962. He had been a New Year's Day Barrymore. In late 1963, NBC quietly gave Lindsey the "Granddaddy of Them All." A year later Mel's Movietone reign ended. Like that, his non-Stripes empire collapsed.

The exception was the Series. It seemed absurd that he would ever leave its spooked-up days and splashing hues.

◆ ◆ ◆

By the early 1960s, the Grand Event was a small boy's Thanksgiving, Christmas, and Fourth of July: radio, smuggled into class; play-by-play, heard by earplug; teacher, feigning rage, craving score. A smile here, raised eyebrow there, told of Perranoski's save, Clemente's double, or McCovey, going deep.

Baseball is now said to weld greed, litigation, and prima donna. By contrast, at ten, unaware of Thomas Wolfe, I knew why he said, "Almost everything I know of spring is in it"—also fall. Bill Glavin attended Albany, New York's, Vincentia Institution. "Each year, the good nuns piped Mel into class over the loudspeaker." Strangers reacted like kin. "'The Duke parked one!' or 'Damn Yankees! Just got out of a jam.' Games were day. All morning you debated it, heard or saw it, then argued till bed."

Glavin was 7 when Burdette thrice beat the Yanks; 11, Ford twice blanked Cincy; 13, Mr. K K'd the Chairman. Mecca was 1958: New York, foiling a 3–1 game deficit. Excused in the sixth or seventh inning, "No one thought of staying outside to play. We'd rush to catch the last couple innings on TV: Sisters, teachers, boys who didn't like sports—even *girls*."

Black and white, the Series was Costas's Emerald City. "It made me so impressed with The Stadium monuments that the first time I walked on the field I was careful not to disturb their plot." Brooklyn's Larry King knew the Bums like the Torah. "My first Series was Gionfriddo, in '47. Then, Snider and Robinson and Mantle." Afterward "the street corner replayed every play of every game."

George Will spent his childhood hallucinating in Illinois. "You'd hear the 'Gillette Blue Blades March' come on the air, and then the camera would pan Wrigley Field," he dreamed. "The Cubs'd be in the Series," vaunting ivy, bleachers, hand-operated scoreboard, and gales off Lake Michigan. "I'm still waiting." Anyone can have a bad century.

At six, the future columnist quizzed his mother on Gionfriddo's catch. "Will the Yankee mommies be sad?" He was happier in 1950 ("I loved the name of [reliever] Jim Konstanty") and 1954 ("Just the syllables 'Dus-ty Rhodes' absolutely transported"). Despite

Eastern swank, Allen seduced, too. "He was a ritual, like a play opening on Broadway—you *expected* it to be in New York." Will especially liked 1957. "That was really neat, because I thought Milwaukee was related to Illinois."

In Galax, Virginia, a future *Reader's Digest* editor grew up near fictional Walton's Mountain. In 1954, pneumonia let Ken Tomlinson see the Jints mug the Tribe.

1958: Gannett's then-third grader Bob Minzesheimer envied Charlie Silverblatt. "He put a transistor radio inside his shirt, ran a wire up his sleeve, and leaned on his hand during math"—only to scream when the Braves Burdette homered.

1961: Another future journalist, Jane Wulf, cheered Maris's Game 3 poke. "This memory is particularly vivid because my brothers and I were excused from raking leaves."

My memory is of a shoe store: Mom, eying Buster Brown; me, No. 9, on the local NBC affiliate. Three days earlier I had become magically ill the morning of Game 1. A generation shared my malady.

The host of TV's *Talking Baseball* went to school three blocks from Yankee Stadium. "With the window open," said Ed Randall, ten in 1962, "a roar told you the Series was underway." In Hayward, California, a small town near San Francisco, Jon Miller, eleven, played the board game Strat-o-Matic, mimicking the PA Voice (Bob Sheppard), organist ("dum-dum-dum-dum," in key), crowd (blowing, like wind), and hometown Giants Hodges.

At home, Miller knew the score. At school, "we'd ask each other about the Series like the world depended on it." Sixty-two's was literally drilled into him, wincing in a dentist's chair. "When Richardson caught Willie's liner, I almost bit his finger off."

Even in Hamilton, Ontario, the Series briefly put hockey in the penalty box. A future humor writer for Ronald Reagan, Bob Hope, and Joan Rivers followed the plot in class. "It was strange," said Doug Gamble. "Learning scores by sign signal only added to the drama." Stranger would have been a Series, out of reach, at night.

"Life used to practically stop," said *Brooklyn Bridge* creator Gary David Goldberg. "The whole country came together—people on farms, factory workers, kids in school—everyone following the progress of the game." We remember. We were there.

On October 13, 1960, leaving school at 2:50 P.M., Glavin reveled: Yanks, 7–4. His bus shortly stopped at a corner. A friend shouted: "9–7, Pirates.'" Bill got home as Maz untied the score. The Series tie still binds.

Like many public men, The Voice wrote a memoir in middle age: 1964's *You Can't Beat the Hours*, by Harper & Row, with former *SPORT* magazine editor Ed Fitzgerald. "There is always something new in baseball," Mel observed. "The Yankees have a new manager named Yogi Berra, the new pitching genius of the game is a good-looking Dodger named Sandy Koufax, the Mets have a new ball-park. The game is never the same and it is always the same"—but for whom, till when?

Allen's Stripes *adieu* garbed flagship WCBS (AM 880 and FM 101.1) and a forty-one-outlet network. It began with three over-timers, including April 18th's, before only 12,543 in Colts-crazed Baltimore. October 1963 seemed remote: Mel was choice, and clear. Jerry Adair "bats 'em right-handed"; Jackie Brandt "is a tough customer in a tight game"; "Johnny [Boog] Powell worries you to death." Robin Roberts and Al Downing paired "age and youth in a pitching duel." Rain had rescheduled a June 16 doubleheader. "Man [how could it match tonight?] I have eaten my fingernails right up to the elbow."

The defense "deployed itself in a fashion." The eighth batter became "the second cleanup man." For sundowners, "yesterday's scores might have been missing in early editions." Not much was missing in The Voice as connecting tissue. "I don't know if they play, 'Run, cheeky, run' in Venezuela. But Luis Aparicio knows how to run." At break Mel crowed, "Get a smile every time with a Ballantine!" The Orioles did, 4–3, in twelve.

Each half-inning Allen gave a line score—"For New York, one run, six hits, no errors"—having sired it circa 1940. "The sponsor wanted me to give a signal so stations would expect a break." On July 4, a latecomer's was good seats still available. "We've got the room," Mel said of The Bronx. "So why don't you zoom? Come out and see the rest of this game [*v*. Minnesota] and all of Game 2."

Recently Ballantine had launched a special Totem Pole display. "Howdy," Allen parodied Sitting Bull. "You totem plenty in self-open cans." On the scoreboard, Boston aced a nine-spot: "the forfeit score [9–0]," he said, doubling back to the September 26, 1942, Polo Grounds. "'Scrap Iron Day,' my only forfeiture. Kids got in free if they got scrap medal to aid the war, but got antsy and rushed the field."

Coleman became "Merry Jerry"; a rundown play, "Rollins to Battey back to Rollins to Klippstein, covering"; the Twins, "denizens of dynamite." One, Tony Oliva, "reminds me of a tall Ernie Banks: quick, strong wrists," lining to left-center field. "He [Mantle] can't get up for that one! Oliva, with his speed, is around second on his way to third!" Allen cried. "Lopez up with the ball! An inside-the-park try for a homer! The throw into the plate! And he's got it!" The Yanks got the game, 7–5.

Go figure. Mel less evoked yesterday's mashed potatoes than The Voice of 1956.

Replacing Houk October 24, 1963, Berra was introduced at the Yanks' 745 Fifth Avenue office, then made the Savoy Hilton for a bubble-gum event. Garagiola introduced him. "Joe," said Yogi, "what's up?" One reply: Houk, named general manager. "[As manager] his players rallied around him like kids around a Good Humor Man," Allen wrote. The GM could hire/fire, though Mel seemed immune. Next July, "Dan Topping heard some of our broadcasts in Florida, and wrote to tell me how good they were. It wasn't his habit to write letters like that."

In August, swept at Comiskey Park, the '64ers fell 4½ games behind. Busing to O'Hare, Phil Linz began playing on harmonica

"Mary Had a Little Lamb." Berra told the shortstop to knock it off. Ignored, he knocked the instrument to the floor. Mel emceed his last "Day" (Elston Howard's) till Mantle's in 1969. That month CBS bought 80 percent of the Yankees for $11.2 million. *Caveat emptor.*

Mick got his 450th homer, dinging lefty/righty a record tenth/final time. On September 26, having passed the White Sox and Orioles, New York won an eleventh straight game. Next day it trailed Washington, 1–0. Howard's blast "just hooked out at the last fraction of a second"; Ford was "working rapidly"; his "pickoff throw got him [Mike Brumley]! They had him a mile!" This Mel tied detail ("For late tuners-in," out-of-town scoring), prose ("Bennie Daniel's Sunday pitch"), and feel for strategy ("A slide away from Blasingame! What a fadeaway by Tresh!").

Mantle hit in the seventh. "Here's a high drive to deep left-center field! Lock going way back! That ball is going, going, gone!" Threads fuse: "[Senators manager] Gil Hodges eying the long ball" at Brooklyn, now D.C. Next inning Nat-turned-Yank Pedro Ramos, K-ing six of seven men, faced ex-Bum Don Zimmer. "He didn't strike him out! There's a drive going to deep left-center! That ball is going, going, gone!: 2 to 1, Washington!"

Maris reached on a ninth-inning two-out muff. The Switcher swung again. "There's a high fly ball along the leftfield line! Chasing it is Hinton!" The ball dropped fair. "Maris rounding third! He's heading for home! Zimmer has the ball! Throwing to the plate! The slide! Safe! The ball game is tied!" Break starred a longtime sponsor. "Camel time is a mighty pleasant time."

For New York, the eleventh inning spurned Pleasantville. Washington filled the sacks. "A hit [Dick Phillips'] to the pitcher [Pete Mikkelsen], and off his glove for a base hit! Lock comes in to score!": Senators, 3–2. Leaving, Mel recalled Topping's letter: vote of confidence, or sleight of hand?

"I think Mel erred," Nelson later said, "in not realizing that many Yankees higher-ups were not exactly fond of him." That September

Allen entered Topping's office expecting to extend his contract. Instead, the owner eyed the floor, puffed one cigarette after another, and told baseball's Caruso that he was through.

"I'm afraid we've got some bad news."

"What's that, Dan?" Mel said.

"We're going to make some changes. We're not going to renew your contract."

Topping left the room. Returning, he began to pace. The Voice sat, immobile.

Finally: "Why?"

"It's nothing you've done, and it's not CBS or the Yankees."

Mel's dominion had lasted a quarter of a century. It ended with a thud, not cause.

Stunned, The Voice conjured Ballantine. Most breweries had built regional outlets. The Yanks expanded its Newark base. Shipping rose. "They started going under, had to cut the budget, and my head rolled," he later said. "If we'd only had time to talk, I'd have taken a cut, done"—softly—"*anything* to work things out."

Next day Barber reached the booth before the game in Cleveland. Allen was sitting in his seat, "staring across the ball field. He didn't speak. I don't think he knew I had come in. I don't think he knew where he was. He was numb. He has protruding dark eyes. They were bulging out so far they looked like concord grapes. He was the saddest-looking man I have ever seen. He was in a nightmare"—the look "sad, deserted. He just couldn't believe it. He was desolate, stricken. And he didn't know I knew. [Topping had told him.] How he got through it, I don't know. It was hard enough for me."

The red light shone. Gently, Red touched Mel's shoulder. He blinked, said, "Hello there, everybody, this is Mel Allen," endured the road trip, and returned to New York. The Voice began phoning publicist Bob Fishel, arguing, pleading, "Please, take it back."

On Saturday, October 3, 1964, the Yanks clinched a pennant long time coming (Game 161) and long time gone (twenty-ninth and last till 1976). Mel was in Worcester, Massachusetts, for NBC TV football (Syracuse-Holy Cross). "Coming up now," Rizzuto introduced him next day, "sorry he wasn't with us yesterday, one of the few clinchers he's ever missed, the Voice of the Yankees, Mel Allen."

He commenced with intimacy: a chance to sum up and say good-bye. "Thank you very much, Phil. A football game! Right now, my little nephew, two years old, is seeing his first baseball game . . . My niece is six . . .You know, a lot of kids have a lot of fun coming to the ball game. Does 'em a lot of good. I really think it does. I saw my first game." Pause. "Oh, by the way, hello there, everybody.

"I saw my first game when I was about their age . . . but I don't remember it. 'Bout 1,200 miles from here. Class A League. But my mother remembers it very well, because my father had to travel 30 miles from the small mining town where we lived to take me. But he had to tend to some business [before seeing the game]. What business he had to attend to, he tended to in a hurry.

"When we came back, Mom was undressing me, and she said, 'Did you have a good time?'

"I said, 'Yes,' and I started talking about having peanuts and soda pop. She knew what had happened": baseball as summer music, nighttime light, and pillow pal. Twelve seconds of silence followed. It seemed like a year.

"Well, we're all set to go [*v.* Cleveland]," The Voice said, finally. "I knew that the clinching would take place the day that I had to do my first football game—if it took place, that is." More silence, then reminiscence, still painful to rehear.

Manager Berra had put ex-Athletic Hector Lopez at third. "I recall one day," Mel began. "He [Lopez] remembers it well, too. There were several balls that were hit to him. More properly, I should say, they were hit through him." A's skipper Lou Boudreau later brought "the entire team out for fielding practice." Below, Phil Linz led off for New York. Indian Duke Sims called time. "A tisket, a tasket," said Allen, "he's lost his big catcher's basket."

Stripe Jake Gibbs hit second, evoking "Mickey Cochrane, the only catcher I knew who batted second. Bill Dickey hit fifth, Gus Mancuso sixth, Gabby Hartnett fourth the same Series [1935] Cochrane hit second for Detroit." Luis Tiant delivered. Roger Bresnahan—"he was a great one"—led off for the 1905 Jints. "It takes two to tango, and he caught some great ones like Christy Mathewson." In the "National League, the Reds and Cardinals" led by a game. The Ballantine scoreboard soon bared a tenth St. Louis pennant.

Suddenly, the ex-teacher segued. "You know, there are many names which become Anglicized, even if they're not publicized, take a different accent": *Mar*tinez became Mar*tin*ez; RAH-mos, RAE-mos; "Tiant, from Havana, delivers to Lopez, from Panama." Each had a Romance lilt, like French: "There was a time when Johnny's forebears pronounced the name Blan-CHARD." Once pitcher Art "Hoot-a-man" taught The Voice "HOW-te-man." "Regardless of the spelling of proper names," said Mel, "it's how you want to call it."

He wanted to thank the globe. "Every year's final game we salute the family": Topping, Webb, and Houk!; publicity, scouting, accounting, and receptionist. Rookie Archie Moore spanked a double. "Around third comes Blanchard to score!"—Yanks, 1–0. Next: security, comptroller, switchboard, ticket director, and game-tying blast. "A high drive hit to deep right! And the ball is into the right-field stands for a homer for Luis Tiant!" As he "trots around the bases, we'll continue to trot around our bases of thanking folks": statistician, TV/radio, doctor, trainer, clubhouse, Western Union, press box men, and "the fine men in blue. We'd like to thank them"—over ninety, in all.

Elvio Jimenez arced to Tito Francona near the rightfield line. "That takes care of just about most everybody, but not everybody. Always miss a few." Mel gave his last line score. "Without these people," he resumed, "you don't do your job." Finally: "As we get ready to move into the fourth inning, all set to move in, Red Barber."

The Redhead asked about Holy Cross.

"They're still talking baseball even during football season up there," said Allen.

"Okay, boy," said Red, not meaning to dismiss. Mel mended, but never healed.

Allen would miss the World Series, a critic wrote, when the Great Salt Lake turned fresh. It began Wednesday, October 7. Monday, The Voice was packing for St. Louis. "Nobody told me I wasn't going to do it. My contract still had a 'lead announcer' stipulation." Instinctively, he phoned the Commissioner's Office: Scooter had replaced him.

Stunned, Allen wrote: "I regret that all the best things in life must come to an end, but I am proud, though, that you [Topping] have been my fine friend." Drowning, he clutched Dan's lifeline— "a rationale," said a friend—of not being fired, just not rehired. "Whatever may have brought about the multiplicity of changes," Mel continued, "as you told me, I appreciate so much your graciousness in granting to me the consideration in bowing out gracefully." Actually, they broke him, needlessly and heedlessly.

SERIES OPENS: YANKS "BENCH" MEL ALLEN! bayed the *News*. An Associated Press photo showed him watching the opener in a rocking chair: "Just another Series fan via video." Bud Furillo eulogized: "The picture tells it all. They've put Allen out to pasture, and the agony the decision caused him is plainly written in the face of the man with the melodious voice"—a casualty of his field. "Allen thought that in order to stay on top, he needed to broadcast all the time. When he wasn't broadcasting, he was making speeches. He was a patsy for everyone's club from War, West Virginia, to Broken Arrow, Oklahoma." Mel feigned a fine sense of *que sera*. "I've been in the business long enough not to be surprised."

Barber was. "Incredibly, Red thought he'd do NBC's Series," said Leonard Koppett. "Not a chance with Phil around." Also doing it: Harry Caray, Joe Garagiola, and the friend for whom Allen had been best man. "In 1961 and '62," said Gowdy, "I did the

All-Star Game with Garagiola and Scully [respectively]. There weren't links like I had with Mel": 1958 Series and first 1959 and each 1960 All-Star Game. In 1964, Curt called a blast his mentor might have aired.

"Here's Mantle . . . facing [the Cardinals'] thirty-eight-year-old Barney Schultz," Gowdy said in Game 3. "The big Yankee crowd roaring now for some action! There's a high drive to deep right! And forget about it! It is gone! The [2–1] ball game's over! Mantle has just broken a World Series record. He now has 16 World Series home runs. He and Babe Ruth were tied with 15 apiece."

The Bombers lost their fourth Series since 1957. The Swifties seventh title trailed only New York's then-twenty. Under small world: Berra was axed, replaced by St. Louis's Johnny Keane. Overnight the Stripes went into mothballs. Mel's closet was about to close.

"Mel Allen cried all the way to the bank, the day he learned he would not broadcast the World Series," wrote Bob Consodine. The *News*'s Red Foley was gentler. "Allen missing from air. Finished with Yankees"—or was he? He could not accept not being their Voice—until he wasn't.

"Allen was too oblivious to notice unhappiness," said the *Newark Star*'s Jim Ogle. "Topping and he'd had run-ins. Even when Dan dropped the bomb, Mel expected it to fade." NBC gave him *College Football Scoreboard* (cohost, Jack Lescoulie) and October 24 and 31 and November 21 play-by-play. "Face saving," Nelson said. The Voice was a conspirator. "I have no reason to think that I will not [rejoin the Yanks]," he insisted. "This [Series] is a rotation of announcers." A team flack cautioned: "I wouldn't want to say so."

In November, Allen, "informed by letter," Ogle wrote, "was given the opportunity to make the announcement." Actually, said Larry, "Fishel was supposed to meet Mel, compose a press release, but kept stalling." On December 17, 1964, the Stripes previewed the Series film at Shor's. Almost as an asterisk, a statement released the ex-M. A. Israel, shocking those who knew what was said of Sophocles: "He saw the world steadily, and he saw it whole." Knowing baseball thoroughly, Mel had conveyed it whole. For what? For this.

Jack Mann scored "giving him anything but the standard mealymouthed explanation. Bus boys are fired every day, but they are usually told by the headwaiter that they dropped too many dishes." Leonard Shecter wrote: "Unlike Arthur Miller's [*The Death of a]* *Salesman,* Allen is a success. But like Miller's salesman, Allen is afraid of being a failure." The heave-ho lived down to expectation. "He had expected it for twenty-five years. 'I have as much security in this business as a light switch going on and off.'" Even Mel found his firing a puzzle. "I frankly don't know why. I'd feel better if I did."

Houk declined to say. "There's no point in going into details as to why we're making the change. I can see no reason for embarrassing Mel or anyone else." Agent Rubin was incensed. "It was insensitive and unprofessional. Every artist has a clause in his contract that he will get five or six weeks notice of termination. He deserved at least that."

The *Times* bannered: RUMORS FLYING SINCE SEPTEMBER. None gave a damn about Mel's honor, chary tenderness, or reluctance to offend. On page one, Val Adams wrote, "The sponsor and Yankees decided it was time." A CBS "informant" said "the Yankees eventually would make public the 'reasons' behind the move."

They never did.

Imagine Dick Vitale or John Madden being canned, abruptly and unexpectedly, except that Allen was bigger in his day and place. As word seeped into print, New York gaped, then mourned.

"Nobody—not Ruth or George Weiss or Frank Crosetti—was as clearly and long identified with the Yankees," said Mann. "He was the Yankees apostle and their apologist . . . the twenty-sixth man." Editorials ripped. Even Ann Landers griped. "You know, I've never understood it," The Voice said later. "Actors leave, they're forgotten. People still writing the Yankees, asking where Mel is": more Tyrone Power than Austin Powers.

"There were no farewell dinners, no fond ceremonies," Ron Powers wrote. "CBS did not even issue an explanation as to why it had consigned one of the most popular play-by-playmen in history to oblivion." Later ruing it, Allen stiffed comment, too. In 1974, Stripes head Michael Burke said only: "He wasn't what he used to be."

Ogle was a house man. Mel, he charged, "repeatedly disobey[ed] direct orders about how the broadcasts should be done, what his role in them was to be." He began to stray, "[tangents] not only more frequent, but getting longer." Allen laughed. "Hell, if the Yankees had objected to my talking a lot, I'd have been fired long ago."

In November 1964, on NBC's *The Tonight Show*, he "didn't commit himself as to his status," said Ogle, "but went into a digression." Next day TV columnist Jack O'Brien said: "After listening to Mel Allen sermonizing, it was difficult to decide if he wanted a job sportscasting or a small parish."

A daily mass-goer had a thought.

A year earlier the Bob Hope of the resin bag had left the Cardinals full-time for NBC TV. Most people take their work, not selves, seriously. Joe Garagiola took himself, not his game.

"Kennedy was, whether for good or bad, an enormously large figure," a writer said of America's first Catholic president. "Historically, he was a gatekeeper. He unlatched the gate and through the door marched Catholics, blacks, and Jews, and ethnics, women, youth, academics, newspersons, and an entirely new breed of politician." Garagiola, a large baseball figure, unlatched a gate for nonrural, -cornpone, and -native stock announcers. He was urban, ethnic, and as barbed as wire.

Nelson called him "the single most ambitious man I ever met," not intending a compliment. On the other hand, Joe later sired the Baseball Assistance Team charity. "I went through life as a [1946–54] player to be named later," said Garagiola. Ordinary on the field, he was extraordinary off.

Joe's mother could not speak English. Dad worked in a brick-yard. Like the Israels, their son learned a salute to the flag, catch in the throat, tear in the eye Americanism. Best friend Yogi Berra lived "a pickoff away" on St. Louis's Dago Hill. Their cosmos was base-ball: the exception, oddly, soccer.

Berra took ill the morning of one game. "You look terrible," said Garagiola. "Why don't you go home?"

"If a guy can't get sick on a cold, miserable day like this, he ain't healthy," Yogi shrugged. Try converting *that* for Mom.

Increasingly, Joe became Berra's ambassador without portfolio. "I'll ask him, 'What time is it?' Yogi'll say, 'Now?'"

"I get lost going to Yogi's home, and call. 'Where are you?' he says. I tell him. He says, 'You're not far away. You come this way. Don't go that way.'"

A woman mused, "Yogi, you look cool in that outfit." Berra smiled. "Thanks," he said, "you don't look so hot yourself."

What a card—or baseball's Charlie McCarthy? "It's *his* humor," said Garagiola, growing wintry. "Yogi thinks funny, and speaks what he thinks."

In 1960, Joe wrote the best-selling *Baseball Is a Funny Game*. By 1964, the Peacock eyed a team not poignant, like Brooklyn; or awful, like Boston; or funny, like the Cubs. "Boy, I'd like to get the Yankees job," Til Ferdenzi quoted Garagiola telling a friend. To Phil Pepe, the Series closed the deal, announced that December: "Work-ing with Rizzuto, he won critical acclaim for . . . entertaining re-porting." Said another writer: "If Allen were famed for being too wordy, Garagiola won fame for finding the right words."

Houk prized Joe's devotion to the quaint and personal. "We are confident Yankees fans will enjoy his warm interpretation of the game." The '64 Amazins outdrew them by 429,959. Shea Stadium's Banner Day featured MONGOLIA LOVES THE METS (in Mongolian), EAMUS METROPOLI ("Let's Go Mets" in Latin), and E=MC$^2$ (Errors equaled Mets times customers squared). Anything they could do, Houk said, stung, the Yanks could do better. Bring those signs and placards down.

"We're not a bunch of stuffed shirts," he insisted. "If that's what they want to do, that's what we'll do." Like a lagging firm, The Major misread his customer. "Baseball ought to be fun"—as if Mel hadn't. "I don't think we'll be running second to anybody in the radio and TV booth"—as if Allen had. "We've got just what we want up there"—as if the listener had been ignored since 1939.

Boston's Ned Martin "always knew the Yankees were a bitchy outfit." A bystander asked when they had turned stupid, too.

ALLEN REPLACED BY JOE GARAGIOLA, said the *Times*, skipping Mel's first name, since you knew it, anyway. Joe's "good wit, no hit," said Ferdenzi, would "salt Yankee baseball with quips, snappy sayings, and maybe an occasional soft shoe." Garagiola vowed humor "if one club is blasting the other team, 13–1." Some found him disingenuous. "With a dynasty, why would you want Ringling Brothers?" said Gowdy. "Who wouldn't focus on the stars?"

Audiotape clarifies memory. Early sixties tape often backs Burke's view. Mel was not always "what he used to be." Mick's penicillin shot, team attendance, The Voice's 1963 Series, his regular-season wax/wane cost. "Team displeasure was cumulative," Red felt. "Everything caught up." Ironically, NBC's and Movietone's absence focused Allen's 1964 Yanks play-by-play. The first part of the decade poisoned his well.

Had they wished, the Stripes could have crafted a brief sabbatical. "At the very least, maybe ease Mel's schedule," said Bob Murphy. "Sometimes you just need a rest to recharge." Houk and Topping couldn't bother, deeming him—The Voice! their public's eyes and ears—a complication, some form of lowlife: new lamps for old.

What kind of people were they? if one may ask: treating a Salieri, to quote Ring Lardner, like a side dish they declined to order, even as Mel congratulated his successor.

"Hope you stay on the job as long as I did," read the first telegram that Garagiola received.

A quarter century later Joe shook his head. "'Christ, Mel,' I told him, 'I didn't know there were nice people like you still around.'"

"When you broadcast for one club for twenty-five years, you have to be good, and Mel Allen was better than good," Young wrote in a paean to human rhythms. "He had music in his voice and the voice was of tireless muscle. He would talk for hours on end with a resonance and sustaining quality that was incredible. On the whole his judgment was mature, although every once in a while Mel would leave the play-by-play hanging."

At fifty-one, "That's pretty young for a man to retire, even in this automated age. They won't hold any benefits for Mel. He made it good and he'll get a day's work here and there because the voice still has the music and the name of Allen means quality."

Who dreamt what lay ahead: hurt, shame, turning inward, but not bitter, then rebirth as a household name, as if The Voice had never been away? ◆

# Down on Your Knees (1965–1972)

or the heck of it, compare cars, clothes, and imported gin: Dick's taste may repel Jane. "Agreed," George Will told a reporter. "Take great musicals. There's *Carousel.*"

"*South Pacific,*" said a writer.

"Just proves the point. Consensus can be a dirty word"—except that by 1965 the Yankees already missed The Voice.

In February, Rizzuto spoke at St. Mary's School in Oneonta, New York, 22 miles from Cooperstown. His first question was "the one probably on all fans' minds," read the hometown *Star.* Why Mel?

"I really don't know," said Scooter. "He was a fine broadcaster. Maybe the brass felt they needed a change."

It began March 21, from Ft. Lauderdale, on WPIX's Yanks inaugural. Kay Gardella wrote: "Joe Garagiola will call the plays for the Yankees in Allen's spot," aiding Coleman, Red, and Phil.

"Before his axing," said Val Adams, "the Yankees said that there no longer is a number 1 man on the broadcast team." Houk expected each to match the Mets. He did not expect his club to resemble theirs.

September 18, 1965: 50,180 fete Mickey Mantle Day. More typical: Frank Howard's grenade off Stripes reliever Steve Hamilton. "It went over the [Stadium's] leftfield roof, but just foul," said Clete Boyer. "You had to see it to believe it." It was harder to believe the Fall. New York flunked .500 for the first time since 1925. Ghouls careened around the tiers.

Its booth was as spooky. "As opposed to the more or less conventional Mets announcers, the Yankees' crew consists of four diverse and clearly identifiable personalities," wrote *Newsday.* "[Yet] fans are still debating the merits of Allen, canned without public explanation. They have had a hard time making the adjustment. Who can forget . . . the boring game in Washington that Allen picked up by singing *Yankee Doodle* between pitches?"

Predictably, the new quartet spurned anything germane to score. Houk replaced Johnny Keane. The '66ers thudded last. On September 22, the day Mike Burke became president, 413 specked the 65,010-seat Stadium. On WPIX, Barber thought it "the perfect place for Burke to start, nowhere to go but up."

Red asked director Don Carney to pan the stands. No shot. Ask again. No go. "I found out [Yanks radio/TV head] Perry Smith was in the control room. He told them not to show the seats." *Report,* he recalled from thirties teletype. "I don't know what the paid attendance is, but whatever it is, it is the smallest crowd in the history of Yankee Stadium, and this crowd is the story, not the game."

Next week, asked to breakfast, Barber, like Allen, anticipated a new pact. Burke skipped sugar: "There is no reason to be talking pleasantries. We have decided not to renew your contract." Red called the press. "I have a record of thirty-seven years of fine work. I am not going to allow Mr. Burke, or anybody, to trifle with it as they did with Mel Allen." The Voice "is still waiting for them to make an announcement, and I wasn't going to wait."

Fired, Red was freed. "I'd become a servant to the microphone. On my own, I'd have gone back for who knows how long." Instead, the next quarter century soldered seven books, six Halls of Fame, and feathers in the cap for excellence, including broadcasting's Pulitzer, the George Foster Peabody Award.

In 1981, this mix of "old courtliness and the flintiness of the utterly independent man," wrote David Halberstam, began weekly National Public Radio *Morning Edition* commentary. Depending on date and mood, he canvassed cats, cooking, or crape myrtle in his Tallahassee yard, once segueing from Geraldine Ferraro to Mary, Queen of Scots, to caddies at the British Open.

Time of discourse: three minutes.

The Redhead skipped his egg timer.

Wife Lylah was often cited, but never heard. Allen's *en famille* had been the Stripes. "He never married anybody but those New York Yankees," said Anna, curtly. A writer asked whether she was happy about his life. "I wish he was a shoemaker. A married shoemaker." She begrudged that, and time.

One night the clan entered an eatery near Esther's home. "No sooner do we walk in the door," Mom rued, "when here comes the kids, the mamas, the papas, the grandmamas, and the grandpapas," craving an autograph. A man raged because Mel asked to check his schedule before agreeing to a speech. "Then this boisterous blonde tries to sit in Mel's lap. It was too much. Me, I wanted to be at home in my kitchen, eating a sandwich with Larry."

On May 28, 1965, Anna, seventy-four, died at Flushing Hospital, near Shea Stadium: said the *Times*, "survived by husband Julius, two sons, and daughter Esther." Mel wrote friends and relatives: "So much of us whom she bore is in turn borne with her departure." Jim Woods and Russ Hodges later talked "about Mel's taking his mom's death so hard," said Poss. Fox, the Yanks, now this: "We'd try to figure what went wrong." For something right, he turned to baseball's once-capital.

By 1963, Braves attendance was a third of 1957's peak. Next year's rose to 910,911. The team shrugged: Only a temporary court order kept it in Milwaukee. "What a mess," Merle Harmon, replacing Earl Gillespie, said. "Before moving to Atlanta [1966], they had to play another year in a city which *knew* it'd lost them": two people in a house, awaiting a divorce.

Merle became the loci of curse, slight, and hate. "If I praised the Braves, people said, 'Don't back traitors.' If I didn't, diehards said, 'Don't keep us from another team.'" The 1965 Braves vied till

September. "Baseball was afraid we'd make the Series and County Stadium would be empty."

Lewis Carroll coined "curiouser and curiouser": (a) A Wisconsin bank and three breweries sponsored WEMP/WTMJ Radio network coverage, "but wouldn't say so publicly"; (b) Atlanta WSB TV/wireless aired seventeen and fifty-three games, respectively. "Milwaukee doing a team it's losing. Atlanta doing a team it doesn't have"; (c) Like an apparition, The Voice reemerged.

In 1954 spring training, a Milwaukee pitcher heard a voice across the street talking to a friend. "I thought, 'Gee, that sounds like Allen,'" said future mikeman Ernie Johnson. "You couldn't miss it"—nor 1965 gossip when Mel joined WSB. "I'd heard he had problems, but nobody wrote saying, 'Get him out of here!'" He did wonder about The Voice's lack of a full-time job.

In 1955, Harmon had visited The Stadium as Voice of the Kansas City Athletics: "first time, I'm quaking." Entering the booth, he thought, "My God, it's him, the most famous man in broadcasting." Smiling, Allen said, "Anything I can do, let me know. We want to make you feel at home." A decade later ABC's new *Game of the Week* chose Merle over Mel.

Undone, not yet remade, Allen returned South. Milwaukee's number 2, Tom Collins, froth as a Miller Lite beer, arrived in 1965 from Schlitz publicity. "Mel was doing ads. I said, 'Hey, why don't you guys put him on [Atlanta] TV?'" They dined at Bookbinders in Philadelphia. "A regular guy, like Merle, just listened and laughed. It'd been nice if he stayed," except the Braves skipped town.

"Mel took Atlanta to stop talk that he no longer could do the job," Harmon explained. "He always flew in exhausted from somewhere, you asked how he kept going." One day Merle invited him to his Milwaukee home. "We had a conversation about life, very personal. Mel poured his heart out. 'Why? The Yankees never told me that I wasn't coming back.'"

Pals communed over steaks, "sitting there, like Ward Cleaver. [Wife] Jeannette and our three kids. For one day we were Mel's family, trying to comfort him": to Merle, a soldier shot through the heart.

Ballantine pulled the trigger: "Times change, there were new trends, the brewery was going under." That was Allen's story, and he stuck to it till death.

Nine times Mel aired a Dodgers Series. On October 2, 1965, he voiced Milwaukee at Dodger Stadium. "The Dodgers seeking a thirteenth pennant. Sandy Koufax seeking a twenty-sixth victory. One out before this place erupts!" Koufax "takes off his cap, runs his hands through his hat, puts the cap back on, pulls at the visor, looking in, gets the sign." A fly sailed to left. "Lou Johnson getting under it! The Dodgers win the pennant [3–1]! And they rush out on the field! They mob Koufax! And pillows start flying out on the field. And in one of the exciting moments in the history of baseball, the Dodgers win their thirteenth pennant!"

L.A. went to Minnesota, opening the Series. After thirteen years—so few, they seem almost mythic—the Braves left Milwaukee for a state where many did not know a soul. Mel did: "Only fifty-two, from next door, an institution," said Harmon. "I couldn't imagine him not getting Atlanta." Team vice president John McHale could.

That June the Braves and White Sox played a Georgia exhibition. At a pregame luncheon the Hose's Milo Hamilton was introduced to a howl. Radio's WCFL Chicago network had knit the South. "They knew my name," Milo said, "or at least my voice."

McHale collared him, bright, glib, and bookish. "That was some welcome you got. You ought to come down here with us next year."

"I'd be interested," said Hamilton, "in just that chance."

Onlookers gasped. How could the Braves bypass *Allen?* Readily, as it occurred. "There were these rumors," a McHale aide said. "Drinking, drugs." Milo was young (thirty-eight), fresh, and handsome. "We wanted a new lease on life."

In New York, The Voice and Team resumed trying to recapture theirs.

Mel wrote an old friend August 27, 1965: "I am again in need of your [Weiss's] counsel. I wonder if I might drop by your home for a few minutes next week upon my return from Milwaukee." On November 9, a giant power failure dimmed the Tri-State area. In suburban Norwalk, a banquet hailed by candlelight its longtime emcee. Gowdy, Nelson, Schenkel, Coleman, and Rizzuto spoke: The firing was the elephant in the room. "It was inevitable," wrote Sam Cohen, "that Allen's [release] would be sort of a 'specter at the feast,' but speeches studiously avoided any reference and instead spoke hopefully of the popular announcer reestablishing himself in the field in which he attained high fame." Only later did Jerry say: "The Yankees nearly destroyed him." Ralph Houk sent a wire. It did not contain a job.

Increasingly, the booth found it one to hawk the Yanks. An exception: May 14, 1967. "Stu Miller's ready! Here's the payoff pitch by Miller to Mantle," Garagiola cried. "Swung on! There she goes! There she goes! . . . Mickey Mantle has hit the [career] 500th home run." The '68ers hit .214 *v.* 1930's .309. Memory mocked the slingshoters in the flesh.

"Many irrationally came to believe Mel was somehow a factor in the Yankees great success after World War II," mused Isaacs. "The reason was what happened after his firing." *Nonpareil* together, they collapsed apart. It would be nice to say that each repaired quickly—but as a former president said, that would be wrong, for sure.

Vanishing, as he had, so swiftly, cryptically, Allen turned to dinners, ads, store and restaurant openings, and KRAK Sacramento's Little League World Series. In 1964, Mel had been an Eminence. By 1966, he was grateful to rejoin WNBC. "Put a veteran sports announcer back in [late-night weekend] business," wrote Matt Messina, "and he's a kid with a lollypop." Still under network contract, "he also brings versatility to *Monitor*" and odd *Game*[s] *of the Week*. As a player, "[occasional NBC partner Tony] Kubek wouldn't go on our pregame show," Mel said. "Now, he's lost his shyness." Soon Allen lost each gig.

That November he and five big leaguers took their eighteen-day trip to Vietnam. Back home, Mel wrote a three-page letter thanking William Eckert—aka "The Unknown Soldier"; as 1965–68 Commissioner, a terrific Lieutenant General—for "the priceless privilege of representing baseball. Reports have [already] begun to trickle into the Special Forces headquarters in Saigon indicating the tour was most successful." Before the official cable, "I thought this general preliminary report would be of interest"—also, he may have thought, a way to woo baseball.

The troupe—"on the move up to fifteen hours a day," wrote Allen—visited the China Sea, Gulf of Siam, Danang, and central steppe land. It visited hospitals in Saigon, neared Cambodia, and got a "captured Viet Cong flag" from sectors "so [remote] smoke grenades were used to show the helicopters where to land." Mel flesh-pressed, showed the official All-Star Game movie, and met General William Westmoreland, Nelson's World War II bud. Soldiers "often got visits from great entertainers but seldom got a chance to talk to them. Baseball was a part of them, a real part of home."

He returned to Miami Dolphins play-by-play, working an exhibition with Barber, was ditched after a year, and later retrieved Miami college football. "On each occasion," said the *Miami Herald*'s Howard Kleinberg, "the knock was that he could not keep up with the play and had a difficult time identifying the players." The baseball Hurricanes let him go after a regional College Athletic Association tourney. "No job lasted long," said later Voice Sonny Hirsch. In 1968, Mel almost took another.

"We had a long talk," Allen said of Charlie Finley, moving the Athletics to Oakland. "But Larry and I'd just bought a Canada Dry bottling dealership in Stamford [Connecticut, moving to nearby Riverside] and I didn't want to walk away."

Mel offered to do the A's if he could live off-season in New York. Finley balked, wanting him year-long to vend. "I couldn't," Allen said. "Anyway, who wants to leave New York?" The Voice, in Oakland? Was Gertrude Stein a baseball fan?

WJW Cleveland was, hiring Mel in 1968. "Remember the sequence," said Barber. "Atlanta fails. Oakland misses. Rumors still fly. Mel takes Indians TV because that's what there is."

In one game, The Voice rendered from memory part of "The Song of Hiawatha." A decade later Jerry Coleman beamed. "Who else could make baseball and Henry Wadsworth Longfellow twins?"

Axed again that fall, Allen began almost a phased bigs withdrawal. "As far as the larger American public was concerned," Powers wrote, "[he] simply ceased to exist." Puzzled, it felt a gentle protectiveness. George Steinbrenner now owned a Cleveland shipbuilding company. "I'd go around the country. Even Yankee-haters missed 'em and Mel on the Series." Baseball missed the Switcher, retiring in March 1969.

On June 8, before 60,008, the Yanks retired No. 7. The Voice introduced him. "There's no one else who could perform this task," emceed Frank Messer. "Mel Allen!" revisiting The Stadium for the first time since 1964. The sound could be heard in Jersey City. "This is one of the proudest moments I've ever had on this hallowed baseball ground," said Mel. "And I'm terribly proud to have the honor to once again call from the dugout one of the all-time Yankee greats. The magnificent Yankee, Mickey Mantle."

Mick's reply eclipsed Commerce, Tulsa, and Spavinaw forming an Okie twang: "I always wondered how someone who was dying could say he was the luckiest man on the face of the earth. Now I know how Lou Gehrig felt." Mel sent a letter to team VP Howard Berke: "Having emceed Babe Ruth and Lou Gehrig, nothing meant more than this." Next year he added Old-Timers Day. "It was amazing," said Steinbrenner. "His ovations'd top everyone's but Mickey and DiMag." Already they topped the Stripes revolving booth.

"In recent years, their announcing team has been shuffled almost as often as the ineffective bull pen," wrote J. Anthony Lukas.

After Barber, "[Rizzuto, Joe, and Coleman] carried on for a season [1967] until Garagiola" joined NBC's "*Today Show* replaced by Messer," stiff and sterile, "brought in from Baltimore."

Coleman left, replaced by hapless Bob Gamere's, "Here it comes, there it goes!" Gamere, in turn, yielded to the bigs first black play-by-play man.

"That first season [1971] I was terrible," said ex-Cardinal first baseman Bill White. "I had no style. The next season I was a little less terrible." None replaced The Voice's grand and unmitigated eloquence, including baseball's then-network prism and progenitor.

From 1953 to 1965, Mel, Red, Bud Blattner, Dizzy Dean, Garagiola, Harmon, Nelson, and Wolff, among others, aired network baseball. In early 1966, gaining exclusivity, NBC expected Gowdy to succeed them. What if his voice was not a fever-swamp? He was fair, did homework, and had a Chip Hilton delivery. Surely, that would be enough.

"The good news is that Curt was thorough," said Blattner. "The bad is that the Good Shepherd'd flunk if only He did play-by-play." Augmenting angst: "[Curt] may not have many downs," said Associated Press, "[but also] not many ups." Just the facts worked in a Republic fused to baseball. They seemed archaic in an anything-but-bore me age.

"As spectacle, baseball suffers on [TV]," Harry Caray wrote. "The fan at the park [talking, drinking, taking Junior to the john] rarely notices the time span between pitches. The same fan at home . . . finds things dull." As new All-Star and Series Voice, Gowdy frowned on spectacle. Mel smiled, like the late sixties and early seventies.

Ultimately, Curt seemed too bland for a hip and inchoate age's "place, environment, relations, repetitions . . . the breadth of . . . being," said Thornton Wilder. Even in exile, bucked by nostalgia and a residual curiosity, Allen—"The Legend," to Tony Kornheiser—meant bigs radio/TV. Had his skill truly towered? Were successors that dull? Did he denote a richer baseball past? How boring was today?

The Voice made Halls of Fame: Alabama, American Sportscasters Association, College Football, Emerson Radio, National Association of Broadcasters, and National Radio and Television Museum. In 1972, the National Association of Sportscasters and Sportswriters opened its sanctorum in Salisbury, North Carolina. A picture, fedora-topped, behind a microphone, read: "Mel Allen, peer of the Nation's Sportscasters."

On the periphery, he did a diaper ad ("There is no joy in Diaperville"), bought country-and-western station WYAM in Birmingham, shilled a Tri-State car rustproof firm (FROM BEER TO RUST, said the *Daily News*), and began a syndicated radio series, *Wake Up the Echoes*, written by ex-*Herald Tribune* sports editor Robert Cooke.

"I tape it in Miami," Mel said of the daily $3\frac{1}{2}$-minute program. He also refound an old mistress/new flame.

"The other evening," wrote Lukas, "while waiting for Harry Reasoner to unravel the news, I was stunned by the simplicities of my youth. Suddenly they were there in the TV commercial before me—the flash of a white arm, the swing of a brown bat, a blurred arc rising into the outfield, a foaming glass of beer and Mel Allen's voice.

"'Remember when 'Purity, Body and Flavor' were as famous as 'Going, going, gone!'? . . . And along with baseball and Ballantine came a pennant every year?'

"Did I remember?" Did he ever.

Soon Ballantine "made a stunning reversal," wrote *Newsday*'s Dave Klein. "Allen's sudden reappearance is a delightful entree into lives." In 1964, he had made a most-for-a-sportscaster $200,000. Now, not for sale: "the play-by-play," Mel said, "that keeps me in the business." To survive, The Voice reconstrued his fall. "Those who were anti-Yankee were glad I was gone. Whatever it was, I was guilty." The Stripes status was even worse.

"They aren't what they used to be," Klein continued. "Listeners stopped listening [after 1964] and when they stopped listening they stopped buying tickets," luring a submillion for the first time since V-J Day: 966,328 in 1972. "Allen has been responsible for their financial decline." Young agreed: "Smartest fan-reclaiming move Yankees can make is rehiring Mel, and they are talking about it."

Play word association. To Scarsdale or Staten Island, Allen spelled a dreamboat past. At the New York Writers Baseball dinner, wrote Isaacs, "of the two dozen baseball personalities introduced, Mel got the loudest ovation. It happens all the time."

The Yanks wavered about age and style. "There are a lot of people who'd like you back," said their general manager.

"Sure would be nice," mused Allen.

"Mel, how old are you?" said Gabe Paul.

John Morrison of Merrimack, New Hampshire, wrote Marilyn and Hy Gardner's *Glad You Asked That* series: "Whatever happened to the once-popular sportscaster Mel Allen?" He's "doing swell," the Gardners said.

They lied.

*Sans* introduction, I called Mel in 1972 from the State University of New York (SUNY) at Geneseo. I was a college newspaper sports editor and was there a chance I could interview him and, if there was, it would be as fine as anything I had known. Later, I learned that he regularly took time to respond "to letters from youngsters in announcing," like early '50s Steinbrenner. "I answer the questions by mail or call them at their home and talk to them." I still think fondly how Allen—"a gentle soul," wrote Isaacs, "with hardly the confidence in himself that people thought"—need not have met me, but did.

On Monday, February 28, floormate George Petrotta and I arrived at the Canada Dry firm in Stamford. "Hello there [doubtless 'everybody']," Mel said. A visitor eyed his broad forehead, jutting nose, and gray toupee, then entered an Oldsmobile, paper cups all around.

Driving, Allen rethought lunch, U-turned, and crossed the inter-
state. "You don't mind if we go to the Golden Gardens, do you?" he
said. Does the cow jump over the moon?

Parking, Mel entered the restaurant. The menu listed egg roll
and mustard sticks and NBC's then-Gowdy and Kubek ("They don't
do much") and New York's cachet ("Almost joined the [1969]
Expos, but I'd miss this place. Anyway, my French ain't good") and
how the Mets nearly called.

"George Weiss wanted me in '66 or '7." The Amazins sponsor
didn't. "'Mel, every time you say "Rheingold" [beer], people gonna'
think Ballantine.'" The Voice seemed vulnerable and thoughtful
and sad and alone.

Onlookers waved, Allen liking the attention, despite, Petrotta
mused, it being "a light year from 21." Afterward he weaved in traf-
fic, ran several lights, and returned to the company, where a truck
filled his spot.

"I've told those guys a thousand times not to park in these
spaces," Mel groused. "They've hit me enough times, so I figure I
owe 'em one." Reversing his car, The Voice hit the truck's rear.

"It's taken a while," he said inside, "but I realize things happen
and you have to live your life." Pause. "It's that this isn't my bag. I
just have to hope my time comes again."

By now, Associated Presser Joe Reichler had become Commissioner Bowie Kuhn's chief aide. "At this point," he later said, "Mel
had lost the incentive to live." Berra urged famously: "When you
come to a fork in the road, take it." Allen's fork seemed a permanent dead end.

Most sought The Reason. A writer told him to publicly deny the
scuttlebutt. "The gossip's not in print," Mel replied. "There's nothing to reply to."

One myth was being gay: a then-career-killer. Even in 1957,
Allen, forty-four, felt obliged to apologize for being single. "It has
created problems and situations, some of which he finds distaste-

ful," wrote Leonard Shecter. "He doesn't think, for instance, it's a proper concern for the public prints. Still, he is forced to talk." It wasn't just Mom. "Everybody in the family seems to spend most of their waking hours trying to marry me off," said The Voice. "I think I must be getting to the point where most girls would consider me too old . . . for anything except a rocking chair."

Nothing suggests that Mel was homosexual. "Just a mama's boy," said Isaacs. "She wanted him to get married, just to no one in particular": At any rate, sex would not have affected him on-air. Allen blamed salary. "That theory doesn't hold water," the *Post* wrote, "because Garagiola did not come cheap." Brother Larry cited Mel's last statistician. "Bill Kane had a limp, played it for sympathy, and would make all sorts of mistakes," earning a flick of Allen's scorecard. "He started calling Mel a tyrant, saying he beat him. Just ridiculous. It all played a role."

Other prattle named disease or heroin. "That doesn't make sense," Koppett observed. "Each's effect would be obvious, debilitating." Harmon had several 1990s ministrokes. "They cause a short-term memory loss. On occasion I'll forget my kids' names for several minutes." Merle's doctor called it hard "to retain anything. That's how it may have been for Allen."

Mel and I often spoke by phone or in person: He was lucid, then errant, like sixties radio/TV. "This argues against strokes," a physician said. "The patient's behavior doesn't vary." Another suspect was less *déclassé* in Mel's than in our politically lockstep time. Peter O'Toole played *My Favorite Year*'s boozy actor Alan Swann. "With Swannie," declared an admirer, "you forgive a lot, you know?" It is said that the Yankees forgave, too.

"You can't name one time he got loaded," Coleman dissented, angrily. "That's garbage." Vecsey recalls Mel at The Stadium bar "with a couple beers. Possibly he'd overdo it, not much." By the 1980s, "Maybe he'd nurse a glass of wine for an entire hour," said *This Week In Baseball* executive producer Geoff Belinfante. "That was it. I don't think he had a problem."

Stan Isaacs fingered the mental, not chemical. "In the end he often couldn't relate in-depth to people. The Yanks wanted him to get some help. He wouldn't, a macho thing." Maury Allen cites September 8, 1964: Bloomington, Minnesota. The pressroom fills before a game. In one corner, Houk and a Twins attendant kibitz. In another, The Voice—"his big voice starts booming, it's loud, it dominates"—recalls Murderers' Row.

Disgusted, Houk shouts an obscenity, walks out, and phones Topping. "He'd had it," said Maury. "Mel was gone. Ralph won't talk about it, even now." Others have.

One day The Voice took ill at Detroit's Cadillac Hotel. Treating him, Tigers team physician Russell Wright thought that Mel had more pills in his bathroom "than I have in my doctor's bag." Later, partner Harry Jones told Boston's Joe Castiglione, "He was a hypochondriac. One pill after another."

Garagiola cracked, "Mel has so many things going for him, if he ever got the flu he'd be a one-man Depression." In 1962, Bud Blattner, Dean's ex-CBS "pod-nuh," joined the expansion Angels. "Mel'd take a pill to get up, a pill to fall asleep. He'd do a game, jet somewhere for an ad, then tape a Movietone. 'Jesus Christ,' I'd say, 'You don't need this. Slow down.' He wouldn't."

That July the White Sox radio team got to gabbing at The Stadium. "Mel'd stand there, the Series himself, with that dramatic voice," said Milo Hamilton. "The strange thing is he didn't act like he knew us." Allen stared across the field, "like he was in another place." Milo whispered, "Gee, Bob [Elson], is that the great Mel Allen?"

Lon Simmons did 1962 NBC Series Radio. "He felt Mel was spaced out," Jon Miller added, "didn't hear a word when Lon spoke to him off-air." Stengel would meander in "a dozen directions, but never lose his point," said Maury Allen. Mel would. "I don't think there's any question that in the end he was on something. It was hard to have a conversation—almost an airy sense."

As we have seen, The Voice's doctor was among President Kennedy's: to Max Jacobson's nurse, Ruth Mosse, "a quack . . . out of his mind . . . a butcher," often seeing thirty patients daily, including Mantle in September 1961. Mel told the Switcher: "He's wonderful, the best there is." Jacobson's shot then struck Mick's bone. Mosse might have warned them: "When he gave an injection he would just spill the contents of his medical bag on the table and rummage around amid a jumble of unmarked bottles and nameless chemicals until he found what he was looking for." Jacobson would then inject himself, spilling "blood all over his whites."

The patient-physician axis hangs on trust. "You depend on a doctor to prescribe," said Maury. "What happens when he *mis*prescribes: worse, when he's crazy? You can get hooked on pills without knowing it." Reason exists to think Mel did.

In 1960, Jacobson, "known to his New York society clients as Dr. Feelgood," wrote *Newsweek*'s Evan Thomas, began treating then-candidate Kennedy's injured back. Next year he injected the now-president in Washington, Palm Beach, Paris, Vienna, and later Berlin, where Feelgood lived in 1920–34.

"I feel much better," Kennedy said after a shot. By mid-1961, wrote C. David Heymann, the President and First Lady had "developed a strong dependence on amphetamines," synthesized as early as 1887, popular by the 1950s, later known as "speed," and finally curbed by Federal law.

In his book, *President Kennedy*, journalist Richard Reeves relates Jacobson prescribing a strange mix of amphetamines, vitamins, and human placenta.

"You don't know what's in that," said Robert Kennedy.

"I don't care if it's horse piss," said his older brother. "It works."

PBS Television's *A Presidency Revealed* tells how the attorney general raided JFK's medicine cabinet, found pills, and had them analyzed by the Food and Drug Administration. At the time, Jacobson, flown from New York by pilot, patient, and presidential photographer Mark Shaw (who later died of amphetamine poisoning), injected Kennedy up to thrice weekly. Irate, Bobby kicked him from the White House.

"Speed" was then felt benign. "Its effect was [really] an exaggerated sense of power and capabilities," said Reeves, "and the debilitating symptoms of classic paranoid schizophrenia." Client Truman Capote didn't care. "You feel like Superman . . . You go seventy-two hours straight without so much as a coffee break . . . Then you crash." Singer Eddie Fisher was another pilgrim: "Jacobson is my God." The Voice might have nodded. "Man, what he can do," he said in 1963. "Those pills, they work."

By 1968, "Dr. Jacobson could not account for quantities of amphetamines to the Federal Bureau of Narcotics and Dangerous Drugs," wrote Reeves. In 1975, the New York State Board of Regents revoked his medical license. Dr. Feelgood died four years later, having destroyed many medical records, including Kennedy's and Allen's, widow Ruth believed.

No evidence proves that Jacobson gave amphetamines to his famous broadcast patient. It does show that a charlatan became Allen's more Hannibal Lecter than Marcus Welby, providing and prescribing, at the very time Mel's life went belly-up.


In 1974, Julius Israel, eighty-five, died in Stamford. "Cancer, liver, kidneys, he just fell away," said Larry. Save siblings, the eldest son was alone. He revisited a fork in the road. "I was near marriage several times," The Voice said, softly. "My mistake was trying to please Mom and Dad. Every time I thought I'd found the right one I'd bring her to the house. The older you get the more you realize that you should have done what you wanted, then told the others."

Grab a Ballantine. Light a White Owl. Freeze-frame this stretch. Each day a card, passerby, or interview evokes fall, void, and stain. Their subject can't escape a snide smile, curled lip, the knowing look. What happened? How could a lion turn leper? People still asked in 1995. "Hell, that's thirty years ago, and I'm still working," said Allen. "If I knew why, I'd be glad to tell 'em, so I could get people off my back."

Mel had nowhere to hide; nobody, help; no one, defend. Yet— this is the thing—he reacted gallantly, even nobly. TV's John Walton says, "Bad things come to all of us. What counts, son, is how you handle 'em." Richard Nixon says, "You won't have Nixon to kick around." Teresa Heinz Kerry tells a columnist "to shove it." Shunning victim-babble, Allen declined to slobber, blame, or rage.

"There is no radio/TV parallel to Mel Allen's story," said Joe Reichler. "Overnight he goes from the planet's most famous sportscaster to falling off a cliff." In response, he grieved, endured, and sought a last outpost of strength.

By this point, The Voice, like Blanche DuBois, relied on the kindness of strangers. Larry returned to Alabama to run WYAM. Mel and widowed Esther moved to a new home at Greenwich's 21 C Weavers Hill. "I was in Thunder Bay [Canada] the other night," Allen said, "and people said how much they missed hearing me doing the games." His life induced William Faulkner: "The past isn't finished. It's not even past."

Allen began *Memories from the Sports Page*, a two-minute daily drive-time radio program in Boston, Chicago, Cleveland, Detroit, Los Angeles, New York, Philadelphia, San Francisco, and Washington. "The face of the man behind the microphone in Studio 5-C of New York's RCA Building on an afternoon last week was familiar," *SI*'s William Leggett wrote in 1975, "but it was not until he opened his mouth that a bystander felt a nostalgic twinge and said to himself, 'How About That!'"

Echoing PBS's *The Way It Was*, the show "[took] a past personality, event, or vignette, and attempts to enliven it with dashes of humor or bathos," Leggett said. "Mostly it is hearing Allen's voice, one of the finest in sports broadcasting history. Once it [got] rolling he dominated the scene."

Airing a segment, Mel said, "I don't like it."

"It is fine," said director Ken Davis.

"I want to do it over," Allen said, and did.

Later Davis said, "Mel, I'm glad you did. It's so much better."

Catapulted back, Leggett recalled The Voice "[being] treated by the Yankees like a skunk at a picnic. When they finally shooed him away, he was hurt and bewildered."

Now, said Allen, "I'm just trying to keep my feet warm and Blue Cross active." On one hand, the last few years of bric-a-brac "wasn't much: Not like I had." On the other, "the response—it was unbelievable."

One morning, he read *TIME* magazine. "It was on the nostalgia wave and I sat up in bed and said to myself, 'I guess I'm part of the wave.'"

Soon Mel mocked Heraclitus's view that a man cannot stand in the same river twice. ◆

# That Old Feeling (1973–1991)

n 1973, a cartel led by George Steinbrenner bought the Yankees for $10.3 million. "Here's why you won't hear me on a soapbox smashing George," Maury Allen said three decades later. "First, he's put my kids through college, helping write my books. Second, the team's worth [an estimated] $1.2 billion now."

Ron Blomberg made history: baseball's first designated hitter. Stripes attendance hit a best-in-a-decade 1,262,103. Mel joined Gowdy and Kubek one Monday *Game*, "NBC having just started," he said, "a celebrity concept." Among others, Ted Williams, Danny Kaye, and Barber also guested. Red was "choppy, tentative," mused Jon Miller. Mel wed "that big voice, great stories, good feedback," planting seeds, he guessed, for *This Week In Baseball.*

Meanwhile, New Jersey's Meadowlands inked the football Giants. "The city panicked," said Harold Rosenthal. "Yankee Stadium seats were too narrow. The infrastructure stank. Suddenly, it'd do anything to keep the Yanks." On September 30, 1973, 32,238, including Babe's and Gehrig's widows, watched Detroit beat New York, 8–5. A $100 million makeover began as the team slummed two years at Shea: "They were in a no-man's land," said Lindsey Nelson. "A situation not unlike Mel's."

One day Alan Hague of New Milford, Connecticut, and a cousin drove to The Bronx. Rubble lay everywhere, including several seats behind the rightfield gate. Hague gave a guard $50. An uncle laughed: "What are you guys going to do with those pieces of junk?" It seemed an allegory for the Bombers past ten years.

◆ ◆ ◆

A then-visitor saw photos, rolling away, row upon row, at Mel's home: "How about that!" one read. "There's a Ballantine Blast! The Yankee Clipper! Springfield Rifle! The Super Chief! Old Reliable!"; with Skowron, after a Series swat; Turley, Howard, and Berra; with Ruth, in light jacket; dark-suited, with the Mick. In 1976, Allen added pitcher Bob Shawkey, who opened The Stadium in 1923. He threw out a first ball at the less retread than refurbished den: Yanks 11, Twins 4, before 52,613 (new capacity: 54,028).

"When you were broadcasting games, you were a considerate and kind person who took time out to help young people," wrote Steinbrenner, inviting Mel to the opener. "I know you did that with the ballplayers and I know you did with me personally a long time ago." Arriving, Allen saw tiers and posts painted blue. New seating under the upper deck almost put you on the field. Sight lines were clearer; aisles, wider; concessions, choicer. Eddie Layton's organ never sounded richer. The rest of The Ballpark's music jarred.

*Pared*: bleachers and original roof facade. *Lost*: to a new inner wall, 450-foot circus catch, inside-the-parker, or belt amid the stones. *Moved*: to new Monument Valley, slabs (DiMag, Gehrig, Huggins, Mantle, and Ruth) and plaques (Barrow, Berra, Dickey, Ford, Gomez, Howard, Maris, Martin, Don Mattingly, McCarthy, Thurman Munson, Reynolds, Rizzuto, Ruppert, Bob Sheppard, Stengel, Pope Paul VI and Pope John Paul II, saying Mass in 1965 and 1979, respectively, and Allen: "A Yankee institution and national treasure.")

Center field was now 408 feet; left-center, 399; right-center, 385. Old pens fell from 402 and 367 to 379 and 353. Lines swelled: left field and right field's 301 and 296, respectively, to 318 and 314. "In the old Stadium, Al Kaline'd perch on the low wall," said Mantle, "leap and spear the ball." Heights varied: left and right, 4 feet tall; left-center and right-center, 8; center, 14. The inner fence was 8: uniform, and dull.

"The old outfield look was beautiful," said Bob Costas. "This reduced the mystique. They could'a rebuilt the stands, kept the dimensions. Instead, they hurt the classic look—but why?" Mel never asked. To him, the new place might as well have been the Parthenon.

"Progress," he proposed. "They made the park fairer and more accessible. Like life, you move on." Some drove, parking at the nearby Grand Concourse. From a train, others eyed right-center field. "The exterior wall became so high," said Costas, "that Yankees fans couldn't see inside," missing the end of the team's longest drought since Brooklyn built Ebbets Field.

New York took the East, met Kansas City in the LCS, and led the fifth and final game, 6–3. The Royals George Brett then hung a three-run dinger. In the ninth, Yankee Chris Chambliss, homering, was greeted like Lindbergh at Orly Field. Allen dismissed the Stripes Series loss. "Those Reds—Bench, Perez, Rose—were nearly as good as we in '61. We were back, at least." Dean Acheson wrote *Present at the Creation*. The Voice was present at the Resurrection.

"Look at Mel's life," said Baltimore's Chuck Thompson. "The threads are unbelievable. The Yankees win for two decades after World War II. Mel becomes their signature. He's fired, and they start to lose," drowning for a decade. "Bingo! They reopen the Stadium, win their first pennant [in twelve years], and again Mel's there"—calling the Bicentennial Yankees, except that few knew or heard.

Since 1946, free television had keyed baseball's local coverage. Rumored, pay cable was rarely viewed. "The problem," said Allen, "was that systems only existed in some places, not others." Satellite could link them, bulging the bigs' stage; baseball, cable's audience. Ted Turner yearned to please—thus, grow.

In 1976, he bought the Braves, upped their coverage, and renamed WTCG Atlanta SuperStation WTBS: "The Braves'll tie the sticks to the big time." Another outpost, SportsChannel Long

Island, seen in a small number of Tri-State homes, hired Mel. "Not play-by-play," said *New York Post* columnist Phil Mushnick. "Just postgame talk [with Jack Sterling] and between-game [twin-bill] interviews."

Having sold his firm, Allen now did Canada Dry publicity. Another gig: emceeing Yanks promotions. "Hey, he's part of Yankees history," huffed Steinbrenner. Mel said, "George is generous. He treats me like family." Then, with a twinge: "After all these years, they still call you the Voice of the Yankees. You can't help but feel good."

In 1976, Brewers Voice Tom Collins saw him for the first time in eleven years. "I run into some people from Milwaukee. I decide to do my pregame show on them—their first impression of Yankee Stadium."

At that moment Allen passed him on the field.

"Hi, Tom."

The cheeseheads gasped. "In their minds, I'm now a big-leaguer," Collins said. "Not because of me. Because I knew Mel Allen."

Still, he felt and looked peripheral: said Barber, "without any direction to his life." Bereaved, but not sullen, The Voice pined for his old.


By 1977, baseball and network television had misstepped a quarter-century dance. "Two ships in the night," said Geoff Belinfante. "Football had a promotional series, *This Week in the NFL.* [Also *NFL Action, Great Games/Great Years, The Men Who Played the Game,* and *NFL Week in Review.*] Baseball wasn't a TV infant. It hadn't even been born."

In 1975, Belinfante worked at Kenyon and Eckhardt Advertising Agency, which bought Robert Landau Associates, whose main client was Major League Baseball Promotion Corporation (MLBPC). Its production company had been W&W Films, owned by Barry and Dick Winick: "great filmmakers," said Geoff, "but not TV guys." Baseball craved a weekly half-hour vehicle of lowlight, highlight, feature, and other swill.

Belinfante helped produce the 1975 All-Star and World Series movies. The Soxaphile was in his Athens: "We're talking Carlton Fisk," arcing his memorable, epochal Game 6 blast. "What a way to break in." The real breakthrough would be television: "Baseball wanted to combat football, but didn't have much credibility." Sooner rather than later, it needed someone who did.

Kenyon bought and began to reformat and renovate old Series film. As host/voice-over, Reichler conjured a longtime friend whose post-1964 TV blackout concerned, not cowed. "Mel was a golden flash from the past," said Kuhn's aide. "But I figured if he was great before—why not now?" Emerson wrote of Napoleon, "He was no saint—to use his word, no 'Capuchin,' and he is no hero in the high sense." To many, this Capuchin was.

First, Mel did an audition tape: "not very good," said senior producer Mike Kostel. "He was in the depths." Writer Mark Durand was shocked. "Mel hadn't shaved. Many thought he was dead. He looked it." Allen then narrated 1976's two-part *This Is Baseball*: still, no series. Pro football put a film crew at its fourteen weekly games. Baseball had seventy. Q: How could you record them without going broke? A: Sony's three-fourth-inch tape video recorder, introduced that winter.

"We bought one per team [then twenty-six], put it in each park's production truck, paid someone to tape off the local TV feed, and copied to standard two-inch format," said Geoff. The plan was cutting edge: a 1990s bromide. Don Carney thought it would cut baseball's throat. "You can't do this," he told Belinfante. "It's never been tried: It'll be technically inferior"—credibility. Allen might conquer doubt: Carney's, and his own.

"It was the perfect marriage," said Geoff. "Mel gave us believability, heck, got us on. We gave him a new life, probably added years to his longevity, provided a validation of his career." Health was an early trial. "He had trouble saying certain letter combinations, so we wrote around them." Another: hearsay about "being a prima donna, hard to work with. With Movietone Mel'd done all his writing. Now we did."

Allen might have sulked. Instead, he thrived—"an older man with a lot of guys around for whom this was their first job out of college."

Their youth was not wasted on The Voice.

Baseball's first highlight series began June 12, 1977, on fifty outlets, including WTBS, WPIX, WGN Chicago, KTTV Los Angeles, and KPHL Philadelphia. "Our first choice was adjacent to a strong local baseball station," mused sales head Terry Kassel. "A close second was the local NBC affiliate, since it preceded *Game.*" *This Week In Baseball*'s cast, said Belinfante, was "barely big enough to play basketball": Kostel and writers Durand and Ouisie Shapiro. One day a stranger phoned, having just arrived from Georgia to seek his fortune in The City. "I saw a show. There were a couple of things wrong with the script."

"Come on in," said Geoff, having never heard of him. The next week Warner Fusselle joined *TWIB*.

Each week tape was flown to New York, taken to a South Hackensack, New Jersey, studio, near the Meadowlands, and logged, viewed, and edited. "Now highlights blitz Direct TV, ESPN, Fox Regional," said Miller. In Seattle, satellite shows the Olde Towne Team. In Shanghai, streaming ties the Cubs and ex-Chicagoan. For a long time *This Week* stood alone. "When I was growing up [outside Detroit]," said the Yankees Derek Jeter, "it was the only chance to see other players besides our home team."

*TWIB*'s spine soon became a metronome: "stuff for each team, a feature, and funnies," said Allen. "Odd-type plays with players running into each other." Bloopers flowed from fluke: Pat Kelly, closing his mitt prematurely, turned a first-show fly into homer. "We're editing as the camera zooms in and Kelly knocks the drive over the fence," said Belinfante. What a vision existed in the Oriole's dazed look.

"Are we going to find things like this every week?" Shapiro wondered. "We soon found odd plays were as funny as the game."

NFL Films head Steve Sabol laughed. "We struggle to find these weird things. You have 'em every day."

Mostly, they had Mel: "our soul," Geoff mused, "with us from the start." Ultimately, no TV sports serial so bespoke one man. Another response was shock—at the very fact of his return. That first year a sometime fan entered her living room. My mother could not have heard The Voice since 1964. "I can't believe it," she said, recalling his country gabble. "Is that Mel Allen?"

How about that! It was.

By then, *TWIB* waved a 3–4 A. C. Nielsen rating. "What synergy," Reichler glowed. "Most outlets we're on at 1:30 Saturday, the game at 2:00." In 1977, MLBPC head Joe Podesta got Kuhn to fold *This Week* into the comissioner's office. "The sport put us on salary," said Geoff. "We were growing so fast the joke was that a kid gets his first tape at the airport and six weeks later's a producer."

Most were anonymous. By contrast, Allen was "eternally grateful to be recognized again after a decade of being banished." Already he had become almost a surrogate to Esther's and Larry's children.

"Dadgummit, I want them to say 'yes, sir' and 'no, ma'am,'" Mel told his brother.

"Even if they do," said Larry, "there's not a kid in their school who'll copy 'em."

"I don't care. They gotta' be good people." Gradually, he again used his great voice like Jascha Heifetz did a violin. "The nuance, inflection, drama came back," said Belinfante. "Part was his wonderful newsreel background, part dramatic training," part that God, Geoff joked, loved The Game.

Yearly Belinfante said: "This is what [salary] we've got for the next season." Allen: "Fine," shaking hands. He never had a contract. Aptly, Mel did have an old friend to talk about. "Holy Cow! Can you believe it?" Scooter bellowed. "*This Week* starts—and after all that time the Yankees win the Series!"

If he played in New York, Reggie Jackson said, "They'd name a candy bar after me." In 1977, he joined the Yanks, whereupon they did. On October 11, ancient foils began the rounders tournament of North America. "How big was it? The [New York-Los Angeles] opener led our *news*cast!" tooted ABC's Cosell. The Apple took a 3–2 set-to lead. Game 6 lit The Stadium.

Jackson's first up pulled Burt Hooton into the rightfield seats. "Reg-gie! Reg-gie!" then put Elias Sosa in Ruthville's lower deck. In the eighth inning, he knocked Charlie Hough's knuckler 450 feet off the centerfield tarpaulin. "Four straight swings!" Cosell brayed. "[Including Game 5] four straight homers!"

Mr. October became Cooperstown '93. In 1978, Mel himself got a call.

Unable to choose between John Gielgud and Ralph Richardson, the Hall of Fame offered each its first Ford C. Frick broadcast award. Induction Day was August 7. A moment of silence hailed members dying in the last year, including Joe McCarthy. Allen and Barber then spoke in alphabetical order. "The Ol' Redhead was the greatest. He should have been here first," Mel demurred. "The epitome of broadcasting: a great, precise broadcaster." The object of his affection noted how "broadcasters made fans out of more people," said Red. "We brought baseball into the home. We made women more familiar with the game."

Ralph Kiner introduced The Voice: "[His] greatest day was a twenty-two-inning Yankee game because it was the first time he had enough time to explain the infield fly rule." Mel began, "Hello there, everybody!" then gave a talk rich with pathos, evoking a restless boy, unaware of himself, yet aware of a larger world.

"I guess I began my career at eleven, when I was a batboy for the Greensboro Patriots. A seed was planted, though I didn't know it," blooming, among other sites, in Alabama. "I got my LLB degree, but it wasn't until now that I realized what it stood for . . . Long Live Baseball."

New York. "A newspaper editor once told me some of the best writing in a paper can be found in the sports section. I am presumptuous to add, some of the best electronic journalism is found in baseball broadcasting."

Cooperstown's 1939 centennial. "It was a great privilege to cover," said the then-CBSer. "Here I am, back home."

Behind Mel hung a plaque: "A dedicated baseball fan, his voice was known to millions. Throughout his career, he was even more popular than many of the outstanding players he covered. Highly articulate, extremely knowledgeable, his broadcasts transcended the drama and excitement of the game in a cultivated, resonant tone—uniquely his own."

The Voice closed on a certain feeling of possibility: "I hope to get a copy and place it in my home right near the front door so that every day when I go out to go to work I'll be able to glance at it and say, 'How about that!'"

It was a phrase Scott Pitoniak had first uttered under a blanket at age seven.

Cooperstown means memory, rolling greenery, and houses built on a human scale. An hour away, in Rome, New York, the future Gannett Company columnist fell asleep with an earplug still attached. "Our information-exploded age won't believe it, but to me my red transistor radio seemed the technological genius of our age."

Ronald Reagan said, "If not us, who? If not now, when?" If not Mel at the mike, said Pitoniak, a "Mantle homer never happened." An official game required 4½ innings. A Stripes' required Allen. "Explaining Yankees history, he became our storyteller" describing Mick's "blond hair" and "bulging biceps": the Voice of authority, "heck, the Voice of God."

Retrieve a time that must now seem atavistic. Cable does not exist. Computers grace only IBM. The VCR and DVD are just letters in the alphabet. "We saw color photos in *SPORT* magazine," a print ESPN. "We had *Game*, books, and magazines. Mostly we had Mel." Scott's fourteen-year-old son mocks Dad's delayed-gratification age. "I take it as a compliment. How can kids know our sense of awe? With no diversions, we got stuff that lasts."

Pitoniak plays nineteenth-century "Vintage" baseball. April 1965 soiled his twentieth. "I couldn't imagine Mel not at Yankee Stadium. It was like a death in the family, like when Mantle left. You followed the team, but it wasn't the same." Yearly Scott and *his* dad attended Old-Timers Day: "our homecoming. We'd drive down the [New York State] Thruway for the players—Kubek, Richardson, Yogi, the Mick—but also to hear Mel."

In 1978, the then-Utica *Observer-Dispatch* columnist interviewed him pre-Induction night. "I had an hour and had just two questions to ask." Pitoniak knew his man.

Next morning the *Times* headlined: MEL ALLEN LEGEND STILL. Each baseball Thursday The Voice overnighted at the Biltmore Hotel. A day later he taped *This Week* in a nearly windowless Manhattan studio used by Alice Cooper and Bruce Springsteen: wrote Tony Kornheiser, "making words come to life." He sang in the hallway, poured coffee he never drank, then settled in the booth. "Coming up on *This Week In Baseball,*" Mel caroled. Outside "four young men [pursued *TWIB*'s] mission. [He] seemed amused by their urgency."

Allen readied. "[His] voice goes up the hill; then tumbles down the other side; he turns it like the volume control on a radio. At times it is magic." Durand nodded: "Mel's very strong these days. He was a little shaky last year when we started the show. Maybe he wasn't confident. But when he gets warmed up, there's nobody better." Kostel liked how the show was taped. "Otherwise, the pace might be too fast." Even Belinfante doubted he could do it live.

"At times his eyes search the cavernous ceilings of the hotel lobby as if looking for the years," Kornheiser wrote. "He cannot believe [1964] had anything to do with his ability, though some say he had lost his touch, that he wasn't crisp enough getting in and out of an inning." Mel donned glasses, half cocked a fishing hat. "I know I can still broadcast games, but the travel, I'm not eighteen or twenty-eight any more." Leonard Faupel was an ex-Ballantine suit. "He seems at peace [not being] a national announcer," if not grasping his past, no longer at its mercy.

That Christmas Mel's card was the Hall Induction program. "Santa Claus came early for me this year with a rare present made more rewarding by the priceless gift of your message of friendship." The Yankees gift had arrived earlier that fall.

Nineteen seventy-eight. The phrase stands alone, needs no explanation, so affixed to the Red Sox that even non-Townies grasp the spoken tone reserved for a drunken spouse or wayward child.

On July 17, 1978, the Yanks trailed Boston by fourteen games. Ahead lay "the apocalyptic Red Sox collapse," wrote Dan Shaughnessy, "against which all others must be measured." A four-game set began Thursday, September 7. The race evened by Sunday: New York, 15–3, 13–2, 7–0, and 7–4—"The Boston Massacre." The Sox fell 3½ games behind, then turned.

October 2 broke crisp and light—the first A.L. playoff since Mel did 1948's. At Fenway, Carl Yastrzemski led off inning two. "Long drive, right field! . . . It is a fair ball, home run! Red Sox lead, 1–0!" cried Ned Martin. New York trailed, 2–0, in the seventh. Jackson's earlier drive toward the Wall had dropped off a shelf. The wind now blew *out*.

Bucky Dent swung. "I saw Yaz looking up," said Sox catcher Carlton Fisk, "and I said, 'Oh, God.'"

On WPIX, Bill White described what he disbelieved. "Deep to left! Yastrzemski will not get it! It's a home run! A three-run homer by Bucky Dent! And the Yankees now lead by a score of 3 to 2!" winning, 5–4, then another LCS and second straight Series.

A decade later, Dent, now a scout, smiled sadly. "Stupid us. We just thought we'd keep winning." The Stripes next title kept till the season of The Voice's death.

◆ ◆ ◆

"I hear Guy Lombardo says that when he dies," mused a wag, "he's taking New Year's Eve with him." As Zelig, Allen threatened to take the Yanks. He aired the first Old-Timers Day in 1947. "We were there to honor Ruth, not start an event. It just became one." In 1979, emceeing, Mel sat with Nos. 5 and 7 on the bench. A year earlier Bob Lemon had replaced Billy Martin. "Presenting," Bob Sheppard told the crowd, "the manager of the New York Yankees again in 1980." Martin took the field to moist palms and open mouths.

"Mickey and Billy were close friends, and Joe befriended 'em as a rookie," said Allen. "You'd think they'd know if anyone would, but hell, they were as amazed by this as me." Ultimately, Mel retired fourteen numbers, including Martin's 1 and 1979's 15 (Thurman Munson). "They'd play in their numbers in the Old-Timers Game, and umps never let 'em walk, no matter how bad the pitcher is. And certain guys, you never let 'em strike out, either."

Language reflects an age. 1966: Stengel makes the Hall, Allen starts a twenty-year Induction Day streak, and onlookers yell, "When the Yanks bringing you back?" A strike meant called or swinging. 1981: It means a fifty-day work stoppage. "What's dumber than the dumbest football owner?" asks Orioles and ex-Redskins owner Edward Bennett Williams. "The smartest baseball owner."

In August, Mel, leaving a Tokyo "replacement game," jibed, "My stories take even longer in Japanese. This strike"—understatement—"I'm in favor of let's talk, not walk." Until his 1975 death, children begged Casey to tell pre-Induction stories at Cooperstown's Otesaga Hotel. "They'd be on the floor, sitting," said Bowie Kuhn. "It was like the blind Homer reciting the folktales of ancient Greece." The Voice became his heir.

Mantle "used to show up with a hangover. I've seen him yawning, without falling asleep, in the on-deck circle. Then he'd hit the ball right out of the park." At Ford's father's bar, "They'd go over there some nights and stay kinda' late. You're not going to stop grown men from doing what they want to do. Just keep it out of the papers," of which the Stripes manager seemed constitutionally incapable.

Once Martin unlocked a cupboard in his office and opened a flask. "Now what kind of trouble is he going to get into later," Allen boomed, "if you start on martinis in the afternoon?"

Mel had usually known what to say. The question was how closely he listened to himself. Increasingly, self-knowledge bloomed. "I love Billy. The players love him. Hell, even George Steinbrenner does. The problem is, does Billy Martin like Billy Martin?"

"If it's Tuesday," goes a film, "this must be Belgium." If it was 1981, it was SportsChannel giving Mel play-by-play. He "has the world's best voice," said analyst Fran Healy. "His sister Esther has the second-best." Mel did voice-overs for General Mills and Eastman Kodak; narrated video like *Babe Ruth: The Man, The Myth, The Legend;* and hosted MSG Television's *Yankees Magazine.* Years earlier, Allen had crooned "Yankee Doodle" in Washington. He seemed pitch perfect July 4, 1983.

"Will he do it? This crowd is standing! This crowd is wild!" Mel said at The Stadium. "The Yankees are leading, 4 to 0, and Wade Boggs, one of the top hitters in the American League, standing between Dave Righetti and a pitcher's dream. Outside—ball one. Three sixty-one is what he was batting going into this game. Wade Boggs—Dave Righetti trying to get him out. Two out. And there's a strike, and it's one and one, and this crowd is roaring! There's Billy Martin, nervous. Everybody on the bench is nervous. Even on the Red Sox bench, they're trying to break it up. Dave Righetti, under the toughest pressure. Will he get it? Wade Boggs swings and misses! Strike two! . . . One strike away for Dave Righetti." Ike must still be president. Suburbia meant Levittown. Patti Page was *au courant.*

"This crowd is going nuts! . . . Everybody at Yankee Stadium is standing and roaring. The Red Sox, trailing, 4 to 0, a runner at second. A foul ball out of play beyond third . . . Dave Righetti, who has permitted only three Sox to reach base, all on walks, has got just about as tough a man to get out as the Red Sox could put up at the plate. It's the ninth inning, one ball, two strikes, two out, Hoffman on second. Boggs takes just outside, ball two . . . The deuces are wild! Two balls, two strikes, two out. Billy Martin, anxious." A listener refetched 1952: "We're past tense, even though we're playing in the present."

"The crowd is standing, forty-thousand-plus people standing and roaring, and Righetti trying to get Boggs . . . And he gets him! A no-hitter, a no-hitter, a no-hitter for Dave Righetti! How about that! He got the no-hitter! Dave Righetti pitches the first Yankee no-hitter since 1956! This is the first no-hitter by a Yankee pitcher since Don Larsen in 1956 in the World Series! The perfect game! How about that!"

Perhaps George Steinbrenner lit a candle, having been born July 4, 1930.

That morning the Red Sox new radio announcer met Allen, educing his 1950s Connecticut boyhood. "Later, when the Sox got good, the area swung their way," said Joe Castiglione. "Before, it was all Yankees," hard to find a Townies fan west of the Naugatuck River.

"You'd go in a store, front porch, near a pool—I loved Barber, there was Phil, but mostly it was Allen." Joe announced fungoes in the backyard like Mel. At Christmas, he requested a beer glass to rehearse pouring the Three-Ring Circle.

Each seventh inning, The Voice opened his WPIX refrigerator: "Can't wait 'till after the game to open my Ballantine." Nearly half a century later the oldest of eight children still confessed to hero worship. Said Castiglione: "Allen's the reason I'm in broadcasting. I'm not here without him."

Mel's "gift of gab" adorned the Stripes: "He'd promote Old-Timers Day. You got a mental picture." A visitor: "He'd relate Jimmie Foxx, which didn't stop opposing fans from hating him." Meal tickets, above all: "Mel'd play up upcoming series and seamlessly sell sponsors." You saw it on the radio.

Lineage helped. "The most distinctive voice in broadcast history," said Joe. "A great vocabulary" from Anna's read-by-rote sustained rally, rout, and rain. "He'd weave stories, so tough to master, never caught short" on a two-strike tale. "A Curt Gowdy was great on nuts and bolts." Mel was a thespian, not technocrat.

"Tuning in in '65, I couldn't believe his firing. Allen had almost become bigger than the product," mused Castiglione. "I wonder how he'd have handled the Yankees fall. As it was, they lost their identity." The age's Boston American League Baseball Company had no identity to lose.

The 1966 Sox dredged ninth. In 1967, 100-to-1-ers wrote "one of baseball's great rag-to-riches stories," said Joseph Durso, by lofting a last-day flag. That July, Joe made his first trip to the Mormon Tabernacle of Catholic New England. "Fenway knocked me out. With Mel gone, not a bad year to change loyalty."

For Phil Mushnick, 1983 was not a bad year to get cable. In April, he had phoned The Voice.

Q: "Could Mel Allen get a job today?"

A: "I honestly don't think I could," Mel said. Even baseball owners rarely listened to radio. "They're either at the game or watching TV. They don't care about ability": only name, not skill.

Depressed, Mushnick called agents, sponsors, and basketball's Marv Albert for a column on local television. "Each said any interviewer no longer even asked about knowledge. It was all cosmetics, looks, your tan": empty suits, and lives.

Phil wondered about Allen's. Talking, he felt grace and grief. "I was in my thirties, and Mel was the legend. Yet he was so grateful to speak with me—needing affection, I guess. It's I who should have said the thanks."

Mushnick's northern New Jersey home was wired Independence Day. "What an entree": Righetti, no-hitting Boston. "Mel's on it, going bonkers." In nearby New Britain, Connecticut, another student felt cuckoo, too.

Pete Weber grew up in an Illinois of farms and fields and boys playing basketball. On his porch, hockey's future Nashville Predators Voice sipped lemonade, caught fire flies, and heard Caray—"my guy. Allen meant U.S. Steel. Mid-America hated the Yanks. Yet you couldn't miss it. Mel was a painter." It helped that for a long time Monet's was not a paint-by-number team.

That July 4, Buffalo's Triple-A announcer eyed TV at the team hotel, again hearing the Ghost of October Past. "I'd had bootleg recordings over the years, but here's the real thing." Pete never forgot Righetti's no-no. "Talk about capturing a moment," banning muted tints for bold pastels.

As usual, Marty Appel was at The Stadium, handling 1968–77 publicity and 1980–92 WPIX TV. "You can look it up," said Casey Stengel. Appel's 1962 eighth-grade yearbook reads: "Mel Allen, step aside." The apprentice wrote him a handwritten letter. A typed reply arrived, "back when each page had to begin from scratch." Marty recited it, meeting Mel on Mantle Day 1969.

The child liked The Voice's making the complex simple. "He'd mention the ump making a fist for a strike": conversing, not condescending. The adult sensed hurt. "I was a stranger, then friend, but the constant was that Mel was no longer doing what he'd been born to do."

For a decade—"through 1975, '76"—one query trailed Appel. "Didn't matter where I was: 'What happened to Mel Allen?'" Supplanting it: "What's it like to work for George Steinbrenner?" Later, Mel often sat in Boss George's box: "Glad to be back," yet self-contained.

In 1987, WPIX's new executive director had a thought. "As long as I do this," Marty told a friend, "I'm going to start every year with Mel: 'Hello there, everybody, on the New York Yankees Network, it's the 1987 Yankees.'"

Allen went the extra mile. "Since we're taping this, why don't I cut as many years as you want?"

Hello there, everybody, in 2525.

◆ ◆ ◆

"*This Week*'s forum made all of this possible," Belinfante said, correctly. "We gave Mel another baseball life for a new generation who hadn't known him." Terry Kassel added: "Mel didn't *do This Week*. He *was This Week*."

By the early 1980s, seven of ten *TWIB* stations were Peacock outlets. "For years the show carried our company," said Kassel. "NBC so loved it they'd deliver our specials to affiliates. People thought it was a network show." *TWIB*'s now-6 to 7 Nielsen rating rivaled syndication's *Wheel of Fortune*. The magazine *This Week* listed nonnetwork shows. "Sometimes we'd make the top five," Geoff said. "Unprecedented for a highlight series."

Belinfante produced HBO's *Race for the Pennant*, ESPN *Baseball Magazine*, regional *Pennant Chase*, syndicated *The Baseball Bunch*, and All-Star and pre- / postseason special. Mel voice-overed most, like *TWIB*'s fifteen-minute wireless version, its script freer than TV's. "We didn't have to tie to picture," said associate producer Bob Smiley. "He'd have you laughing. Go to break, return, and he had you crying. You never knew where he'd go."

Ultimately, Alabama's Hamlet went to language.

"You'd say, 'Hey, that's a nice blue sky.'"

"'Nice blue-gray,' he'd qualify, especially if something was bothering him." Usually Mel brightened. "Sorry, boys," he said, leaving, "for practicing my law."

By 1984, fourteen bigs teams used *TWIB* as a radio pregame show. "It ran into talk junking traditional," said writer John Bacchia, "got hard to place," dying in 1986. The studio abutted 42nd Street and Ninth Avenue. "Mel'd be wearing a SportsChannel jacket. He'd finish with us, then get a limousine."

One day The Voice waited in the lobby. The receptionist left at 5:00 P.M. A visitor approached. Not recognizing Mel, John Candy asked directions. Allen began to talk. Slowly, a How about that! gleam filled the actor's eyes.

"You're Mel Allen," he said: one original, to another.

◆ ◆ ◆

Warner Fusselle knew baseball's original. "Talk about timing," he said. "Leaving the South for New York, I taped a Miami-Clemson baseball game Mel did, figuring I'd never hear him otherwise." Soon he wrote, directed, and even pinch-narrated for The Voice.

Allen could be, in Bob Prince's term, "disputatious." The *All-Star* Game turned All-*Star* Game. "It's from when he started," said Warner. "You emphasized players—stars." The perfectionist vaunted uncommon sense. A line read, "Out west in Kansas City." Mel read the riot act. "New York's not the country. Kansas City's east if you're in Utah."

Fusselle's first taping began at 9:00 A.M. Durand had written an all-night script. "He's outside in the hall, still editing, some lines are in pencil, hard for Mel to read": Abruptly Allen walks out. "Oh, no, where's he going?" says a colleague. The bathroom, as it happened. Warner blanched. "He could have just as easily left. We gotta' do this right."

At Movietone, Mel synched time to text. "I like knowing how many seconds I've got for each sentence," he told Fusselle, who reassured him. "Just read it at normal speed." Allen balked. Finally, Warner "invented time. I'd say, 'Twelve and a-half seconds.' To pacify him, I'd make it up."

Wilson Pickett was a rock and soul artist. Warner wrote: "[The Royals Willie] Wilson can really pick it."

Mel changed the line to "Wilson can really pick 'em up and lay 'em down." Fusselle observed that this lost something in translation.

"Trust me, Mel. It'll work. Please do it our way." Allen did, not necessarily liking it. "Man, what am I reading? You got me doing crazy things."

Even unaware, he stoked *touché*. One tease used the Beatles. A Darryl Strawberry catch became "Strawberry Fields Forever." Ad-libbing, Mel smartly closed the segment: "Yeah, yeah, yeah." Ringo Starr seldom sounded better.

◆ ◆ ◆

In 2001, Fusselle joined the Class A Brooklyn Cyclones. "It's minor league, and I know times change." Still, picture the Voice of Brooklyn Baseball! "You think of Red, Vin, Desmond. I hope Mel—nobody called him Allen—would be proud." The Voice was proud of the eighties. His 1963 rain monologue "may have been the final straw," said Coleman. Two decades later Allen again held forth on SportsChannel. "It's raining. He talks for one and a-half hours," said Healy, Mel's sidekick with Rizzuto, White, Messer, and Bobby Murcer. Glad to have him, few complained.

Kevin Bass, Tug McGraw, and later Mike Piazza claimed the "world's best Mel imitation." Roy Epstein was a then-new *TWIB* producer: At spring training, "people everywhere yelling, 'Say hello to Mel.'" Said Reichler: "'Jesus,' players say, 'wait till Mel gets a hold of *that* one!'" To *Sports Illustrated*, "He is back where he belongs, an old campaigner, a keeper of tradition. If baseball is back, Mel Allen must be, too. Salaries and cities and even grass may change, but Allen, the venerable Voice of Summer, remains forever the same.

"'Hello, everybody, this is Mel Allen!' he says at the start of every Yankee game on cable TV. The voice is rich, thick, and Southern, to many the most recognizable in baseball. When you hear it, it's summer again, a lazy July or August afternoon with sunlight creeping across the infield. For years he was a forgotten man, but it has all come back to him in abundance. Like the game itself, Allen is timeless," even retrieving his once-drop-dead event.

In October 1982, the Peacocks had Mel air "promo spots" for their new prime-time schedule. "The idea," said director Harry Coyle, "was to coincide with the World Series," still seamlessly affixed to Allen. Next year The Voice narrated his first Classic highlight film since 1962. "Man, I 'bout jumped out of the booth, to do the Series": back at its periphery, if not hub.

Ronald Reagan helicoptered to Baltimore for the 1983 opener. Todd Cruz scores: "The [Orioles] do a little cruising." Philly's Gary Matthews dings: "The man called Sarge has taken charge." Steve

Carlton strained; Pete Rose doubled; Joe Morgan fell near home. "In coming so close," Mel punned, "the Phillies have fallen short." Ron Powers wrote: "The voice was never more resonant"—or was that 1984?

Detroit's "Jack the Cat [Morris threw] a finicky five-hitter"; "[Chet] Lemon turns in sweet glovework"; Goose Gossage was San Diego's "longtime ace. But in this case, the Tigers have a trump of their own"—Kirk Gibson's clinching homer. Motown became only the fourth team to lead its league or division each day. "Unlike my rebirth, not an overnight sensation," Mel chuckled.

"The taste must be sweet," said the *Daily News*. It was.

About this time Chris Schenkel inducted "the dean of all broadcasters" into college football's Hall of Fame. In Nantanya, Israel, Mel joined the Jewish Sports Hall of the Wingate Institute. The National Association of Broadcasters tapped him and radio's 1940s Sky King, Earl Nightengale, whose plane, "Songbird," evoked The Voice. Accepting, Mel scored "today's description of play." An incident told why.

Rose Bowl, 1952. "For color we're going to put [49ers quarterback] Frankie Albert on with you," says an NBC producer.

What should I do with him? Allen asks. A bulb goes on. "When he has something to say relevant to his playing days, I'll have him raise a hand."

Grudgingly, Mel grasped a gamesman's survival. "I hate this, but if you get Tom Smith, that doesn't excite a fan. But Tom Seaver, gee whiz, the network figures you can overlook mistakes, maybe crudeness, in the early going."

In 1984, he went back to Alabama's Farrah Law School, accepting a chair and quoting a Chinese writer: "'Today, we are afraid of simple words like goodness and mercy and kindness. We don't believe in the good old words anymore because we don't believe in the good old values anymore'"—to Mississippi's William Faulkner, "the old verities and truths of the heart."

Less hifalutin, Dick Young proclaimed "The Comeback Kid! His voice—that wonderful, unmistakable voice—is all over the place. It's Mel! As in Mel-lifluous." The headline read: PUBLIC REDISCOVERING "VOICE OF THE YANKEES."

The *News* columnist recalled 1961. "You could be three rooms away from your seat and you knew the Yankee game was on because you knew that unique voice. [Re]born at seventy-one," Allen could "again be the biggest thing in the Big Apple, the way he was before the Yankees quietly let him go." Young was wrong.

One reason was the principal: Mel's "wanderings"—his quaintism—could mime a mouse on a computer. Reggie Jackson asked about Gehrig. The Voice hit the start button. "You know Reggie, he doesn't care about being polite," said Jon Miller. "Off-air he says, 'What the hell you talking about?'" Another: Cable knit New York glacially, its penetration below radio's and free TV's. Further, Steinbrenner hired seventeen announcers between 1980 and 1989, dimming identity. "With one team for radio and two, TV," said Tony Kubek, "no one would own the stage like Mel." Also, the Apple increasingly found Yanks wireless fine.

"It's not that they don't miss Mel," Mushnick cautioned. "People just got used to White and his pal. Homework? Stick around? He's the Scooter!"—not paid by the fact or pitch.

A ninety-year-old woman writes a card. "I'd better answer before it gets too late," Phil reasons. "She might not be with us the whole game"—going to bed or the beyond, who knew?

The camera spots a lovely teenage girl. Rizzuto: "She reminds me of that old song, 'A Pretty Girl Is Like a Memory.'"

White: "Scooter, I think that's 'Melody.'"

Phil: "Really. How do you know her name is Melody?"

Rizzuto starts waving from the second deck. "You know, Mussolini used to do this." A visitor arrives from San Jose. "San Jose? I love San Jose. What's that song?" Someone begins the Dionne Warwick tune, "Do you know the way . . . ?" Scooter amends: "No, it isn't San Jose. It's Phoenix."

A Hindu "or Indian or something" wrote "beefing about that Holy Cow. He said in India the cow is sacred, and I shouldn't say such a thing."

Love that Phil. If it's sacred, he said, what's wrong with "Holy Cow"?

"Some guys just click," Rizzuto rhymed. Allen clicked with Hodges. Tim McCarver renewed Ralph Kiner. Scooter unlocked White's wit. In turn, Bill—to Phil, always "White"—became Abbott to his Costello.

Rizzuto starts reading a long list of birthdays. White interrupts: "Hey, don't you have a name in there that doesn't end in a vowel?" Phil recalls putting grits in a pocket his first time South. "It looked like oatmeal. I didn't know what to do," nor did the Stripes, fourth or worse in 1982 and 1987–89.

By George: The White Sox Tom Seaver won game 300 in The Bronx. "He did a press conference, then a single one-on-one," said Epstein. "We got it because of Mel." Martin chugged a fifth (firing). The Yanks hit bottom for the first time since 1966. "Until then Mel and they'd paralleled," said Nelson. "Up in the fifties; down in the sixties; both coming back." Ballantine pitched "full-bodied taste." Mel now seemed more able-bodied than his team.

"I can play it square or I can play it round," John Connally said. "Just tell me how to play it." In 1986, having tried writing lyrics— "Let's play ball, play ball, you all," one began—Johns's Music Man narrated magic/manic rap. "Here's the windup, the pitch, the count, 3 and 2 / He swung that stick, and that ball flew / Man alive, what a drive! / A grand-slam homer. That ain't no jive."

The Boss's tune was jack, inking a $30 million deal with WABC Radio. Newcomer Hank Greenwald "hated it when people introduced me as 'Voice of the Yankees.' There was only one 'Voice of the Yankees,' and it wasn't me." Born in Detroit, he was really a New Yorker. "My greatest thrill wasn't seeing Mel at The Stadium, or even walking into it. It was walking out and finding my car was still there."

For a decade, baseball had been there as *This Week*'s daddy. "This was before today's video, DVD, hundreds of program-hungry stations," said Belinfante. "We were a six-, not twelve-, month business, with as many employees as the Commissioner's Office." In 1985, new commissioner Peter Ueberroth, ruthless, a bottom-liner, 1984 Summer Olympics boss, axed them all. "We had a lot of salary, health care, insurance costs. Plus, we were younger, long-haired, didn't really fit in." Nerve ends stung.

MLBPC became Major League Baseball Productions, turning *TWIB*'s name, studio, and equipment into Phoenix Communications: "a bird rising from the ashes. To the public it looked the same," said Geoff. "But on our own, we had to spend more time on the financial side just trying to stay alive. It made it harder." How hard, Mel in the 1990s was to learn.

In 1986, he chucked SportsChannel. "They wanted me for one hundred games a year. Man, I'm seventy-three: too much." Weight rose, face pouched, eyelids puffed. "I'd just grab food, no consideration for health." A 1989 checkup turned wake-up: Allen's cholesterol had soared. Next day Mel called heart specialist, former Yankees third baseman, and now A.L. president Bobby Brown.

"Who should I talk to?" he said.

"Houston used to have the best doctors," said Brown. "But they're getting on. This'll seem strange, but maybe the best is your home town: the University of Alabama at Birmingham. I've seen their procedures." Mel, brother Larry said, was careful. "If Bobby'd said Alaska, he'd been on his way to Nome."

Allen promptly phoned UAB. "I know I'm supposed to be operated on," he said, "but I've got some speeches in the next month."

"Cancel 'em," said Dr. Lou Pacifico. "If you can grab a flight today, get here." In November, Mel had quadruple bypass heart surgery, healed at Larry's home, found fitness, and lost twenty pounds. "I take my pills, exercise on a treadmill," and soon looked his best since, say, 1959.

April 30, 1990: The Stadium hails—what else?—a record. No one had done seven decades of play-by-play. "One day it hit me," said Fusselle, phoning the WPIX director. "'All he needs is one game for the record.'"

"Can he do it?" said Appel, recalling The Wilderness.

"Of course he can," and did.

Rizzuto preceded Mel's 1½ innings *v.* Oakland. President Bush sent a letter: "Abner Doubleday may have created baseball, but you created baseball play-by-play." An ex-boy of summer nodded, born near Ebbets Field.

"He surrounded you in stereo at the beach or in the parks," George Vecsey wrote, "from car windows and apartment houses. In the days of the humble portable radio," Allen was a megaphone. The Voice of the Yankees had been his "Voice of Doom. He belongs to us all now, aging Brooklynites, Yankee fans who remember the glories of Dickey and Yogi and Elston, and new generations, discovering the great game."

Each day *TWIB* bounced off the decks. "We come early to the ballpark to catch batting practice, and that same voice, still more black-eyed peas than bagels, resounds from gigantic speakers, hardly necessary in this case." The *Times* columnist cited 1964. "If he had one gram of malice, he might gloat at outlasting the regime that jettisoned him, but he's going too good for that."

Vecsey revived colleague "John Drebinger, a merry old gent, seeing Mel at The Stadium bar, ostentatiously turning down his hearing aid, and saying in a stage whisper, 'Oops, here comes that fucking Allen.'"

"Nobody laughed harder than the target," who deserved a codicil, and found it in the last decade of his life.

In 1990, the State University of New York at Geneseo launched the annual Mel Allen Scholarship, his first outside Alabama, for a student stoked by language. "How about that!" said The Voice. How could he not, after a lifetime of recital?

SUNY's Doug Lippincott was a Braves fan. "When Milwaukee lost 1958's final game, I ran upstairs and cried," he wrote in the Upstate New York *Clarion*. Meeting Allen, "it doesn't seem so bad anymore. I wish that Hank Aaron, Eddie Mathews, [and] Warren Spahn had been in the van with Mel and me. Maybe they'd feel better."

All three made the 1956 All-Star Game, telecast by Allen, at Griffith Stadium. In 1991, making B'nai B'rith's Sports Hall of Fame, Mel trekked 2 miles from Mantle's first tape-measure blast. Larry King introduced me. Introducing The Voice, I quoted a lawyer whose filibusters, like Mel's, were equally ad-lib.

"What quality matters? Branch Rickey mused. Wealth? 'A man can be rich today and broke tomorrow.' Health? he continued. 'A man can be robust today and stricken tomorrow.' Looks, or status; rags, or charm? Rickey went down the list—naming traits; then, dismissing them.

"Finally, he came to what would sustain a life 'through all its problems, its disappointments, its fears, its sorrows. Out of infinite kindness,' Rickey said, 'grows real understanding and tolerance and warmth. Nothing can take the place of such an enduring asset.'

"This is what Mel Allen has given me; and thousands who have met him; and millions who have not but are secretly thrilled by his name." Age instructs. It also frees. Allen replied on an antic, much-his-own-man, bring-down-the-house note.

"I stand here because my father gave me some great advice, may his soul rest in peace," he began. At age fourteen or fifteen, Mel heard "about the birds and the bees, and my father said, 'Oh, by the way, I never want you to go and see a burlesque show.'"

Hooked, The Voice "somehow or another stole into a burlesque show, and as usual, my father was right. I did see something I ought not to have seen.

"My father."

Having made the Grand Hyatt ballroom laugh, Mel recalled Old Reliable, in 1942, about to go to war.

Detroit's Dizzy Trout was pitching at The Stadium. Suddenly, the PA Voice blared: "Ladies and gentlemen, this is the last time that you will see Tommy Henrich in a Yankee uniform for the duration . . . "

The crowd burst a lung. Henrich stepped into the box, yelling, "Come on, Dizzy, throw the ball."

Trout cupped his hands: "Stand there and listen to it, you SOB. You'll remember it as long as you live."

Allen paused. "That's how I feel tonight. I'll remember it as long as I live." ◆

# Been to Canaan (1992–1996)

n myth, Abraham Lincoln, playing town ball, learns of his 1860 presidential nomination. "I am glad to hear of their coming," he lauds its committee. "But they will have to wait a few minutes to have another turn at bat." Liking baseball, Lincoln loved laughter more: "Without it, I think my heart would break." Humor made him unusual: a politician funny on purpose. Not trying, Mel often was.

"Sometimes you look over the script ahead of time," he said of *This Week In Baseball*. A favorite bit concerned Alaskan baseball. "An eighty-three-year-old tradition features the Hawaii Islanders against the Alaska Goldpanners!" chirped Allen deadpan. "Penguins admitted free."

Eyeballs rolled. The ad-lib stayed. "You get crazy 'cause you know somebody's gonna' say, 'Oh, for God's sake, you ruined that take. Now we've gotta' do the take over again, but leave that out.' Sometimes, you know, you leave it in." Increasingly Phoenix Communications found laughter rare.

In 1985, MLBPC's Baseball Newsatellite in Stamford began downlinking each TV game. "Three times daily we sent a thirty-minute feed of local highlights, interviews, and features to stations signed up around the country," said Geoff Belinfante. "Use it on evening sportscasts, morning reports, whatever," auguring 24/7 coverage that changed and curbed *TWIB*.

"Our first ten years, we were the highlight outlet," Roy Epstein noted. "Today, you get 'em from all over each night. It makes our job tougher." The show had "been text, no sound bites, no calls," said writer Jeff Scott. "Now we write less, so Mel speaks less, which means what he says counts more." The staff spent 250 hours a week tracking footage. The Voice's taping session then began.

"You ready in there, Mel Torme?" a director said.

Mel still used a single light, framed by headphones, humming between takes. "He has a good feel for what we do," added John Bacchia. "Sure, he'll ad-lib a few 'How about that[s]!' But he's demanding, not here just to read copy"—it being preferable to what Belinfante had to read.

Since the 1960s, pro football had used NFL Films to gloss interest. "They got the league's long-term financial commitment," said Epstein. "Football knew it could be a powerful propaganda tool." Even at *TWIB*'s peak, baseball was clueless about what it had. Among others, "Chub Feeney and Lee MacPhail [1970–86 N.L. and 1974–84 A.L. president, respectively] didn't grasp how we could sell baseball," rued Belinfante. "We'd bang our heads against the wall. What we did with one hand behind our back was remarkable."

Who would negate such a nest egg? Baseball's dumber-than-dumbest football owner. CBS TV paid $1.04 billion for 1990–93 bigs regular-/postseason exclusivity. The catch was *Game*: Columbia didn't want it. "I hadn't seen it coming," mourned Robert Redford in *The Natural*. Allen hadn't of the sport NBC first telecast in 1939.

"Never crossed my mind," he said. "Why kill your best way to reach the public?" Suddenly, you could hear Styx, fly to Paris, or enroll in Arthur Murray's, but not regularly watch network ball. "I wouldn't see a game for a month," Peacock Marv Albert mocked its sixteen-game schedule, "then didn't know when CBS came back on." Ratings plunged. For many lacking local and/or cable television, the bigs vanished, not unlike sixties Mel.

At a 1988 Christmas party, one CBS exec wore a Cardinals hat. By 1992, pining to shed baseball, he wore a cap styled "One more year." NBC Sports Dick Ebersol grinned: "I assume [its] baseball strategy has to be a big disappointment." *Sans* anchor, *This Week* lost markets, moved to weak outlets in others, and had a 1–2 rating. "Instead of WNBC New York at 1:30 P.M.," said Mel, "we're on an independent after midnight."

NFL highlights blanket television. Negotiating, pro basketball makes ABC air its kids show *Inside Stuff.* By contrast, Belinfante learned of *Game*'s end in the papers. "With it following us, an awful lot of people watched our show." Now, like the Flying Dutchman, *TWIB* panted for safe port.

"Already we were changing from highlights to features. Now we had to begin over again just to avoid being out of sight, out of mind." To a child, a like fate cursed October. At twelve, Bill Glavin memorized the Yanks 1963 roster. At fifty-two, he couldn't name his last seen *in toto* Series game.

"My kids have never watched a final out. They don't know how it was." Allen could have told them, if they could have found him on TV.

In 1969, the Mets won the all-day-games Oktoberfest. "I had a 90 average and a radio to my ear," said Dave Lilling, then fourteen. "My teacher let me slide." In 1971, NBC telecast its first Series primetimer for working people. Next year all weekday coverage repaired to night. Since 1985, the Fall Occasion has wholly been prime time. "Baseball's deserting kids was like smoking," said Mel. "By the time you see the problem, the damage is done."

Ring Lardner called the event the World Serieux. The grounder under Bill Buckner; Kirk Gibson limping like Walter Brennan, fouling like Hank Aguirre, and dinging like the Babe; or Joe Carter, homering to end 1993, left many in the dark. The 1996–2000 Yanks took four Series. Arizona won a classic Classic. Anaheim, Florida, even Boston cut wild cards. How many saw all, or part?

"Is baseball serious about engendering a love affair with the next generation when children are in bed, preparing for school?" wrote the Chicago *Tribune*'s Bob Verdi, thinking not. Mel had livened. In 1992, the antipodal first outside-U.S. Classic ended after midnight. The *New York Post* interviewed twenty-three "self-described fans": Only one saw the *ninth* of its eleven-inning close. What did the Series convey to a ten-year old? Said George Will: "Probably that the NBA season is here."

Prime time meant to swell TV viewership. It shrunk, under the Law of Unintended Consequences. In 1980, 130 million saw all or part of the Series. Ninety million did in 1993. CBS's twelve to seventeen-year-old and overall LCS audience fell 24 and 20 percent, respectively. In a 1964 Harris Poll, 48 percent named baseball their favorite sport. Thirteen percent did twenty-nine years later. "How did the sport become a second-rate TV draw?" asked *TV Guide*. Out of sight, and mind.

Nielsen Media Research listed a typical year (1991) of network sports events: college/pro football, 22 percent; college/pro hoops, 20; golf, 18; multisports, 11; baseball, 5. "Because baseball forgot the fan," said The Voice, "the fan forgot baseball." Actually, it tried to forget a culture that seemed unable to stomach class.

Mojo rising. Remember a time before elbow-in-the-rib scatology? When cool and base differed? When a wiseacre deserved contempt, not praise? Boy, those were the days. "In our youth," Jon Miller said of the 1950s and early 1960s, "baseball fit the age": unslambang and -cutting edge.

Dan Rather spent each Sunday at a minor-league game "in the time-honored silent communion between father and son." Rudy Giuliani grew up a block from Ebbets Field. "Dad put me in stripes with a Yankee cap on my head." Tom Brokaw put his boyhood park above Versailles, the Hermitage, or Czar's Winter Palace. Pat Boone wrote "Joan" on his bat, then homered for a grade-school love: attitude, as adjective. By the nineties, in your face was noun—and king.

"Man, ain't stuff on TV or at the movies I'd let a pervert watch," Allen said. Taunt and trash could make the bigs seem prehistoric. Instead of leavening a less Andy Hardy than Andy Dick age, they tried to mime. "I hate this damn screeching PA during innings. Give me a real park and grass, day ball, and ump who makes the pitcher and batter move, and it's great." Many would have settled for Voices who buoyed the game.

Joseph Alsop wrote, "If I feel that there were giants in the Roosevelt years, I claim the right to say so." The two Jacks, Buck and Brickhouse, the Old Commander and Redhead, were not giants, exactly or even only, but family. The Gunner and Nelson were, too, but dead by the early nineties. Caray, Buck, Thompson, and Gowdy followed. Rizzuto and Harwell retired by 2002.

"Somewhere in a small town in the country, when you talked about the team," said ESPN's Gary Thorne, "[the broadcaster] pictured the game for them night after night." Today's heirs include Bob Uecker, Milwaukee's catcher in the wry; Harry Kalas, synthesizing Philadelphia's hope and fatalism; Miller, Coleman, Marty Brennaman, Herb Carneal, a Dave Niehaus, a Dave Van Horne. Most, alas, taste vanilla, not meringue.

"When I started, we didn't have models," said Harwell. "Now guys train at radio school and college," sounding programmed and alike. To Barber, radio/TV "have forgotten about the most beautiful thing I know next to human love, and that's the English language." Mel's age communed by wireless. Video's lacks "radio's background," Red noted, "to paint word pictures." Some even prefer other sports, thinking baseball nothing special.

A thirty-five-year-old doesn't instantly become a Pirates fan. "You have to follow it from childhood," said Miller. Baseball's rhythm reveals a fraud. On the other hand, lifelong study lets the Voice chat around a fire: The listener can tell. Despite, not because of, broadcasting, baseball has recouped much lost nineties popularity. A decade ago, that appeared improbable, at best.

"It'll come back," Allen vowed. "It always does." Then, some oddly linked him to its malaise.

"How old is he? Eighty?" asked White Sox owner Eddie Einhorn. "That's some connection to the young." His view was the exception.

◆ ◆ ◆

*The Great Gatsby* termed style "an unbroken series of perfect ges-
tures." Mel's changed little, and were as knotty as his career. Leaving radio for TV's *TWIB*, Bob Smiley liked Allen's low maintenance
in a high-ego field.

"Would you make a copy?" he might say.

"Would you do me a kindness and get a cup of coffee?"

Mel's old-world bolt—"the fedora, galoshes, overcoat," said Jeff
Scott, "always precise, deliberate"—could try a rawer peer. "Get to
the bottom line!" Steinbrenner huffed. Mused Smiley: "Allen could
spend fifteen minutes comparing rye bread versus marble."

One *This Week* gofer-turned-assistant asked about an HBO special. "Do you have ten minutes to talk about Casey Stengel?" said
Steve DeGroot. "Mel reacted like a lifelong friend."

By 1991, DeGroot headed a production company—and Fox released the film *Sleeping with the Enemy*. Future Hall of Fame publicist
Jeff Idelson empathized, having worked for the Red Sox and Yankees: "like changing sides as the Cold War grew frigid."

Idelson's 1989–92 Stripes were 288–359. "I'd tell Red Sox
groups, 'Hey, I did my part. You guys just didn't cooperate.'" Born
in suburban Boston, he edited *Yankees Magazine*. "Meeting Mel, I
started shaking more than for Mantle."

*TWIB* later profiled Jeff's two-head Janus. "I gave a copy to my
father, a Yankees fan," who broke down. "To have his son hailed by
Allen—too much. Mel'd come into my office, we'd talk for an
hour": the ex-officer still a gentleman.

Jim Rogal became *TWIB* writer in 1984: "Greeted on the street
for the thirty-seven thousandth time, Mel'd be as courtly as the
first." Even a broadcast wannabe raised on Vin Scully found the
ex-enemy of his ex-team a friend.

At eight, Charley Steiner found the future in a fungo game a block
from his Brooklyn home. Donnie Sorensen, "an experienced veteran of eight or nine," said to hit the ball, then run to first base

(elm tree), second (towel), third (another elm), and home (cardboard). Steiner was nothing if not literal, racing to the tree, towel, tree, and "home. I mean *home*. All the way to my *house*. I couldn't figure why everyone was chasing after me, laughing, screaming, and telling me I was running the wrong way."

Daily he absorbed Scully, "carefully, even clinically." In 1958, the Bums moved the wrong way—west. Teamless, the Dodgerite switched leagues. "No audio streaming. In L.A. they were as good as dead." Mel was alive. "A baseball announcer must have a distinctive voice. Not deep, like an opera singer, just transcend the crowd." Allen's could: "perfect pace, pitch, and sound." Charley missed each October 13, 1960.

"My piano teacher wouldn't excuse me to see Game 7. In broken English, she asked, 'What's the World Series?'" Maz cost him a $1.00 bet. "He swings, and I'm playing 'On Top of Old Smokey.'" Mel's play began in April: "off-season, just filling time." Hockey was alien; NBA, Peoria; NFL, not Big-Game America. "Allen's firing evoked Brooklyn—a loss. I wasn't angry, just a void."

In 1975, the Bradley graduate, twenty-six, working in Connecticut, met Stengel at a banquet table. "I'd been in Davenport, Iowa, and Casey's first year in baseball had been Rock City. We're talking, and Mel's name came up." Casey formed a downward wrist. "The gay smear. God help him, that's what Mel fought for years."

Charley joined ESPN, which assigned a 1988 "great broadcaster series. I'd spend a day with, then report on, each." Radio journalist David J. Halberstam visited Barber. "I'd asked for twenty minutes for a story. We were connecting." Red then checked his wristwatch. "Young man, your twenty minutes are up."

In Tallahassee, Steiner hit Barber's wall. "Gracious, but an edge you couldn't penetrate." Holy Cow! He flew next to Chicago. "Caray was its emperor. Unbelievable appeal." Finally, Charley drove to Greenwich: Allen "on the other side of his prime," but paternal and curious: like meeting the Wizard, except this Oz was no fraud. "I went there with a reverence, but Mel's irreverence put me at ease."

In December 1992, two months after Barber's death, Allen, Steiner, and Miller shared an American Sportscasters Association dinner head table. "They showed a tribute to Red," Jon said. "Part of it was an old kinescope of he and Mel sitting in the booth at Ebbets Field before Game 7 of the 1952 World Series."

Miller eyed The Voice, "who had tears welling in his eyes. I longed to know what memories had been unearthed about those long-ago days when Mel and Red were baseball broadcasting's Kings."

Jon looked away, then back at Mel on the dais. "He was crying. Suddenly, I'm crying, too."

Like many men, Allen thrived on habit. In 1960 he made the Custom Tailors Guild "America's Best Dressed Men" list. "Coordinated, crease, had a tie, always folded into his pocket," Epstein said three decades later. "Set your clock by it." Ibid., taste. "Each week we'd have lunch sent in. No fancy stuff: Mel had a grilled cheese with tomato sandwich."

He remained curiously ignorant of who he was. "There's a reason Mel cried when Gehrig patted him on the knee," said Fusselle. "Lou was a hero. Mel couldn't imagine himself in that league." Warner cried: "You could have been a senator! A Huey Long! With that voice you could be president!"

Allen lifted an eyebrow. "President of *what?*"

Rogal had written for Associated Press. "Famous folks didn't wow me, but when friends heard who I worked with they went nuts." The subject was too consumed to note. "With so many games," said Kostel, "we needed more time to view them": Unlike *NFL*, *TWIB*'s tape preceded script. Eight seconds of Don Baylor tape required an eight-second text. "This meant a voice-over must be perfect. Mel was": e.g. accent, fact, and grammar.

"We'd spend fifteen minutes," said Rogal, "on an 'a' or 'an.'" Most voice-overs sip water, clear the throat, and read unseen. Allen demanded to see each 6½-minute segment. "He'd plan where to be serious, funny, have inflection," mused Epstein. Later: "'Let's go back and start the Pirates segment'—taped two hours earlier. Mel wanted to get it right."

He also wanted to trust—but how? Past being prologue, Allen warily eyed a newcomer. "When we started together he tested me," said Rogal. "Once Mel got comfortable, he became more willing to be collaborative" after their "beautiful friendship" nearly died stillborn.

Rogal's second taping passed three hours. "Mel, please do it this way," he finally said, pressing the studio button to speak. Wearily, Jim told a colleague: "If [The Voice would] just read it the way we want, we can get this done."

To his horror, the button stuck. Allen heard every word.

"*What* did you say?"

"Nothing," Rogal lied, wilting.

"Yes, you did. I heard you."

Jim felt five years old. "Mel, I'm sorry. I'm just frustrated."

"Anything you have to say, say to me," said Allen. "We'll work this out together," and did, with what he called "my bright young men."

The term teenager first graced 1945's the *New York Times*. To Mel, *TWIB*'s cast seemed as old. "We didn't recall the Yankees firing," said Kostel. "There was no stigma with us": instead, loyalty, even awe.

In 1986, Epstein first met Allen on the stage of Arroyo, Lyle, and Gossage. "The Stadium bullpen, ninety degrees, and Mel's taping a thirty-second spot for Rolaids Relief 'Man of the Year.'"

Three takes pleased all but the novice. "Not supposed to say a word," Roy noted a bead of sweat on Allen's chin. Mel stared. "He knew I was looking out for me—and for him."

A picture shows Epstein's two-year-old daughter, Lindsey, lapping popcorn on The Voice's lap. A Christmas photo bares Kostel's three children embracing him: Uncle Mel. When Mike's father died, Allen stayed two days at their home. "Here we're grieving, and he's cheering us." Always, stories: McNamee, Ruth, Stengel, "our Jewish godfather going on about the Cardinal."

Through 1963, Mel took the annual World Series film to Rome's North American College. "When [New York Archdiocese head] Cardinal Spellman found out," said Belinfante, "he asked Allen to talk to the seminarians": also, troops in Berlin, Naples, and the U.S. Sixth Fleet. Unlike Pope Pius XII and John XXIII, many advisors didn't know Mel was Jewish. "So many Christians have been good to me," he said, leaving for the Vatican, "I want to give something back."

He got back at TV's annual National Association of Television Production Executives (NATPE) syndicated convention. "What a cynosure," said Terry Kassel. "He'd be mobbed." Amazingly, her dad had owned Birmingham's shoe store Mel worked in as a teen. Now *Dallas*'s Larry Hagman, Chuck Connors, and Ralph Edwards crossed the room to greet him. "They're celebrities, seeking another one." A pre-white Bronco O. J. Simpson bear-hugged Allen. "Forget race or sex. Mel'd connect."

Desi Arnaz would "splain a thin'" or two. Carmen Miranda's come-on was a befruited head. *The Cisco Kid* made English elementary. Broadcast Latinos had been prop, joke, or foil: Not to Allen. Juan Vene was *TWIB*'s Hispanic Voice. "I can still hear," said Kostel, "Mel's roar for 'How about that!' in Spanish. '*Mi casa es su casa*' means 'My house is your house.'" The Voice no longer had to enter through the bigs back door.

He never had to at *TWIB*. "We'd watch as he made it up the stairs," said Epstein. Until 1994, Mel drove to the studio. "We finally got him a car because we were worried. We wanted to take care of him."

Try finding that in TV Land today.

What goes around. In 1991, SUNY at New Paltz used Mel's voice-over for a *Damn Yankees* reprise. The 1993 Alabama Alumni Association feted "The Star Who Rose from Birmingham." That April the Smithsonian Institution—to Allen, meaning dinosaur bones—hailed the octogenarian. "I guess that makes me a dinosaur." Reagan telegrammed: "[You] helped define the art of sportscasting."

Nixon joined "you and your entire audience in saying, 'How about that!'" Added Bush: "Your unique style and colorful descriptions allowed fans miles away from Yankee Stadium to see." A thousand people filled the Museum of American History.

Next year ESPN's highest-rated Christmas show, *Voices of The Game*, opened with Mel's play-by-play. The close spliced Barber, Scully, Caray, and Nelson, U.S. flag, vendor at Wrigley Field, boy with binoculars, and catch with his American Idol—Dad. Yankee Stadium, in winter, superimposed Allen. "Line drive to deep right. Horton is going back, and the ball is going, going, gone!" He seemed a timeline: "boats against the current," wrote Fitzgerald, "borne back ceaselessly into the past."

Artificial turf: "Cobb and Gehrig didn't need it. I don't like anything artificial, including preservatives [and surely steroids]." Designated hitter: "It eliminates something that was very exciting, watching managers employ strategies." Maturity: "It is a responsibility players should realize. Unfortunately, a few of them don't." Empathy: "We used to travel by trains. There was greater togetherness. And I don't say that 'cause I'm an old codger—which I am."

In *The Show*, baseball's then-official magazine, boats paddled to postseason: "All winter," Allen said, "it gives you something to remember." Mr. October meant Reggie Jackson, Ford, and Lefty Gomez (6–0, in five Series). Classic, as career helper: Martin and Bobby Brown (.339 and .439, respectively). Damper: "Gil Hodges didn't get a hit in [1952's] seven games. They were lighting candles for him all over Brooklyn." Might-have-been: Ernie Banks, in a Series. "When he said, 'Let's play two!' it wasn't a phrase."

Most come-hither Series: 1938 Yanks-Cubs. "I was thrown on, without having broadcast a baseball game." Funny: Bob Prince, missing Maz's belt. Showy: Same. "One swing, and a champion." Best moment: Yogi, in Larsen's arms. "There was talk Don came to the park with a hangover. I know there were days he did." Saddest: Mantle, "with his greatest Series in 1960, and afterward he's crying." Best team: "This sounds dumb, but maybe those Yankees."

Series: "Any seven-gamer with the Dodgers [1947, 1952, and 1955–56] or Milwaukee [1957–58]."

Biographer Ronnie Dugger wrote of Lyndon Johnson: "It was all there, the whole history of the period." Documenting and disseminating history, Mel would have preferred to skip the Yanks decade before 1993.

That July 11, Nora Randall died two days before the All-Star Game. Hearing Allen, her husband had told their son to listen. The pupil now aired TV's *Talking Baseball.* To Ed Randall, Mel meant teaching it.

Randall *fils* began taping five straight shows at Baltimore's Oriole Park at Camden Yards. Leaving, he felt someone tug his arm. "I just want to say I really like your show,'" said Mel, aware of Nora's death. "Trying just to navigate through the world," Ed felt "stunned—like an apostle knew my name."

The '93 Bombers finished second. On August 12, 1994, their .619 percentage led the league. "Holy Cow!" rasped Rizzuto of the players strike. "What huckleberries! The season ends!"—baseball's first *sans* Series since 1904. Stripes announcer Kubek quit in disgust. Colleague DeWayne Staats fled to ESPN. *TWIB* did a wrap-up show. "The Series was gone," said Scott. "Mel was furious." To Epstein, "He couldn't believe baseball's meanness. He felt personally betrayed."

In 1989, John Sterling joined Yanks radio. Was he Allen's heir, Bob Gamere *redux,* or somewhere in between? "A terrific talent, enormously popular," said sidekick Michael Kay. Barbed Phil Mushnick: "Pompous, an inventor of fact."

Sterling Time, and the quarreling is easy.

In Dallas, mourning was.

Boozing and chasing, Mantle had gone dry, slowed a fast-lane life, and urged "kids, [to] please don't be like me." In 1994, Bob Costas interviewed him on NBC TV's *Dateline.* The Switcher was warm and penitent. The show pealed respect and love.

"As he's talking," said Bob, "I'm thinking of holding my father's hand in deepest center field at Yankee Stadium and saying to Dad [he died at forty-two], 'Is this where Mickey Mantle plays? Is this where he stands? Can Mickey Mantle throw a ball from here all the way to home plate? Can Mickey Mantle hit a ball here?'" Allen, of course, knew.

In July 1995, The Voice taped *TWIB*, awoke at 2:00 A.M. that weekend, and passed blood. Feeling "kind of woozy," he called a doctor, who ordered an ambulance, found an ulcer like Julius's, and put Mel in intensive care. "I don't know if doctors were kidding, but they said I lost half my blood." At that instant, Mantle lay in a Texas hospital. "I was shocked, but wasn't surprised from the standpoint of knowing he drank a lot and knowing the whole history."

Allen relived 1951: the Yanks and Jints, trading training sites. "I close my eyes, it's Phoenix, and I see the expression on Casey's face when he roared, 'That boy hits balls over buildings!' What can I say? It's very sad."

Doctors installed a pacemaker, staunched bleeding, and released Mel after a two-week stay. The other patient got a telegram. "'Hang in there,'" wrote The Voice. "Mickey will know those three words will mean as much as sitting down and writing one beautiful paragraph."

The Achilles Okie died August 13, at sixty-three. Costas spoke at a memorial. "We wanted to crease our caps like him, kneel in an imaginary on-deck circle like him, run like him, head down, elbows up." Allen watched at home. "All I wanted," Bob said, not knowing it would be telecast, "was to be worthy of the family."

Returning to New York, he was mobbed by passersby. "You don't feel boastful at a time like that, just gratified, that it was something that Mick hopefully would have liked." What Mel would have liked was his childhood game of pepper and politesse.

On September 6, 1995, ESPN visited Camden Yards. The Angels were retired in the fifth inning. The game turned official, its crowd going nuts. "Baseball had just had the strike," said Allen, "and, boy, talk about needing good news"—Cal Ripken Jr.'s 2,131st straight game.

Objectively, he said, recalling Gehrig, "records are made to be broken. Having known somebody who set this record, and lasted so long, and played in the circumstances and his leaving the game and his untimely passing, you think in terms of Lou, a record that's made to stand. So my answer is, 'God bless Cal Ripken. More power to him.' That's part of life, doing more than someone else. Lou would be the first to urge him on." Cal repeatedly tipped his cap. Mates finally yanked him from the dugout for a hand-shaking high-fiving peregrination around the park. The warehouse banner changed from "2-1-3-0."

Next month the big leagues ended the second and last year of an in-house/pray for a profit ABC/NBC contract. "You wonder how anything would be worse [than CBS]," Mel joked. "Then you get The [1994–95/invisible till July/no national or day coverage] Baseball Network," carving the new Division Series and LCS into areas of "natural" interest. The N.L. went dark in Boston. In St. Louis, the A.L. never made a peep. Neutral markets fell to one or the other league. What you saw depended on where you lived.

"Yes, sir, that's baseball: America's regional pastime," *Sports Illustrated* wrote. "Such an abomination is The Baseball Network that in Seattle, where people don't cross against a red light on the emptiest of streets, fans booed whenever the Kingdome PA announcer made mention." TBN's tagline screamed "Catch the Show!" Allen twitted its regular season. "What kind of show cancels a twenty-six-week season's first fourteen weeks?"

In 1996, baseball went back to the future: Fox, reviving *Game of the Week*; NBC, splitting the postseason and All-Star Game. Fox was not your father's baseball network. Alas for Mel, neither was *Game.*

"Being Irish means laughing at life," said a ballad, "knowing that life will break your heart." Being Irish was a lark *v.* TV, say, in 1954. If lucky, you had a statistician, monitor, and wire to the production truck. Forty years later, "Things [for the viewer] are as primitive," said Fox executive David Hill. Quick cuts, miked bases, walls, and players recast coverage. The Fox Box listed score, inning, out, ball, strike, and base runner. Even finer was *TWIB* again having somewhere to hang its hat. "We'll have a lot of Fox affiliates, club flagships, and regional cable," Belinfante said in 1996: 117 outlets, including twenty-nine of the top thirty markets. *TWIB* would again precede *Game*. Phoenix couldn't wait. "The Tyakutake Comet comes around once every 15,000 or so years," a promo read. "But in the earth-bound world of Baseball, the year 1996 plays witness to a once-in-a-lifetime occurrence. It's the 20th season of *This Week In Baseball*, and *TWIB* is going all out to celebrate this occasion!"

A "witness to and chief chronicler of 20 years of Baseball, the show has become an important part of Baseball and American culture," it said. In 1977, "*This Week* revolutionized sports: for the first time, [local] highlights edited into a national program." Going "beyond," it would air "behind-the-scenes stories and flashbacks" through "*TWIB* Notes," Comedy Central cast, bloopers, "footage unavailable on ESPN, CNN, or any local sports report," and "one and only Mel Allen." The ad trilled: "How About That!"

Having voiced Phoenix's *The Eternal Game, History of Baseball*, three Series, 120 team videos, and 570 *TWIB*[s], Mel could not make its soufflé rise twice. Debuting as late as June, Fox's sixteen-game slate often vanished in September. "*Game* not being weekly hurt," said Belinfante. "Unlike NBC, Fox couldn't reinforce." A cultural divide stained, too. Mel was generic; Fox, youth-crazed. Crowed Hill: "[On *Game*] no more dead guys!" The more immediate problem was The Voice's health.

On Opening Day 1996—"Like daffodils," Mel said, "like life after a dead winter, like things sprouting out of the ground"—*Times* critic Richard Sandomir visited Greenwich. He liked Allen's modesty: the old-hat townhome, how Mel drove Esther's Taurus, "retain[ing] the freshness of another era, when voices with a respect for the language reigned." Above all, "[his] voice was resonant, still capable of stirring your senses even if he's just calling down to you from a second-floor window, 'Is that someone down there?'"

Sandomir was too young to recall the Yankees. Driving, The Voice atoned. "He starts doing play-by-play. 'He's passing him on the left!' became 'How about that! A parking space!'" The passenger was amused—"it was adorable"—and touched.

Richard Ben Cramer wrote that Joe DiMaggio loved fame—but not its midwife, celebrity. Mel, felt Sandomir, needed both. "He enters a restaurant, and people shout out. Even with *This Week*, there was a void. We talked a lot, but so little about today."

Ballantine's Len Faupel e-mailed Sandomir about his column. "Why can't people accept Mel's firing just as Ballantine cost cutting?" Hell, Allen would have shrugged: People gonna' think what they're gonna' think.

In 1996, the Smithsonian thought enough to invite Mel to join John Kenneth Galbraith, Tom Bakke, Tom Shales, Benjamin Hooks, Betty Friedan, Victor Navasky, and Stephen Ambrose for that fall's *American Life: The Fabulous Fifties*. The series would include "TV's Fabulous Fifties," "Elvis and His Music," "Blacklisting," "On the Brink of the Women's Movement," and "Play Ball!" recalling Mick, Mays, and Wayne Terwilliger with the author.

Then, in April, The Voice caught a virus from an infection. Fusselle temporarily replaced him. By late May, Allen read a script. "It didn't go well," said Belinfante. "Something was missing. The intonation and nuances were there. But the vocal quality wasn't. He didn't have the resonance." Geoff calmed him. "He was frustrated, but I said, 'Look, when you're strong enough, come back to work.'" Mel forgot the Yanks, Movietone, NBC: His job was still there.

The two friends met for the final time Wednesday, June 12, at Luberto's Restaurant in Hackensack. "They made a big deal about him, he enjoyed it, signed a ball," said Belinfante. "We'd been through so much, the start, open heart surgery. You just figured he'd go on."

That Sunday—ironically, Father's Day—Allen watched baseball in his second-story room: Stripes 5, Cleveland 4. At 6:00 P.M., Esther called, heard silence, and found The Voice dead on the bathroom floor. Reeling, she phoned emergency 911. A policeman contacted Larry in Alabama. At ninety, Herbert Hoover said, "I outlived the bastards." Shunning bile, Mel, eighty-three, had none to outlive.

Stunned by his death, Belinfante thought that hoping for another Allen was like believing the earth was flat. Next day flags flew at half-staff at the house, a writer said, that Mel made part of a million living rooms. Posters scrawled NEVER FORGOTTEN! THE VOICE! FREDDIE "SEZ": A YANKEE VOICE, MEL ALLEN, HOW ABOUT THAT! The Yanks wore an armband, lined up near the dugout, and put hat over heart. The scoreboard read: "So long, Mel, we'll miss you."

New skipper Joe Torre recalled visiting Vietnam in 1966: "If they [troops] didn't know what [he] looked like, they knew what he sounded like." Bob Sheppard said: "May we ask you to spend a few moments in silent prayer as we remember Mel Allen: in his time, the best-known sports announcer in America."

Jon Miller summarized: "Idol. World Series history. All-time great. *This Week In Baseball.* How about that!" At Shea Stadium, Ralph Kiner felt at sea. "I mean, how do you react? Greatest broadcaster who ever lived." Future Mets skipper Willie Randolph said: "That voice, I mean, it's Heaven." Ordained Heywood Hale Broun: "He only had to speak to evoke the Yankees." Scooter likened Mel to Pavarotti or Nureyev— "a master. I'd never have become a broadcaster without him. He taught me everything," even unlearning "Ath-a-letics."

On June 19, a Wednesday, Rizzuto, looking ashen, filed into Stamford's Temple Beth-El with Ford, Berra, DiMag, Joe Pepitone, and Steinbrenner. Arthur Richman, a writer, ex-Yanks brass, and friend, said, "He never tried to impress anyone with his importance." Rabbi Joshua Hammerman echoed: "To silence his voice would have been to silence his soul."

Esther, Larry, and Mel's four nieces and nephews stood for Robert Merrill's "America the Beautiful." The mahogany casket was carried to the family plot next door. Rain flirted with the ritual. For once not willing it, The Voice was again alone. ◆

# Epilogue

ulogy, or fortuity? The 1996 Yankees took their first title since 1978. The '98ers won a league-record 114 games, finished 125–50, and swept the Series. Next year the usual suspects (Stripes) took the usual parade (down Manhattan to City Hall). "This stuff," said Torre, "never gets old." New: in 2000, the first Subway Series in forty-four years. "Bernie [Williams] back! Away back! He's there! He makes the catch! Ball game over! World Series over!" said John Sterling: for baseball's Capella, three straight titles, fourth in five years, and twenty-sixth overall.

Without Allen, *This Week*'s constellation dimmed, more waif of a moon than bright noon sun. "Some didn't know Mel as Voice of the Yankees," said Belinfante. "Through our show, he became the Voice of Baseball," dying "as we tried to shed our darkness of the '90s." *TWIB* aired a tribute, made ex-shortstop Ozzie Smith host, then junked him for California-based Buzz Brainard. A fedora-topped Mel claymation helped in 2000–01.

"Welcome to *This Week In Baseball*," Allen's taped voice began, ending "That's all, folks, join us next week." How about that! Mel *had* become a dinosaur. Said Joe Castiglione: "It's like he never died."

ESPN's Sean McDonough missed the original. "Can't replace it. It's why the program has plunged." *USA Today*'s Stephen Borelli "pouted if I missed it or caught only the show's final few minutes. Every Saturday, I turned on the TV, climbed into a big easy chair in my parents' living room, and onto the lap of . . . my surrogate uncle for the next thirty minutes." However "untrue it was," Mel made baseball seem "a calm, easygoing place where everybody got along."

Critics did, judging him. "He was everything a sportscaster should be: quick, smart, descriptive, and exuberant," said Sandomir. "Mel's greatness will not be puffed up in death: in life, even Yankee-haters would acknowledge his stature." To Sterling, he rivaled "Sinatra, or Crosby, or Astaire." Costas chanted "Hello there, everybody!" Broadcaster Roy Firestone confessed to having loathed the Stripes. "Every loss we gloried in how bad Allen felt. Every win was Mel's win. Every broadcast of the victory was somehow transferred to Allen's being."

Berra recalled a Sunday in Detroit. "I looked at the booth, Mel waved, and instead of waving I pointed to the bleachers and homered. People didn't believe it. But it's true." To Mel, "The Moose [had been] on the loose." Skowron grew quiet. "Never a front-runner. He'd say hello no matter how you played." Hank Bauer allowed to still being called "Man of the Hour." A golf volunteer told of driving from Stamford to New Jersey. "All the way I didn't go over 45 miles an hour," said Barry Cogan. "I didn't want to miss any of his stories. If you're over forty, that voice is the most identifiable you've ever heard."

In the *Daily News*, Pete Coutros retold Allen's opening a bottle and pouring Ballantine into a Pilsner glass to sign off. "It was a ritual repeated hundreds of times, more uncanny with each repetition: the pour, the foam threatening to overflow the glass and then, as if on command, the foam stopping dead in its tracks."

He asked the secret. "Gotta' coat the glass with butter!" said The Voice. Reminiscence became a way to catch its subject at peak tide.

At Major League Baseball Productions, now-head writer Jeff Scott related being asked if he would write for Mel. "For a long time, I said no," finally agreeing. "It was so intimidating. How could you capture him?"

Each week Allen took the freight elevator to a third-floor studio. At 9:45 A.M., "he appeared from the clouds, shed a contraption for his throat from a medical bag he had," read script, watched the see-through, and began. "Taping," said Scott, "we'd be done by 11:00." Leaving at 3:00, The Voice watched the mix—"in itself, unusual. Most actors don't care"—told "Mel Tales," and turned humor on himself.

One night American Sportscasters Association president Louis Schwartz phoned to discuss dinner.

"What you callin' me for?" Allen snapped. "The Yankees are on TV."

"Yeah, I know," Lou said, "but hell, they're leading, 14 to 1."

"You can't be too careful. Call me when it ends." Scott rued some terming Mel's solitude, isolation; reserve, arrogance; dignity, aloofness; sentimentality, tripe. He knew better. Moved by text or talk, The Voice "would often reach out and daub at his eyes."

At *Newsday*, Steve Jacobson, a boyhood Dodgers fan, retrieved a long-ago spring training. Bedridden, forbidden to read, the measles patient stared at the ceiling "[till] there was Allen's voice. And wasn't that wonderful, the surviving icon of our lives when there really was no television." Mel painted the palm trees behind St. Pete's Huggins Field, "which I'd never seen," but forever would. Like Barber, he "taught us we were New Yorkers, and we should have some class. New Yorkers wouldn't throw things at great players. We learned that from [them]."

At Harvard College, a Zoology professor was stunned by the "surprising depth of my sadness [caused by] the extinction of a philosophy as much as the loss of a dear man." Mel's "immense appeal," said Stephen Jay Gould, lay not in flair or tone but two yarns from the teacher's youth. "They have stayed with me, one for its integrity, the other for its antic humor. One exemplifies the high road, the other, an abyss, however charming." Each bared God breaking the mold *before* He made The Voice.

In 1952, Mantle, twenty, trying to replace DiMag, struck out at The Stadium. The crowd began to boo. Dismayed, Mel yelled at a caroler, "Why are you booing him?"

"Because he's not as good as DiMaggio."

On-air, Allen "let him have it," Gould said, "delivering a fero-cious dressing-down to the fan for his indecency."

The other tale yoked No. 7, too. "Why, that ball was just foul by a bottle of Ballantine beer!" Mel would say. Once Mick hit down the line. "Folks, that ball was foul by no more than a bottle of . . ."—The Voice stopped, then bayed—"No, that ball was foul by the ash on a White Owl cigar!"

Here lay "a man of grace and integrity, a shameless huckster of charming originality," the professor mused. "But above all a man who could only be his wonderful cornball self—Mel Allen, the inim-itable human Voice of the Yankees."

In *Julius Caesar*, "The elements [were] so mixed," wrote Shake-speare, "that Nature might stand up and say to all the world, 'This was a man!'" One balladeer, Gould wrote, had prophesied another.

On November 4, 1996, the Center for Christian-Jewish Understand-ing at Sacred Heart University held a memorial service at a place— "The Yankee Stadium of cathedrals," said The Voice—where language soared and faith softened sorrow and the past always whis-pered. "Why a Mel Allen tribute at St. Patrick's Cathedral?" asked Center associate director Rabbi Joseph H. Ehrenkranz. "He was an ambassador of goodwill."

Larry chronicled Mel often speaking the same weekend at church and temple. Future Yanks announcer Suzyn Waldman sang the National Anthem; Merrill, again "America"; cantor Nathaniel Benjamin, the Twenty-third Psalm. Archbishop John Cardinal O'Connor presided. Pews packed Scooter, Costas, Dick Enberg, and Don Dunphy.

Broadcaster Marty Glickman "always respected his ability to re-spect the opposition." Gowdy was more personal. "Where would I be without Mel Allen? Maybe a fishing guide in Wyoming." No one mentioned 1964. "I grind my teeth when I heard those rumors," Curt had said. "I lived with that man. They were vicious." A former neighbor, Bill Ries, made the chapel smile. One night Allen came to dinner. "He talked so long the turkey burned."

The beer was Ballantine, Coutros wrote. "The voice was champagne. Yesterday, in the Hub of Catholicism in the metropolitan area, the quintessence of Mel Allen . . . *rebbe* more than rebel . . . was lovingly laid to rest. As though to irrevocably flush the strains of Dixie from his consciousness, he became the Voice of the Yankees, retroactively incurring the wrath of Scarlett O'Hara," inveigling, overwhelming, but never profaning a listener.

In death, like life, Mel made baseball good company.

When Frank Sinatra sang, "There used to be a ballpark," he bespoke shrines—it may off-put: no other word will do—passing from parent to child the joy of rooting for the home team. Announcers could, too, as I found feting Allen in 1990 at Upstate New York's Geneseo State University, its turf rolling and unbroken, pleasant, almost golden.

I had seen politicians hailed, but not like this: Mel, flanked by teenagers and seventy-somethings, many in tears, falling back on his suzerainty as a Voice. You could be a Generation X'er and know Allen from *This Week In Baseball;* Baby Boomer, the Series, Rose Bowl, or Movietone; senior citizen, pre-Good War Yanks genesis.

Later, the Grand Old Man of Broadcasting called it "maybe the most emotional evening of my life." Improbably, he had reclaimed a place as high as before his exile, in love with his work, yet always afraid it would end.

"America is the land," wrote Norman Mailer, "which worships the great comeback." Watching this kind and shy, stoic and heroic, solitary but, at last, not unhappy man, I thought of Roy Hobbs in *The Natural.* Mel Allen is "the best there ever was." ◆

# Sources

Brief portions of this book have appeared in slightly different form in *Voices of The Game.*

Grateful acknowledgment is made for permission to reprint excerpts from the following.

*FDR: A Centenary Remembrance,* by Joseph Alsop, copyright the Viking Press, 1982. Reprinted by permission of Thames and Hudson Limited.

*Miami and the Siege of Chicago,* by Norman Mailer, copyright the Viking Press, 1969. Reprinted by permission of Thames and Hudson Limited.

*North Toward Home,* by Willie Morris, reprinted by permission of Houghton Mifflin, 1967.

*President Kennedy,* by Richard Reeves, reprinted by permission of Simon & Schuster, 1993.

*Rhubarb in the Catbird Seat,* by Red Barber with Robert Creamer, reprinted by permission of Doubleday & Company, 1968.

*When It Was a Game,* reprinted by permission of Home Box Office, 1991.

Play-by-play commentaries in *The Voice* are reprinted with the permission of the Commissioner of Baseball's Office. Grateful acknowledgment is also made to: ABC Television, CBS Radio, Major League Baseball and its thirty teams, Mutual Radio, and NBC Radio and Television.

# Bibliography

Allen, Mel. *It Takes Heart,* with Evan Thomas. New York: Harper & Brothers, 1959.

___. *You Can't Beat the Hours,* with Ed Fitzgerald. New York: Harper & Row, 1965.

Alsop, Joseph. *FDR: A Centenary Remembrance.* New York: Viking Press, 1982.

Angell, Roger. *Five Seasons.* New York: Simon & Schuster, 1978.

Barber, Walter (Red). *The Broadcasters.* New York: Dial Press, 1970.

___. *Rhubarb in the Catbird Seat,* with Robert Creamer. Garden City, New York: Doubleday, 1968.

Berry, Henry. *Boston Red Sox.* New York: Rutledge Books, 1975.

Borelli, Stephen. *How About That! The Life of Mel Allen.* Champaign, Ill.: Sports Publishing, 2005.

Broeg, Bob. *Super Stars of Baseball.* St. Louis, Mo.: Sporting News Publishing Company, 1971.

Buck, Jack. *That's a Winner!* with Bob Rains and Bob Broeg. Champaign, Ill.: Sagamore Publishing, 1997.

Castiglione, Joe. *Broadcast Rites and Sites,* with Douglas B. Lyons. Lanham, Md.: Taylor Trade Publishing, 2004.

Chester, Giraud, Garrison, Garnet, and Willis, Edgar. *Television and Radio.* New York: Meredith Corporation, 1971.

Coleman, Ken. *So You Want to Be a Sportscaster?* New York: Hawthorn Books, 1973.

Cosell, Howard. *Cosell.* New York: Playboy Press, 1973.

Costas, Bob. *Fair Ball: A Fan's Case for Baseball.* New York: Random House, 2000.

Creamer, Robert. *Babe.* New York: Simon & Schuster, 1974.

Cullinane, Joe. *Face to Face.* Denver, Colo.: JaDan Publishing, 2002.

Durso, Joseph. *Yankee Stadium.* Boston: Houghton Mifflin, 1972.

Enright, Jim. *Chicago Cubs.* New York: Rutledge Books, 1975.

Falls, Joe. *Detroit Tigers.* New York: Rutledge Books, 1975.

Firestone, Roy. *Up Close,* with Scott Ostler. New York: Hyperion, 1993.

Gammons, Peter. *Beyond the Sixth Game.* Boston: Houghton Mifflin, 1985.

Gowdy, Curt. *Cowboy at the Mike,* with Al Hirshberg. Garden City, New York: Doubleday, 1966.

Greenwald, Hank. *This Copyrighted Broadcast.* San Francisco: Woodford Press, 1997.

Halberstam, David. *Summer of '49.* New York: William Morrow, 1989.

Harmon, Merle. *Merle Harmon Stories,* with Sam Blair. Arlington, Tex.: Reid Publishing, 1998.

Harris, Jay S. *TV Guide: The First 25 Years.* New York: Simon & Schuster, 1978.

Hirshberg, Al. *What's the Matter with the Red Sox?* New York: Dodd, Mead, 1973.

Hodges, Russ. *Baseball Complete.* New York: Grosset & Dunlop, 1952.

———. *My Giants.* Garden City, New York: Doubleday, 1963.

Holmes, Tommy. *The Dodgers.* New York: Rutledge Books, 1975.

Honig, Donald. *Baseball's 10 Greatest Teams.* New York: Macmillan, 1982.

———. *The American League.* New York: Crown, 1983.

Kahn, Roger. *The Boys of Summer.* New York: Harper & Row, 1971.

Keegan, Tom. *Ernie Harwell.* Chicago: Triumph Books, 2002.

Lewine, Harris, and Okrent, Daniel. *The Ultimate Baseball Book.* Boston: Houghton Mifflin, 1979.

Lipsyte, Robert. *SportsWorld.* New York: Quadrangle, 1975.

Mailer, Norman. *Miami and the Siege of Chicago.* New York: Viking Press, 1969.

Major League Baseball Promotion Corporation. *Baseball: The First 100 Years.* New York: Poretz-Ross Publishers, 1969.

___. *The Game and the Glory.* Englewood Cliffs, N.J.: Prentice-Hall, 1976.

___. *This Great Game.* New York: Rutledge Books, 1971.

Manchester, William. *One Brief Shining Moment.* Boston: Little, Brown and Company, 1983.

Mathews, Garret. *Baseball Days.* Chicago: Contemporary Books, 2000.

McNeil, Alex. *Total Television.* New York: Penguin Books, 1980.

Metz, Robert. *CBS: Reflections in a Bloodshot Eye.* New York: Playboy Press, 1975.

Michener, James A. *Sports in America.* New York: Random House, 1976.

Miller, Jon. *Confessions of a Baseball Purist,* with Mark Hyman. Simon & Schuster: New York, 1998.

Morris, Willie. *North Toward Home.* Boston: Houghton Mifflin, 1967.

National League. *A Baseball Century.* New York: Rutledge Books, 1976.

Powers, Ron. *SuperTube.* New York: Coward-McCann, 1984.

Reeves, Richard. *President Kennedy.* New York: Simon & Schuster, 1993.

Reeves, Thomas. *A Question of Character.* New York: The Free Press, 1991.

Reichler, Joseph. *Baseball's Great Moments.* New York: Bonanza Books, 1983.

Reidenbaugh, Lowell. *Take Me Out to the Ball Park.* St. Louis, Mo.: Sporting News Publishing Company, 1983.

Rosenthal, Harold. *The 10 Best Years of Baseball.* New York: Van Nostrand Reinhold Company, 1980.

Seidel, Michael. *Ted Williams—A Baseball Life.* Chicago: Contemporary Books, 1991.

Shaughnessy, Dan. *The Curse of the Bambino.* New York: Penguin Books, 1991.

Smelser, Marshall. *The Life That Ruth Built.* New York: Quadrangle/New York Times Books, 1975.

Smith, Robert. *Illustrated History of Baseball.* New York: Grosset & Dunlap, 1973.

Smithsonian Exposition Books. *Every Four Years.* New York: W.W. Norton and Company, 1980.

Stockton, J. Roy. *The Gashouse Gang.* New York: A. S. Barnes, 1945.

Thompson Chuck. *Ain't the Beer Cold!* with Gordon Beard. South Bend, Ind.: Diamond Communications, 1996.

Vecsey, George (ed.). *The Way It Was.* New York: Mobil Oil and McGraw-Hill, 1974.

Vincent, Fay. *The Last Commissioner.* New York: Simon & Schuster, 2002.

White, Theodore H. *In Search of History.* New York: Harper & Row, 1978.

___. *The Making of the President 1960.* New York: Atheneum, 1961.

Wolff, Bob. *It's Not Who Won or Lost the Game.* South Bend, Ind.: Diamond Communications, 1996.

Wood, Bob. *Dodger Dogs to Fenway Franks.* New York: McGraw-Hill, 1988.

# Index

# About the Author

Curt Smith is a best-selling author, award-winning radio commentator, columnist, documentarian, and Senior Lecturer in English at the University of Rochester. He wrote more speeches than anyone for former president George H. W. Bush. Smith is also considered America's leading baseball radio/TV historian.

Smith's books are *The Voice: Mel Allen's Untold Story, Voices of Summer, What Baseball Means to Me, Storied Stadiums, Our House, Windows on the White House, Of Mikes and Men, The Storytellers, A Fine Sense of the Ridiculous, Voices of The Game, Long Time Gone*, and *America's Dizzy Dean*. In 2008, The Lyons Press will publish his thirteenth book, *Pull Up a Chair: The Vin Scully Story*. Says *USA Today*: "Curt Smith shows that writing can be art."

NBC's Bob Costas adds: "Curt Smith stands up for the beauty of words." He hosts XM Satellite Radio and National Public Radio affiliates *Perspectives* series; analyzes politics for Rochester, New York's CBS/Time-Warner TV; and is columnist for Upstate New York's *Messenger-Post* papers, Major League Baseball's official Web site MLBlog.com, and *Jewish World Review*'s PoliticalMavens.com.

Raised in New York, Smith was a Gannett reporter and *The Saturday Evening Post* senior editor before joining the Bush White House in 1989. Among speeches for the forty-first president were the State of the Union; "Just War" Persian Gulf speech; and USS *Missouri* address on the fiftieth anniversary of Pearl Harbor. Smith later headed the ex-president's 1993–98 speech staff, writing Bush's moving 2004 eulogy to President Reagan at Washington's National Cathedral. Said Margaret Thatcher: "I have enjoyed his marvelous work."

In 1993, Smith hosted a Smithsonian Institution series based on *Voices of The Game.* Associated Press and the New York State Broadcasters Association later voted his radio commentary "Best in New York State." He wrote ESPN-TV *Voices* documentaries, helped write ABC/ESPN's *SportsCentury* series, aired the popular WISN Milwaukee *Mid-Day Milwaukee* and WHAM Rochester *Curt Smith Show,* and hosts programming at the National Baseball Hall of Fame and Museum.

Smith has written for, among others, *Baltimore Sun, Baseball Weekly, Boston Globe, Newsweek, New York Daily News, New York Post, New York Times, Reader's Digest, Sports Illustrated,* and *Washington Post.* He has appeared on numerous local and network radio/TV programs, including ABC's *Nightline,* Armed Forces Radio, British Broadcasting Corporation, *CBS This Morning* and CBS Radio, CNN Radio/TV, CNBC-TV, ESPN Radio and TV *SportsCenter,* Fox TV News Channel, MSNBC-TV, and Mutual Radio with Larry King.

The 1973 State University of New York at Geneseo graduate has been named among the "100 Outstanding Alumni" of New York's SUNY system. He is a member of the prestigious Judson Welliver Society of former White House speechwriters; Museum of Broadcast Communications and National Radio Hall of Fame committee; Baseball Hall of Fame Ford C. Frick Award broadcast committee; and SUNY at Geneseo and Rochester, New York, Frontier Field Halls of Fame. Smith lives with wife Sarah and their two children in Rochester. ◆